Country Home Cooking

Compiled by Marjorie Rohrer
7382 Mount Clinton Pike
Harrisonburg, VA 22802
540-867-0007

ISBN-10: 1-60241-003-8
ISBN-13: 978-1-60241-003-9
Published by: Books of Merit Publishing
Printed by: Campbell Copy Center, USA

Artwork by: Marilyn Eberly
Layout by: Shirley Byler

*Every effort has been made to credit the writers of various poems and quotes,
but many remain anonymous.*

Country Home Cooking

Dear readers and fellow cooks,

The idea for a collection of favorite recipes began in 1999 when we were winding down after twelve years of operating a home based food business.

Several dozen young women, my parents, friends and family members assisted us during those busy years and this is a tangible remembrance of those days spent working together. Our helpers contributed their favorite recipes and I asked my mother, Esther Rohrer, to include our family favorites from her handwritten cookbook.

During the years since then, the project has grown to include my own favorites also. Many of the recipes are original, and the rest of them are variations of other cooks' good recipes. As you use them, feel free to alter the seasonings and ingredients to suit your own taste. That's what makes cooking interesting and fun.

I am grateful to my sister, who drew the illustrations and front cover, and to several good friends who typed the recipes.

My wish is that each of you who use this book will consider it a pleasure and a privilege to share your love for your family and friends through good home cooking.

– Marjorie Anna Rohrer

"Spread love everywhere you go; first of all in your own house…
Let no one ever come to you without leaving better and happier.
Be the living expression of God's kindness; kindness in your face,
kindness in your eyes, kindness in your warm greeting."
– Mother Teresa

Table of Contents

Just for Today

Just for today – I will live through the next twelve hours
   and not try to tackle all of life's problems at once.
Just for today – I will improve my mind. I will learn something useful.
   I will read something that requires thought and concentration.
Just for today – I will be agreeable. I will look my best,
   speak with a pleasant voice, be courteous and considerate.
Just for today – I will not find fault with a friend,
   relative or acquaintance.
   I will not try to change anyone but myself.
Just for today – I will do a good turn and keep it a secret.
   If anyone finds out, it won't count.
Just for today – I will have a plan.
   I might not follow it exactly, but I have it.
   I will save myself from two enemies – hurry and indecision.
Just for today – I will do two things I don't want to do,
   because I need the discipline.
Just for today – I will believe in myself. I will give my best to others
   and feel hopeful that others will give their best to me.

Anonymous

Breads and Breakfasts

Doughnut Day

In a farmhouse kitchen warm and cozy,
it's early morn, and Mom is busy
     mixing up her doughnuts.
Yeast and water, sugar, shortening,
eggs and nutmeg, flour and flavoring
     all go in the doughnuts.
Now it's time to get Dad's breakfast,
drink some coffee, mail some letters
     while the dough is rising.
Punch dough down and wash the dishes,
sweep the floor, and get iron skillet
     out to fry the doughnuts.
At nine o'clock she's rolling dough,
practiced hands move to and fro
     cutting out the doughnuts.
Trays of doughnuts hide the table,
the grease is hot, the glaze is ready—
     time to fry the doughnuts.
Dad comes in to check her progress,
smells the coffee, takes his hat off,
     reads the news and eats a doughnut.
Golden doughnuts are placed in rows
awaiting all the lucky folks
     who will get to eat them.
Now comes the part that we like best;
since we five kids have left the nest,
     we still enjoy Mom's doughnuts.
I know she puts a lot of love
into each batch that she stirs up;
     that makes them extra special.
Dad will hitch the horse and buggy;
Mom fills it with trays of doughnuts—
     and they're off to see the neighbors.
Friends and family, mailman, shut-ins,
busy mothers with young children
     all receive those doughnuts.
The day is done, the doughnuts gone,
     Mom saves just one or two.
She's made a lot of people glad-
     That makes her happy too.

                    – Marjorie Rohrer

Breads and Breakfasts

Cake (or baking powder) doughnuts were developed in the New England states many years ago, possibly to enjoy with fresh warm maple syrup. They were originally shaped like nuts – thus the name doughnuts. The Pennsylvania Dutch women later added the holes.

WHOLE-WHEAT CAKE DOUGHNUTS

2 eggs
1 cup sugar
¼ cup melted butter
1 cup buttermilk
2 tsp vanilla
2 cups whole-wheat flour
2 cups all purpose flour
4 tsp baking powder
¼ tsp soda
½ tsp salt
1 tsp nutmeg

Combine eggs and sugar. Beat well. Add butter and buttermilk. Add rest of ingredients and stir until blended. Roll out dough and cut as usual. Fry in deep hot fat at 360°. Glaze while still hot. Quick and delicious.

BUTTERMILK DOUGHNUTS

2 cups sugar
3 eggs, beaten
1½ cups warm, mashed potatoes
⅓ cup butter, melted
1 cup buttermilk
6 cups sifted all-purpose flour (can use some whole-wheat)
4 tsp baking powder
1½ tsp baking soda
1 tsp salt
1 tsp nutmeg

Add sugar to eggs. Beat until well mixed. Stir in potatoes, butter, and buttermilk. Add sifted dry ingredients and mix only until flour is completely moistened. Chill dough at least 1 hour. Roll ⅓ of dough at a time on lightly floured surface to ½-inch thickness. Cut with a floured cutter. Let rest 10-15 minutes. Fry in deep hot fat (360°). When doughnuts are golden brown, lift out, drain on paper towels, and cool slightly. Roll in powdered sugar or dip in doughnut glaze.

– Maria (Eberly) Horst

MOM'S DOUGHNUT GLAZE

½ cup water
1 Tbsp gelatin
2½ lbs powdered sugar (10 cups)
½ tsp salt
1 tsp vanilla
½ cup water (or more)

Soften gelatin in ½ cup water. Melt over low heat while stirring to dissolve gelatin. Combine all ingredients, adding water to desired consistency. Dip hot doughnuts. (The gelatin keeps the glaze from soaking into your doughnuts.)

A friend in need is a friend indeed.

Mom's Doughnuts

It was a little tricky getting this down on paper, because Mom seldom measures her ingredients when she makes doughnuts. This is her closest "guesstimate."

3½ cups warm water
1 Tbsp sugar
1½ tsp ginger
3 Tbsp yeast
1½ cups instant potato flakes
2 cups hot water
1 cup sugar
2 tsp baking powder
1 Tbsp nutmeg
1 Tbsp salt
1 Tbsp vanilla
1 Tbsp lemon extract
3 large eggs, beaten
1 cup Crisco shortening
2 cups whole-wheat flour
9-10 cups bread flour, use more if needed

Combine first 4 ingredients in your largest mixing bowl. The sugar and ginger help boost the yeast activity. Stir potato flakes into hot water. Measure sugar, baking powder, nutmeg, and salt and add to softened yeast mixture. Stir in flavorings, eggs, shortening and mashed potatoes, beat well. Begin adding flour, stirring with a spoon until dough is ready to knead by hand. Add flour until dough is smooth and satiny. Cover and let rise. Punch down and roll dough on generously floured surface, cutting and placing doughnuts on cloth lined trays. Let rise and deep fry in 350° hot shortening. Glaze and drain on wire rack.

*The most important ingredient of all good home cooking—
love for those you are cooking for.*

MAPLE NUT TWISTS

1 cup warm water
2 Tbsp yeast
½ cup butter, softened
¼ cup brown sugar
¼ cup dry milk
1 tsp salt
2 eggs, beaten
About 4 cups flour

Dissolve yeast in warm water. Add rest of ingredients and stir in flour gradually and knead until dough is smooth. Let rise until doubled, divide dough into 3 pieces. Roll each third into a 14" circle. Spread a circle on a 14" greased pizza pan and top with half of filling:

Maple Nut Filling

1 cup chopped nuts
½ cup sugar
½ cup brown sugar
2 Tbsp flour
2 tsp cinnamon
½ tsp maple flavoring
¼ cup melted butter

Place second 14" circle on top of first, and spread with remaining filling. Put third circle of dough on top of filling. Beginning at edge of pan, cut dough into 20 wedges, leaving center uncut. Twist each wedge 3 times and let rise again. Bake at 325° about 20 minutes. Ice while warm.

Maple Cream Icing

1¼ cups powdered sugar
1½ Tbsp butter
3 Tbsp half and half cream
Pinch of salt
½ tsp maple flavoring

He that hath a bountiful eye shall be blessed;
for he giveth of his bread to the poor.

– Proverbs 22:9

QUICK Cinnamon Buns or Sticky Buns

½ cup warm water
1 Tbsp yeast
1 cup buttermilk or sour milk
3 Tbsp vegetable oil
¼ cup sugar
½ tsp salt
1½ tsp lemon (or vanilla) extract
¼ tsp soda
2½ to 3 cups flour

Sprinkle yeast over water. Stir and let set 5 minutes. Heat milk. Add oil, sugar, salt, and extract. Add flour and soda to milk mixture. Stir in yeast and water. Mix well. Roll out on floured surface. Spread with melted butter, sugar, and cinnamon. Roll up and cut. Place in greased pan and let rise until double. Bake at 350° for 18-20 minutes.

Syrup For Sticky Buns

½ cup butter
1 cup brown sugar
½ cup light corn syrup
1 tsp vanilla
pinch of salt

Combine all ingredients in saucepan. Heat and stir until sugar dissolves. Boil 1-2 minutes. Pour into greased 9x13 pan or three 8" pans. Top with nuts if desired. Put cinnamon buns on top and let rise. Bake at 350° for about 30 minutes. Remove from oven and invert into another pan while still warm.

The recipe that is not shared will soon be forgotten,
but ones that are shared will be enjoyed by future generations.

CINNAMON BUNS OR DOUGHNUTS

4 cups warm water
2 Tbsp yeast
1 cup margarine
½ cup potato flakes
¾ cup sugar
½ cup brown sugar
2½ tsp salt
½ cup dry milk
3 eggs
1 tsp nutmeg
1 tsp cinnamon
4½ to 5 lbs flour

Soften yeast in warm water in large bowl. Add potato flakes, then rest of ingredients except flour. Mix in flour. (You may need to adjust amount of flour to make your dough handle well.) For doughnuts, add 2 tsp vanilla, 2 tsp lemon extract, (and use 2-3 cups whole-wheat flour if desired.)

For cinnamon buns, make a cinnamon-sugar mixture with equal parts brown and white sugar and enough cinnamon to suit your taste. I use one Tbsp cinnamon per cup of sugar. Divide dough into 4 portions. Roll each into a large rectangle. Brush with melted butter. Cover with cinnamon-sugar mixture, roll up, and cut. Place in greased pans and let rise until doubled. Bake at 350° until done (20-30 minutes). Don't over bake.

Makes 4 dozen large doughnuts or 6 dozen cinnamon buns.
Use the syrup recipe on pg 11 to make sticky buns.

Creamy Cinnamon Bun Icing
2 ½ lbs powdered sugar
½ lb butter (soft)
¼ cup dry milk
½ cup water (+ 1 Tbsp if needed)
1 tsp salt
1 Tbsp vanilla

Combine all ingredients, adding water gradually. Beat until fluffy.

Caramel Bun Icing

1 cup brown sugar
½ cup butter
pinch of salt
¼ cup milk
1¾-2 cups powdered sugar

Melt butter. Add brown sugar and salt. Stir over low heat for 2 minutes. Add milk. Bring to a boil. Cool to lukewarm and add powdered sugar.

Doughnut Glaze

2 lbs powdered sugar (8 cups)
½ tsp salt
¾-1 cup boiling water
2 tsp vanilla

Mix until smooth. Dip hot doughnuts in glaze. Let drip on rack (or on a wooden spoon handle placed over a bowl).

For a Contented Life

HEALTH enough to make work a pleasure.
WEALTH enough to support our needs.
STRENGTH to battle with difficulties and overcome them.
GRACE enough to confess our sins and forsake them.
PATIENCE enough to toil until some good is accomplished.
CHARITY enough to see some good in your neighbor.
LOVE enough to move you to be useful and helpful to others.
FAITH enough to make real the things of God.
HOPE enough to remove all anxious fears concerning the future.

QUICKY STICKY BUNS

Dough

¾ cup milk
½ cup water
¼ cup butter
¼ cup sugar
1 tsp salt

Combine and stir over low heat until mixture reaches 130°. In a large mixing bowl combine:

1½ cups flour
1½ Tbsp yeast

Pour warm milk mixture over flour and yeast and stir a minute or so to moisten yeast. Then beat vigorously for 3 minutes. Stir in by hand:

1 egg beaten
1¾ cups flour
Cover and let rise 30 minutes. Meanwhile make topping.

Topping

¾ cup butter
1 cup brown sugar
1 Tbsp water
1 Tbsp light corn syrup
1 tsp cinnamon
pinch of salt

Cook over low heat until butter melts and sugar dissolves. Pour into a greased 9"x13" pan. Sprinkle 1 cup chopped pecans or walnuts over syrup. Spoon dough over syrup in about 20 dips, and let rise 30 minutes. Bake at 350° until done, about 25-30 minutes.

–Suetta (Rohrer) Horst

Life is like a ladder, every step we take is either up or down.

FUNNEL CAKES

1¼ cups flour
¼ tsp salt
1 tsp baking powder
½ tsp soda
2 Tbsp sugar
1 egg
⅔ cup milk
Oil for frying

Combine dry ingredients. Beat egg. Add milk to it. Stir in flour mixture, beating until smooth. In large skillet heat ½ inch of oil to 375°. Using a small funnel (⅜" opening), hold finger over bottom; fill with batter. Let batter drop in spiral and crisscrossing motion into hot oil, the size of a large pancake. Fry until golden, turning once. Remove and drain on a paper towel. Dust with powdered sugar, and serve hot. A sprinkle of cinnamon tastes good, too.

APPLE FRITTERS

2 cups apple slices
1 cup flour
1 tsp baking powder
½ tsp salt
2 Tbsp sugar
1 egg beaten
⅔ cup milk
Oil for frying

Combine all ingredients, except apples and stir until smooth. Stir apple slices into batter and drop pieces into hot oil (350°-360°) in a deep skillet. Fry until golden brown, turning once. Drain on paper towels. Sift powdered sugar over top and serve warm.

When I was young, our family and relatives would take turns having a "nut picking" social. We'd gather in each home on a late fall evening to crack and shell nuts for holiday baking.

The highlight for the youngsters was helping to make and eat fresh apple and banana fritters, after the nuts were all picked out.

Biscuit Mix (Bisquick)

8 cups flour
⅓ cup baking powder
1 Tbsp salt
2 tsp cream of tartar
3 Tbsp sugar
1½ cups dry milk
2 cups Crisco shortening

Mix dry ingredients. Cut in shortening until mixture has the consistency of cornmeal. Store in a cool place. To measure mix, pile into a cup and level off the top with a knife. Makes 13 cups mix or 4 dozen biscuits.

Biscuits

3½ cups Biscuit mix
⅔ cup milk or water

Stir milk into mix, just enough to moisten Add more liquid if needed. Roll out ½" thick on floured surface. Cut. Bake on ungreased pan at 375° for 10-15 minutes. Makes 12 large biscuits.

Cheese Biscuits

Add 1 cup shredded cheddar to dough. Brush with melted butter and sprinkle with parsley and garlic salt before baking.

A man's reputation is only what men think him to be.
His character is what God knows him to be.

YEAST BISCUITS

3½ cups warm water
3 Tbsp yeast
¾ cup sugar
4 tsp salt
1 cup potato flakes
½ lb margarine
¼ cup dry milk
2¾ lbs Occident flour (7-8 cups)

Mix as usual for yeast breads. (see page 23) Cover and let rise. Roll out on floured surface and cut biscuits. Put on baking sheets and let rise until doubled. Bake at 350° until lightly browned. Makes a soft biscuit that will not crumble like a baking powder biscuit.

These freeze well, and make a good ham biscuit. Recipe makes 6-8 dozen 2" biscuits. Four pounds shaved country ham will fill 100 (2") biscuits.

PIZZA BREAD

Use Yeast Biscuit dough for crust. Press ⅓ lb dough into a 9" pie pan. Top with a thin layer of pizza sauce. Sprinkle with oregano and basil flakes. Top with grated mozzarella or cheddar cheese. Let rise until puffy. Bake at 350° for about 20 minutes.

BACON CHEESE PINWHEELS

Using Yeast Biscuit dough, roll out a portion of dough into a long rectangle, as if to make sweet rolls. Sprinkle with a generous amount of crumbled bacon and grated cheddar cheese. Roll up and seal edges. Cut into ½" slices and place, not touching, in a greased sheet pan. Let rise until doubled. Bake at 350° until a light golden brown. Good eaten warm or cold.

Christian character is not an inheritance,
each person must build it for himself.

ITALIAN FLATBREAD

Dough

1 Tbsp yeast
1 cup warm water
1 tsp sugar
2 Tbsp oil
1 tsp salt
2½ to 3 cups flour

Topping

⅓ cup Zesty Italian dressing
¼ tsp garlic powder
¼ tsp dried oregano
¼ tsp thyme
Dash of pepper
¼ cup Parmesan cheese
1 cup mozzarella cheese

Mix dough ingredients and let rise until doubled. Press into a greased 14" pizza pan. Spread with Italian dressing. Combine seasonings with cheeses and sprinkle on top. Bake at 400° until done. Cut into wedges and serve warm.

Variations: We like to use Colby or cheddar cheese. Any kind is good. Italian seasoning may be used in place of the four herbs.

– *Sharon (Wenger) Good*

SOUTHERN SPOON BREAD

2½ cups milk
1 cup sour cream
1 Tbsp sugar
1½ sticks melted butter
1 lb corn muffin mix (or 2 boxes Jiffy corn muffin mix)
2 eggs, well beaten

Combine milk and sour cream, beat until smooth. Add sugar, butter, muffin mix, and eggs. Blend well and pour into greased 9" bake dish. Bake at 350° about 40-50 minutes. Serve with a spoon.

HUSHPUPPIES

1 cup flour
1 cup cornmeal
2 tsp baking powder
1 tsp salt
½ tsp pepper
½ cup minced fresh onion
1 egg, beaten
1¼ cups milk
Oil for frying

Mix dry ingredients, add onion. Add milk to egg, and whisk into cornmeal mixture. Spoon dough into hot oil (375°) and fry until golden brown. Oil should be at least 1 inch deep. Serves 10-12.

CORNMEAL ROLLS

⅓ cup cornmeal
½ cup sugar
2 tsp salt
½ cup shortening
2 cups milk
1 Tbsp yeast
¼ cup warm water
2 beaten eggs
4 cups flour (approximately)
melted butter and cornmeal for garnish

Sprinkle yeast over warm water. Cook cornmeal, sugar, salt, shortening, and milk in medium saucepan until thick. Cool. Add yeast mixture and eggs. Beat thoroughly. Add flour to form soft dough. Knead well on floured surface. Place in greased bowl. Let rise. Roll out to 1 inch thickness. Cut with biscuit cutter. Brush with melted butter and dust with cornmeal. Place on greased cookie sheets. Cover and let rise. Bake at 375° for 15 minutes. Makes 18 rolls. This dough may be refrigerated for several days.

– Mary Ethel Wenger

LIGHT WHEAT ROLLS

2½ cups flour
1 cup whole-wheat flour
1 tsp salt
¼ cup sugar
1 Tbsp yeast
½ cup shortening
½ cup hot milk
½ cup hot water
1 beaten egg

Combine 2 cups flour, salt, sugar, and yeast. Stir in shortening, milk, water, and egg. Beat 2 minutes. Add remaining flour and knead. Let rise until double, form rolls, and let rise until double again. Bake at 350° until golden. Makes 18 rolls.

– Anna Knicely (Amos)

MOLLIE'S SQUASH ROLLS

1 pkg yeast (1 Tbsp)
1½ cups warm water
1½ cups cooked mashed squash
1 tsp salt
½ cup sugar
½ cup margarine
2 eggs
7½ - 8½ cups flour

Sprinkle yeast over water in mixing bowl and let set. Meanwhile heat squash, salt, sugar, and margarine in saucepan until margarine melts. Beat eggs into yeast mixture. Be sure the squash mixture is not too hot before you add it to the yeast mixture. (You wouldn't want to kill the little yeasts!!) Mix well. Mix in the flour. Knead, punch, and mash at least 130 times. Let rise until double. Punch down and form into spheres a little larger than golf balls. Place ¾" apart in greased pan(s). Let rise until double. Bake at 350° for 20-25 minutes.

– Lois Y. Wenger

A little of the oil of courtesy will save a lot of friction.

MAKE-AHEAD CRESCENT ROLLS

1 cup warm water
1 Tbsp dry yeast
1 Tbsp sugar
3 eggs, beaten
½ cup sugar
½ cup soft shortening
1 tsp salt
5 cups flour

Beat together water, yeast, 1 Tbsp sugar, and eggs and let stand 10 minutes. Add remaining sugar, shortening, and salt. Finally add flour and knead until smooth.

Place in large covered container and refrigerate overnight or up to one week. Divide dough in half. Roll each half in 12-in circle and cut into 16 pie wedges each. Roll up each wedge, starting at wide end. Place in greased baking pans and let rise 2 or 3 hours or until double. Bake at 350° for 12 to 15 minutes. Butter tops. Makes 32 rolls.

Variation: You may roll dough to ½" thickness and cut with a biscuit cutter. A delicious soft roll.

– *Marilyn Eberly*

A Recipe to Pass Along

Spice a day with laughter.
Mix with a happy song.
Add a pinch of friendship,
As you go along.
Stir in lots of loving,
It makes no difference where.
Fold in daily toil
And flavor with a prayer.

CORNBREAD

1 cup flour
¼ cup sugar
1 Tbsp baking powder
¾ tsp salt
1 cup yellow cornmeal
1 egg, beaten
1 cup milk
5 Tbsp butter, melted

Mix first five ingredients, stir in the rest. Bake in greased 8x8 pan at 425° for 20 minutes. Serve with butter and honey.

– Audrey and Amanda Wenger

CINNAMON RAISIN BREAD

2 cups warm water
1½ Tbsp yeast
¼ cup sugar
1¼ cups raisins
1½ tsp salt
6 Tbsp margarine
2 Tbsp dry milk
2 tsp cinnamon
5 – 5 ¼ cups white flour

Mix as usual for breads (see page 23) adding raisins after yeast and sugar. Knead until smooth. Shape into 2 loaves. Let rise until doubled. Bake at 350° for 25-35 minutes.

And Jesus answered him, saying, It is written,
That man shall not live by bread alone,
but by every word of God.

– Luke 4:4

MIXING & BAKING YEAST BREADS

On most recipes, unless other directions are given the following method may be used:

Soften active dry yeast in warm liquid, 110°. Add shortening, sugar, salt, etc. and stir to blend well. Add grains or other ingredients. Then begin stirring in flour, mixing and kneading until dough is smooth, elastic, and satiny to the touch. Cover and let rise in a warm place until dough doubles in size. Shape into desired size loaves, rolls, etc. and place in greased pans. Lightly grease loaves, let rise until doubled, and bake in preheated oven at 350° until done. *

Adding a little ginger or buttermilk powder will help the yeast to work well. To extend the shelf life of your breads add a little lecithin (made from soybeans) or powdered milk.

All recipes use all purpose white flour unless noted otherwise. I use unbleached Occident brand flour. Most grocery and bulk food stores sell bread flour, which is milled from hard (high protein) wheat, so it has more gluten strength than all purpose flour. Gluten is the "glue" which makes dough elastic when it's kneaded. Knead bread a little longer if using bread flour. If you wish to, you can add wheat gluten to your recipes for breads of all kinds. (Add about 1 Tbsp for every 3 cups of all purpose flour).

Flour varies in moisture content; so in recipes using lots of flour, reserve some, and use only if needed in your yeast doughs, etc. Flour is like a sponge. In the winter when houses are warm and dry, flour is dry and can absorb more moisture than in the humid days of summer. You'll likely need a little less flour for winter-time baking, especially in breads and sweet doughs.

*Determining when bread is done can be tricky, especially when making dark wheat breads. After baking the suggested amount of time, check to see if loaves are browning to your liking. Take a loaf from the oven and quickly turn it out of the pan into your gloved hand. Tapping the bottom of the loaf and getting a hollow sound usually signals it is baked. A quick and easy way is to insert an instant-read thermometer into the center of the loaf. When it reaches 190°-200°, the bread is baked. Remove from pans to cool immediately. For a soft crust you may grease loaves again.

Give us this day our daily bread. – Matthew 6:11

CHEESE BREAD

2 cups warm water
1 Tbsp yeast
¼ cup sugar
1 Tbsp salt
¼ cup minced onion
⅓ cup margarine
6 cups white flour
¼ lb grated sharp cheddar cheese

Mix as usual for bread. (see page 23) When all the dough is satiny and smooth, slash deeply with knife and sprinkle cheese over dough and knead just enough to "capture" all the cheese. Shape into 2 loaves. Let rise. Bake at 350º until done.
Variation: Add 2 tsp herbs (thyme, oregano, parsley, etc.).

DILLY BREAD

1 Tbsp yeast
¼ cup warm water
1 cup cottage cheese
2 Tbsp sugar
2 Tbsp butter
2 tsp dill weed (or seed)
1½ Tbsp minced onion
1 tsp salt
¼ tsp soda
1 egg
2¼-2½ cups bread flour

Dissolve yeast in water. Combine with rest of ingredients, adding flour last. Let rise, shape and bake as usual at 350º for 40-50 minutes. Makes 1 loaf. Tastes real good with spaghetti, lasagna, soup, or casseroles. Also good toasted , or for sandwiches.

Work is the yeast that raises the dough.

OATMEAL BREAD

4 cups boiling water
2 cups quick oats
½ cup butter
1 cup water
3 Tbsp yeast
1 Tbsp salt
½ cup honey
½ cup sorghum molasses
1-2 cups whole-wheat flour
7-9 cups bread flour

Pour boiling water over oats. Let set awhile to cool, stir in butter. Soften yeast in 1 cup warm water. Add salt, honey, and molasses. Stir in oatmeal. Add flour gradually, kneading until smooth. Let rise and shape into 4 or 5 loaves. After loaves have doubled, bake at 350° until done, about 30 minutes.

HONEY WHEAT BREAD

2½ cups warm water
2 Tbsp yeast
½ cup honey
⅓ cup oil
1 Tbsp lecithin
2 Tbsp wheat gluten
2 tsp salt
3-4 cups whole-wheat flour
3-4 cups white flour

Mix and bake as usual for bread. (see page 23) Makes 2 large or 3 small loaves.
This bread may be made with all whole-wheat flour.

– *Marilyn Eberly*

Singing to the Lord is like riding an elevator—it gives you a lift.

White Bread and Rolls

2¼ cups warm water
1 Tbsp yeast
⅓ cup sugar
½ cup shortening
1 Tbsp salt
½ cup dry milk
6-6½ cups flour

Mix as usual for bread. (see page 23) Shape as you wish after dough has risen once. Let rise again, bake at 350° until done. Makes 2 dozen dinner rolls or two loaves.

Milk and Honey White Bread

2½ cups warm milk
1 Tbsp yeast
½ cup honey
½ cup melted butter
2½ tsp salt
8-9 cups flour

Dissolve yeast in warm milk. Add honey, butter, salt, and half of flour. Beat well. Add rest of flour and knead until smooth. Let dough rise, then shape into two loaves. When loaves have doubled, bake at 350° for 35-40 minutes. Makes good rolls too.

God meant the Bible to be bread for daily use,
not just cake for special occasions.

POTATO BREAD

½ cup warm water
2 Tbsp yeast
½ cup honey
1 Tbsp salt
1½ cups warm milk
½ cup butter
2 eggs
2 cups mashed potatoes
8 cups (or more) flour

Mix as usual for bread. (see page 23) Makes 3 loaves. A good way to use leftover mashed potatoes. Bake at 350° until done.

HEARTY GRAIN BREAD

4 cups warm water
3 Tbsp yeast
½ cup sorghum molasses
½ cup brown sugar
4 tsp salt
1 cup shortening
1 cup cracked wheat or any grain mix
3 cups whole-wheat flour
8-9 cups bread flour

Mix as usual for yeast breads. (see page 23) Knead well. Let rise until double. Shape into 4 loaves. Let rise until loaves have doubled in size, and bake at 350° for about 30 minutes.

Bread with a friend makes any meal a feast.

SOURDOUGH BREAD

Starter

2 cups warm water
1 Tbsp yeast
1 Tbsp sugar
½ cup potato flakes
2 cups flour

Stir yeast and sugar into water in a large bowl. After 10 minutes or more, stir in potato flakes and flour. Beat until smooth. Cover loosely and let set 12-24 hours at room temperature.

Bread:

sourdough starter
2 cups warm water
1 Tbsp yeast
⅔ cup sugar
4 tsp salt
½ lb margarine
10-11 cups white flour

Dissolve sugar and yeast in warm water. Add salt and soft margarine. Stir in the entire sourdough starter and begin adding flour until dough is stiff enough to knead by hand. Shape into 4 loaves and let rise in bread pans until doubled. Bake at 350° for about 30 minutes.

If you your lips would keep from slips,
Five things observe with care:
Of whom you speak,
To whom you speak,
And how, and when, and where.

Spelt Bread

3 cups warm water
½ cup oil
½ cup honey
1 Tbsp yeast
1 Tbsp salt
3-3¼ lbs. spelt flour

Mix and bake as usual for bread. (see page 23) Makes 3 loaves. The dough for this bread will be sticky and hard to handle. Use a little extra flour to help shape the loaves.

Spelt is an ancient grain grown in the Middle East since before the time of Christ. In Ezekiel 4:9 KJV "fitches" is spelt. It is a relative of wheat and can sometimes be eaten by those who are allergic to wheat. I like spelt bread for its rich, nutty flavor. The loaf tends to be crumbly because spelt is lower in gluten than wheat or barley.

Light Wheat Bread and Rolls

3 cups warm water
2 Tbsp yeast
1 Tbsp salt
3 Tbsp sorghum molasses
½ cup brown sugar
¾ cup shortening
3 cups whole-wheat flour
8-10 cups bread flour
Mix as usual for bread. (see page 23) Makes 3 loaves or 3 dozen dinner rolls. The molasses and brown sugar make this bread extra tasty. This bread is similar to Hearty Grain Bread on pg 27.

Only a baker can make dough and loaf.

100% WHOLE WHEAT BREAD

Sponge

2 cups water
2 tsp yeast
2 cups whole-wheat flour

Other Stuff

2 cups warm water
2 Tbsp yeast
¼ lb margarine
2 Tbsp oil
½ cup honey
1Tbsp salt
7-7½ cups whole-wheat flour

Combine the water and yeast for the sponge and add the flour. Cover loosely and let set for 2-12 hours (I often let it set overnight, but if I'm in a hurry 2 hours is long enough). Combine the rest of the ingredients as usual for bread. (see page 23) Stir in sponge. Add flour until dough can be kneaded by hand. Shape into loaves. Let rise until doubled, and bake at 350° until done. Makes 4 loaves.

PITA POCKET BREAD

1¼ cups warm water
1 Tbsp yeast
1 Tbsp sugar
1 tsp salt
3-4 cups flour (white and whole-wheat)

Dissolve yeast in water. Add sugar, salt, and 2 cups flour. Beat well. Add more flour until smooth. Cover and let rise an hour or so. Knead and shape into 10 balls. Let set 10-15 minutes. Roll each ball into a 5" circle. Place on ungreased baking sheets. Let rise until puffy. Bake at 500° for 5-10 minutes.

Wrap fresh-baked pitas in a paper towel and put them in a brown paper bag for 15 minutes. This keeps them from turning into crackers as they cool. Cut pitas in half and open each pocket to stuff with sandwich fixin's.

FRENCH BREAD

1 Tbsp yeast
⅔ cup warm water
2 cups hot water
2 Tbsp butter
4 tsp sugar
2 tsp salt
6-6½ cups bread flour

Stir yeast and warm water together and let set 10 minutes. Combine other ingredients in large bowl and stir until butter melts. Add 4 cups flour (high gluten bread flour works best) and beat until smooth. Stir in yeast mixture.

Gradually add 2-2½ cups more flour. Dough should be very soft. Let rise until doubled. Punch it down. Let rise again. This long rising time gives French bread its special flavor.

Grease a large baking sheet and sprinkle cornmeal where loaves will be placed. Shape dough into 2 or 3 long loaves. Cut diagonal slits across top. Let rise until double. Bake in 400° oven about 35-40 minutes. Serve warm. For a more traditional French loaf, you may leave out the butter and sugar. It will still be delicious, but won't stay fresh as long.

Garlic French Bread

Cut thick slices, spread with butter, and sprinkle with garlic salt, and parsley if you wish. Heat in oven until crispy.

God bless my little kitchen, I love its every nook;
and bless me as I do my work, wash pots and pans and cook.
As we partake of earthly food, the table for us spread,
we'll not forget to thank Thee who gives us daily bread.

– Amen

HOT CROSS BUNS

2½ cups warm water
½ cup sugar
2 Tbsp yeast
1 tsp cinnamon
2 tsp salt
½ tsp nutmeg
½ cup dry milk
¼ lb margarine
1 tsp orange extract
1 cup raisins or currants
6 – 6½ cups flour

Mix as usual for yeast raised doughs. (see page 23) Let rise. Shape into 1½" balls and put in greased pans. Let rise until doubled. Bake at 350° until done (20-25 minutes). When cooled, make an X on each bun with an icing of powdered sugar, a pinch of salt, vanilla, and milk.

BLUEBERRY MUFFINS

2 cups flour
½ cup sugar
1 Tbsp baking powder
½ tsp salt
1cup fresh or frozen blueberries
1 cup milk
1 egg, slightly beaten
⅓ cup melted butter

Preheat oven to 350°. Combine dry ingredients in large bowl. Stir in blueberries. Measure milk in a 2 cup measure and add egg and melted butter and stir to combine. Make a well in center of dry mixture and pour in milk all at once. Stir quickly with fork, just until moistened. Mixture will be lumpy. Fill muffin cups ⅔ full. Bake at 350° for 20-25 minutes. Makes 18 muffins.

Muffin Tips

The secret to making tender muffins is to mix the batter just until blended. Over-mixing makes them tough and full of holes. Use an ice cream dipper or cookie scoop when dipping muffin batter.

OATMEAL MUFFINS

1 cup oatmeal
1 cup buttermilk
⅓ cup butter
½ cup brown sugar
1 egg
1 cup flour
½ tsp salt
1 tsp baking powder
½ tsp soda

Combine oatmeal and buttermilk and let set 15-45 minutes. Cream butter and sugar. Add egg and oatmeal mixture. Stir in dry ingredients. Bake at 350° for 15-18 minutes. Makes 10-12 muffins.

– *Neva Horst*

SIX WEEK BRAN MUFFINS

1 cup boiling water
3 cups All-Bran cereal
½ cup vegetable oil
1 cup raisins
3 eggs
2 cups buttermilk
1½ cups sugar
2½ cups flour
2½ tsp soda
1 tsp salt
1 tsp cinnamon

Pour boiling water over a cup of cereal. Cool awhile. Add vegetable oil and raisins. Beat eggs until light in mixing bowl. Add buttermilk and sugar. Beat to blend. Stir in dry ingredients, raisin mixture, and the 2 cups of dry All-Bran. Refrigerate batter up to 6 weeks and use as needed. Fill muffin tins ⅔ full. Bake at 350° until done (about 20-25 minutes). These can be made without raisins, and you may use up to half whole-wheat flour.

SOFT PRETZELS

1 Tbsp yeast
1 tsp white sugar
1¼ cups warm water
¼ cup firmly packed brown sugar
½ tsp salt
3-3¼ cups bread flour
3 cups water
3 Tbsp baking soda
pretzel salt
2 Tbsp butter. melted

Combine yeast, sugar, and warm water. Let stand 5 minutes. Combine yeast mixture, brown sugar, salt and bread flour in large bowl. Stir in extra flour if needed to make soft dough. (May use part whole-wheat flour.) Turn dough out onto lightly floured surface. Knead until smooth (about 3 minutes). Cover and let rest 20 minutes. Cut the dough in desired size and roll into 12-15 inch rope. Shape into pretzel shape. Combine soda and water in saucepan and make hot. Dip each pretzel into mixture, drain on a towel temporarily, and place on greased baking sheet. Sprinkle with salt. Let rise until doubled. Bake at 475º for 6 minutes or until golden brown. Brush with butter. Serve immediately. Makes 6 large or 12 small pretzels.

Cheese sauce or mustard sauce is good on pretzels. (See recipes on page 297) For variation, coat buttered pretzels with a cinnamon-sugar mixture. Delicious!!

– *Marilyn Eberly*

*Whatever you dislike in another person
be sure to correct in yourself.*

CHEESE STICKS

1 cup all-purpose flour
1½ tsp baking powder
½ tsp salt
2 Tbsp butter or margarine
⅔ cup shredded sharp cheddar cheese
⅓ cup cold water

Mix flour, baking powder and salt in medium bowl. Cut in butter or margarine with pastry blender until mixture is crumbly. Add cheese. Toss until well blended. Sprinkle water over mixture and mix lightly with fork until pastry holds together and leaves the side of the bowl clean. Roll on a floured surface into a 12 x 10-inch rectangle. Use a pizza cutter to cut in half lengthwise; then cut each half crosswise into ½" strips. Lift strips one at a time, twist and place 1-inch apart on an ungreased cookie sheet. Bake at 425° for 10 minutes or until lightly golden. Makes 4 dozen. Good with soup or salad.

Recipe for a Good Day

Take two parts of unselfishness,
And one part of patience, and work together.
Add plenty of industry;
Lighten with good spirits,
And sweeten with kindness.
Put in smiles as thick as raisins in plum pudding,
And bake by the warmth which streams from a loving heart.
If this fails to make a good day,
The fault is not with the recipe but with the cook.

Zucchini, Pumpkin, or Banana Bread

3 beaten eggs
2 cups sugar
2 tsp vanilla
2 cups shredded zucchini or mashed cooked pumpkin or
  mashed bananas
1 cup oil
3 cups flour
½ tsp baking powder
1 tsp soda
1 tsp salt
2 tsp cinnamon
1 cup chopped pecans or walnuts

Mix all ingredients together. Pour into greased and floured loaf pans. Makes 2 large or 4 small loaves. Bake at 325° until done.

Lemon Bread

1 large lemon
1 Tbsp grated lemon peel
1½ cups flour
1 tsp baking powder
¾ tsp salt
½ cup vegetable oil
1 cup sugar
2 large eggs
½ cup milk
½ cup chopped nuts, or ⅓ cup poppy seeds

Glaze:
3 Tbsp fresh lemon juice and ¼ cup sugar

Grate lemon, cut and squeeze juice, reserve 3 Tbsp for glaze. If any juice is left, add it to your ½ cup measure and fill with milk for bread batter. Combine flour, baking powder and salt. Set aside. In mixing bowl beat sugar and oil, beat in eggs and lemon peel. Add flour mixture and milk, stir in nuts. Pour batter into 3 small greased loaf pans. Bake at 350° about 35 minutes (toothpick inserted in center should come out clean). Combine sugar and lemon juice for glaze. With a fork poke holes in hot loaves after baking and slowly spoon glaze over loaves in the pans. After 10 or 15 minutes, remove loaves to cool. Wrap in plastic wrap to seal in moisture.

CRANBERRY NUT BREAD

2½ cups all purpose flour
1½ tsp baking powder
½ tsp soda
1 tsp salt
1¼ cups sugar
1 cup fresh orange juice
¼ cup oil
1 Tbsp orange rind
2 eggs
1 cup fresh cranberries, chopped
1 cup pecans or walnuts

Combine flour, baking powder, soda, and salt. Blend the sugar, juice, oil, rind, and eggs in a bowl. Add dry ingredients and mix. Stir in nuts and berries. Grease and flour 4 small or 2 medium loaf pans. Bake at 350° until done, but don't overbake. This recipe also makes good muffins.

ITALIAN COFFEE CAKE

2½ cups flour
¾ cup sugar
1 cup brown sugar
1 tsp salt
¾ cup oil
1 tsp baking powder
1 tsp soda
1 tsp nutmeg
1 egg
1 cup buttermilk or sour milk
1 cup chopped nuts or sunflower seeds
1 tsp cinnamon

Combine flour, sugars, salt, and oil to make crumbs. Set aside ¾ cup crumb mixture. To crumbs remaining, add baking powder, soda, nutmeg, egg and milk. Mix well. Pour into greased and floured 10 x 15 pan. Mix together nuts, cinnamon, and reserved ¾ cup crumbs. Sprinkle over batter and bake at 350° for 20-25 minutes.

ORANGE BOWKNOTS

Dough
¼ cup warm water
⅓ cup sugar
1 Tbsp yeast
1 cup hot milk
½ cup butter
¼ cup orange juice
2 eggs, beaten
2 Tbsp grated orange peel
½ tsp salt
5 cups flour

Glaze
1-2 Tbsp orange juice
1 tsp orange rind
1 cup powdered sugar

Combine water, sugar, and yeast. Let set 10 minutes. Mix milk and butter. Add orange juice and eggs. Stir in yeast mixture and add rest of ingredients. Knead until smooth. Let rise until double. Roll out ½" thick in a 5x12 rectangle. Cut ½" strips and tie into a loose knot. Put on baking sheet and let rise until double. Bake at 350° until done. Drizzle with orange glaze. Makes 24.

—Mary Bendfeldt (Eric)

Six Things We Need for a Successful Life:

❖ *Sincerity*

❖ *Courtesy*

❖ *Humility*

❖ *Wisdom*

❖ *Integrity*

❖ *Charity*

APRICOT DANISH

Use orange dough (as in Orange Bowknots) or plain sweet dough and roll into a large rectangle. Cut into 3" squares and put a teaspoon or two of apricot filling in center. If you'd like something really grand, spoon some cheese filling in it, too. Fold dough over and seal. Let rise and bake. Glaze with orange glaze (see Bowknots) or Danish Drizzle.

Apricot Filling

You may cook dried apricots (diced) or canned apricots (mashed). Cook until liquid is about gone. Thicken with clearjel if you'd like to speed things up. Add sugar to taste.

Cheese Danish Filling

1 egg
½ cup milk
8 oz cream cheese

Beat egg. Add milk and cheese and beat until smooth.

Danish Drizzle

2 egg whites
¼ cup water
2 tsp vanilla
pinch of salt
2 cups powdered sugar

Beat egg whites until stiff and add remaining ingredients.

– *Mary Bendfeldt (Eric)*

Happiness is like honey—you can pass it around,
but some of it will stick to you.

OVERNIGHT PANCAKES

1 Tbsp dry yeast
¼ cup warm water
4 cups flour
2 Tbsp baking powder
2 tsp baking soda
2 tsp sugar
1 tsp salt
6 eggs
1 quart buttermilk
¼ cup vegetable oil

In a small bowl, dissolve yeast in water. Let stand 5 minutes.
Meanwhile, in a large bowl, combine dry ingredients. Beat eggs,
buttermilk, and oil. Stir into dry ingredients just until moistened.
Stir in yeast mixture and refrigerate overnight.

We have fried all the pancakes and frozen some. They warm well
later. The batter refrigerates very well.

– *Esther Burkholder*

BELGIAN WAFFLES

4 eggs, separated
2 cups milk
½ cup melted butter
1 tsp vanilla
3 cups flour
1 tsp salt
2 Tbsp sugar
1 Tbsp baking powder

Beat egg yolks. Add milk, butter, vanilla and dry ingredients. Beat
well. Fold in stiffly beaten egg whites. Bake in waffle iron. Serve
with your favorite toppings: warm maple syrup, sausage gravy, fruit
and whipped cream, etc. Makes 4 large waffles or 8 small ones.
Good for supper, too!

*Junk: the things we keep for years,
and then throw away just before we need them.*

COUNTRY MORNING PANCAKES

2 eggs beaten
2½ cups buttermilk or 2 cups milk
½ tsp soda
2 tsp baking powder
1 tsp salt
1 tsp cinnamon
1 cup whole-wheat flour
1 cup oatmeal
1 cup white flour
2 Tbsp brown sugar

Add milk to eggs in mixing bowl. Stir in dry ingredients until evenly mixed. Use nonstick spray or grease in skillet. Fry as usual.

This was a favorite of the girls that worked in my home. We enjoyed them covered with blackberry sauce, warm maple syrup, or crushed strawberries and whipped cream, (with lots of hot coffee on the side). Yummmmm! Worth getting up for!

APPLE PECAN PANCAKES

1 cup flour
2 tsp baking powder
½ tsp salt
1 tsp cinnamon
2 Tbsp brown sugar
¾ cup plus 2 Tbsp milk
2 eggs, separated
1 tsp vanilla
½ cup finely chopped, peeled apple
½ cup finely chopped pecans

In a bowl, combine first 5 ingredients. Stir in milk, egg yolks, and vanilla. Add apples and pecans. Beat egg whites until stiff, fold into the batter. Fry in hot, greased griddle. Serve with maple syrup.

If there were more self starters, the boss wouldn't have to be a crank.

STUFFED FRENCH TOAST

12 slices white bread
8 oz cream cheese
2 cups fresh or frozen blueberries
8 eggs
2 cups milk
½ cup brown sugar
½ tsp salt

Put 6 slices bread in greased 9x13 pan. Put sliced cream cheese over bread and sprinkle berries on top. Cover with remaining bread. Beat eggs, add milk, brown sugar, salt and a pinch of cinnamon if you wish. Pour over all. Chill overnight. Bake at 350° for 50-60 minutes until golden. Serve with Blueberry Sauce.

Blueberry Sauce

1 cup sugar
pinch of salt
1 cup water

1½ cups blueberries
3 Tbsp cornstarch
½ cup water

Bring sugar, salt, water and berries to a boil. Blend cornstarch and ½ cup water and stir into berries. Cook until thickened. Serve over French Toast. Serves 6-8.

FRENCH TOAST FOR ONE

1 large egg, beaten
¼ cup milk
¼ tsp vanilla or orange flavoring
1 tsp sugar
pinch of salt
cinnamon or nutmeg
2 slices bread

Melt 2 tsp butter in a skillet. Combine ingredients and pour into a shallow pan over bread. Place bread in hot skillet and fry until toasted, turning once. Serve hot with syrup or jelly, for a satisfying breakfast. (This is especially good when made with a multigrain bread.)

Where there's smoke, there's toast. ☹

GEORGIA FRENCH TOAST CASSEROLE

2 Tbsp dark corn syrup
½ cup butter
1 cup brown sugar
1 loaf bread
6 eggs
1 tsp salt
1½ cups milk

Combine first 3 ingredients and simmer until melted and syrupy (but not too long). Pour into 9x13 pan. Layer bread double over syrup. Mix eggs, salt, and milk and pour over bread. Cover and refrigerate overnight. Bake uncovered at 350° for 45 minutes.

– Dorothy (Shank) Wenger

SUNDAY CREPES

*Crepes are very thin pancakes, and are fun and easy to make. They can be served with whipped cream or cottage cheese and fruit for breakfast, or as a dessert. They can be wrapped around cooked chicken or ham, and covered with a creamy sauce for a light supper. Combine honey, butter and pecans, or fill them with vanilla pudding and top with chocolate sauce or fruit. The possibilities are many. Just use your imagination. My favorite filling is cottage cheese and strawberry jam.
2 eggs
1 cup milk
1 cup flour
½ tsp salt
1 or 2 Tbsp sugar (for sweet crepes)
2 tsp orange juice concentrate (for sweet crepes)
2 Tbsp melted butter

Combine all in a bowl and beat well for a minute. Heat a nonstick skillet and grease it lightly. Pour a scant ¼ cup batter in hot skillet and tilt pan to make a 5" or 6" crepe. Thin your batter if it doesn't spread easily to make a very thin crepe. Turn with a spatula when light golden brown. Put filling down the center and roll up crepes. These keep several days in fridge (unfilled). Warm them up for a quick meal.* (Crepes rhymes with grapes)

WELSH RABBIT (CHEESE SAUCE) AND TOAST

Long ago the peasants in England (Wales) were not allowed to hunt on the noblemen's estates. While the rich folk dined on rabbit, the peasants enjoyed their "Welsh Rabbit."

4 cups milk
½ cup flour
¼ cup butter
½ tsp salt
dash of pepper
½ tsp dry mustard
½ tsp Worcestershire Sauce
4 cups cubed Velveeta cheese

Heat 3 cups milk in a heavy saucepan. Make a batter of 1 cup milk and the flour. Stir it into hot milk and continue stirring over medium heat until thickened. Add remaining ingredients. Stir until cheese melts. Add more milk if it seems too thick. Serve over toasted homemade bread or biscuits, chopped hard-boiled eggs, or broken crackers. Tastes good with applesauce.

–Charlotte Rohrer

EGG CHEESE PATTIES

4 eggs, beaten
1 Tbsp grated onion
⅓ cup flour
salt and pepper to taste
1 tsp baking powder
⅓ lb sharp cheddar cheese, grated

Mix all together. Dip large spoon of egg mixture into hot shortening. Brown well on both sides, turning once. Serve with jelly, syrup, hot sauce, relish, sausage gravy, etc. Makes 12.

–Mary Rohrer (Raymond)

Be like a postage stamp, stick to one thing until you get there.

BREAKFAST BAKE

4 slices bread, cubed
1½ lbs pork sausage
1½ cups grated cheddar cheese
9 eggs, beaten
3 cups milk
1½ tsp dry mustard
1 tsp salt

Put bread cubes in greased 9x13 pan. Brown sausage and sprinkle over bread. Top with cheese. Beat eggs, and add milk, salt, and mustard. Pour over all. Refrigerate overnight. Bake at 325° for 1 hour, uncovered.

Variations: You may use ham, or bacon instead of sausage. Any kind of cheese may be used. A little chopped onion is good too.

❖ *To check your egg casseroles for doneness, use a quick-read thermometer in the center. (160° is done)*

BREAKFAST CASSEROLE

6-8 slices bread
1 lb cheese, grated
onions, mushrooms, bacon, ham, peppers, tomatoes, etc.
8 eggs
3 cups milk
1 tsp salt
1 tsp dry mustard

Cut bread into 1 inch cubes. Place in greased 9x13 pan. Sprinkle cheese over bread, then assorted veggies and meats. Beat eggs, add milk and seasonings, and pour over all. Refrigerate 6 hours or overnight. Bake at 325° for about an hour. Serves 8-10

Prayer is the oil for the daily grind.

FARMER'S BREAKFAST

1 lb bacon, fried and crumbled
1 small onion, chopped
2 cups chopped ham
10 slices bread, cubed
1 cup cooked, cubed potatoes
3 cups grated cheddar cheese
8 eggs
3 cups milk
1 tsp dry mustard
1 tsp salt
1Tbsp Worcestershire sauce
¼ tsp pepper

Fry onion in a little bacon grease. Layer first six ingredients in greased 9x13 dish. Combine beaten eggs, milk and seasonings. Pour over all. Refrigerate overnight. Bake uncovered at 325° for an hour. Serve with applesauce, juice and coffee.

–Austin and Marie Eberly

BREAKFAST PIZZA I

1 8-oz container Crescent rolls
½ lb sausage
½ cup chopped onion
1 cup shredded cheddar cheese
2 Tbsp minced red or green pepper
4 eggs lightly beaten
¾ cup milk
½ tsp salt
½ tsp oregano
⅛ tsp black pepper
1 cup shredded mozzarella cheese

Spread roll dough into greased 9x13 pan. Sauté sausage and onion in skillet. Drain and sprinkle over dough. Sprinkle cheddar and minced pepper over sausage. Combine the eggs, milk, and seasonings until well blended. Pour over mixture in the pan. Sprinkle mozzarella on top. Bake at 350° for 25 minutes. Makes 6 servings.

– Melinda (Wenger) Knicely

JANE'S GOOD BREAKFAST DISH

1 stick butter
1 cup Bisquick
1½ cups cottage cheese
½ lb shredded cheddar cheese
2 Tbsp onion, chopped fine
1 tsp parsley flakes
½ tsp salt
6 eggs, lightly beaten
2 cups milk
Chopped spinach or broccoli, optional

Melt butter in 9x13 bake dish. Mix all ingredients and pour over melted butter in dish. Bake at 350° for 40 minutes.

BREAKFAST PIZZA II

1 large pizza crust, unbaked

Press crust on bottom and sides of 10 x 15 pan. You may use your favorite recipe, or one half Stromboli dough on page 70.

½ lb bacon, fried and crumbled
2 cups shredded cheddar cheese
4 eggs, beaten
1½ cups sour cream
2 Tbsp chopped fresh parsley

Sprinkle bacon and cheese evenly over crust. Combine eggs, sour cream, and parsley until blended. Pour over crust and bake at 350° for 20-25 minutes.

– *Charlotte Rohrer*

Friendship is to people what sunshine is to flowers.

St. Louis Breakfast Eggs

2 Tbsp butter
½ cup chopped peppers
8 beaten eggs
salt
pepper
pinch onion salt
celery salt
dry mustard
Worcestershire Sauce
dash milk
several slices of Velveeta cheese
sliced tomatoes
hot pepper sauce

Sauté peppers in butter in skillet. Combine eggs, milk, and seasonings. Pour into skillet and stir while cooking over medium heat. Top with Velveeta cheese, slices of fresh tomato, and a little hot sauce. Goes good with tortilla chips for a hearty meal.

—Jesse Rohrer

Baked Omelet

6-8 slices bacon
¼ cup minced onion
8 eggs, lightly beaten
1 cup milk
1 Tbsp fresh parsley
1 tsp salt
¼ tsp pepper
1 cup shredded cheddar cheese
1 cup shredded Swiss cheese
1 Tbsp flour

Fry bacon. Reserve 1 Tbsp grease in skillet. Sauté onions. Combine eggs, crumbled bacon, milk, salt, pepper, onions, and parsley. Combine flour and grated cheeses. Add to egg mixture. Pour into a greased 1½ quart casserole and bake at 325° for 40-50 minutes.
Variation: Add grated cooked potatoes into egg mixture for a hearty dish.

Swiss Alpine Quiche

2 - 9" unbaked pie crusts
1 pint cooked, drained broccoli
2 cups cubed ham
2 cups shredded Swiss cheese
3 Tbsp minced onion
2 cups warm milk
3 eggs beaten
⅛ tsp salt
⅛ tsp pepper

Layer first 4 ingredients in pie crusts. Combine rest of ingredients. Pour over all. Bake at 450° for 10 minutes and then at 325° for 30 minutes. Serve hot. Serves 6-8.

Variation: You may use crumbled, fried bacon or sausage instead of ham, and asparagus or mushrooms instead of broccoli.

Quick Quiche

Using suggestions from the above recipe, prepare 3 cups of filling ingredients. Put vegetables, meat, and cheese in a well-greased pie plate. Mix a topping with:

1 cup Bisquick (see recipe on page 16)
2 cups milk
4 eggs
½ tsp salt
pinch of pepper

Pour over all and bake at 350° for 30 minutes.

*I go for square meals, but I find with regret
That the squarer they are, the rounder I get.*

POTATO AND EGG SCRAMBLE

2-4 slices bacon
2 cups thin sliced raw potatoes
1 tsp salt
4 eggs beaten
¼ cup milk
dash of pepper

In a skillet, fry bacon until crisp. Remove bacon and add potatoes. Sprinkle with salt and fry over medium heat, stirring occasionally until potatoes are browned. Cover and cook over low heat until potatoes are tender. Combine eggs, milk, and pepper. Pour over 'taters and fry slowly, stirring occasionally until eggs are set. Top with crumbled bacon. A sprinkle of grated cheese will top it off. (You may use leftover boiled potatoes instead of raw).

POTATO PANCAKES

4 medium size raw potatoes
2 eggs, separated
1 tsp salt
dash pepper
2 Tbsp flour
¼ - ½ cup minced onion
3-4 Tbsp oil

Grate potatoes. Beat egg yolks. Stir into potatoes. Add dry ingredients and onion. Beat egg whites until stiff and fold into egg mixture. Heat the oil in a griddle. Drop batter by large tablespoonsfull onto griddle and brown both sides until crispy and done. These are good topped with salsa for a light meal, or Super Sausage Gravy and fried apples for bigger appetites.

You know you're getting up there in age
when it takes you longer to rest than it did to get tired.

BAKED OATMEAL

½ cup white sugar
½ cup brown sugar
⅓ cup vegetable oil
2 eggs beaten
2 tsp baking powder
1 tsp salt
½ tsp cinnamon
1 cup milk
3 cups quick oats
½ cup raisins, blueberries or grated apples, optional

Mix sugars, oil and eggs until smooth. Add rest of ingredients in order given. Mix well. Pour into greased 8x8 pan. Bake at 350° for 25 minutes. Serve warm with milk.

– Sharon (Wenger) Good

OATMEAL SUPREME

2 cups oatmeal
½ cup cornmeal
⅓ cup oat bran
⅓ cup wheat bran
⅓ cup Hot Ralston cereal
¼ cup wheat germ
raisins

Combine dry ingredients and put into a quart jar. When you want to eat some, heat water and raisins to boiling. Stir in dry mix and cook a little bit. (Ratio of water to oatmeal mix is about 2:1) Serve with milk and brown sugar.

– Lois Y. Wenger

Age is a matter of the mind,
if you don't mind, it doesn't matter.

Honey Granola

6 cups oatmeal
½ cup brown sugar
½ cup nuts or seeds
½ cup oat bran
¾ tsp salt
½ cup coconut
¼ cup (or more) wheat germ
1 cup oil
2 Tbsp water
½ cup honey

Mix dry ingredients and wet ingredients separately. Then mix together and spread on baking sheets. Bake at 325° for ½ hr, stirring occasionally.

–Elizabeth Rohrer

Melissa's Granola

12 cups quick oats
4-6 cups rolled oats
3 cups coconut
2 cups grape nuts
6 cups Rice Krispies
2 cups wheat germ
3½ cups brown sugar
½ cup maple syrup
4 tsp vanilla
2 tsp salt
2 cups oil
1 cup water

Stir first 6 ingredients together. Combine last 6 and pour over dry mixture. Stir. Bake in 250° oven for 1 hour or until crispy. Add almonds, sunflower seeds, pecans, apricots, cranberries, etc.

–Melissa (Rohrer) Wenger

Hurry is the mother of most mistakes.
Haste makes waste.

MARYBETH'S GRANOLA

10 cups oatmeal
2 cups chopped nuts
1 cup coconut
¼ cup wheat germ
1 tsp salt
4 tsp cinnamon
¼ cup brown sugar
½ cup melted butter
½ cup honey
2 tsp vanilla

Combine first 7 ingredients in large bowl. Mix remaining ingredients to make a sauce. Pour over the dry ingredients, and mix well. Spread on large baking sheet and bake at 250° for 1 hr, stirring occasionally. May add 2 cups raisins or dried fruits of your choice after baking.

– Clarke and Marybeth Eberly

CHEESE GRITS

4 cups water
½ tsp salt
1 cup quick cooking grits

Bring water and salt to a near boil. Stir grits into water with a wire whisk and mix until lumps are gone. Reduce heat, simmer 5 minutes, stirring occasionally. Stir in:

1 Tbsp butter
½ cup grated cheddar cheese
¼ lb Velveeta cheese, cubed

Serves 12-14. A Southern favorite that will stick to your ribs.

A coincidence is a small miracle,
where God prefers to remain anonymous.

SIMPLE SCONES

Scones are a rich, sweet, and flavorful biscuit; often served with hot tea or coffee.

2 cups flour
1 tsp baking powder
¼ tsp soda
⅓ cup sugar
½ tsp salt
8 Tbsp <u>cold</u> butter (1 stick)
1 large egg, beaten
½ cup sour cream

Mix dry ingredients and cut in butter with a pastry blender or fork to make crumbs. Add the goodies you have chosen to flavor your scones. (See list below.) Lightly stir in egg and sour cream to moisten crumbs. Form 2 balls, turn each out onto a floured surface and shape with hands, into an 8" circle. Sprinkle generously with coarse sugar if you like. Cut dough into eight wedges and place on greased cookie sheets with space in between. Let set 10 minutes. Bake at 375° until lightly browned, 15-18 minutes. Serve warm with butter, jam, lemon curd, Devonshire cream or other toppings.

Variations: Add ¾ cup dried cherries and 1 tsp almond flavor; or use any other fruits: craisins and orange zest, apples and cinnamon, raisins and vanilla, pear and fresh ginger.
For a non-sweet scone, omit most of the sugar, and stir in 1 cup grated sharp cheddar and 2 tsp chopped fresh thyme or dill.

<u>Toppings for Scones, Muffins, Etc.</u>

<u>Mock Devonshire Cream</u>
8 oz. soft cream cheese, or whipped cream
¼ cup powdered sugar
½ cup sour cream

Blend all together until creamy.

The best vitamin for making friends is B-1.

Lemon Curd

4 eggs
2 cups sugar
½ cup butter, melted
1 cup lemon juice
3 Tbsp grated lemon peel
⅛ tsp salt

Beat eggs in top of double boiler. Add rest of ingredients and stir over simmering water until mixture thickens, and reaches 160°. Pour into heated jars and seal. Store in fridge. Good for topping scones, muffins or pound cake, and for lemon tarts.

TEA PARTY MENU IDEAS

All recipes can be found within this book.

Savory Bites

❖ Creamy soups and chowders
❖ Tiny sandwiches: egg salad, pimento cheese, chicken salad, ham biscuits
❖ Cheese sticks, bacon cheese pinwheels
❖ Shrimp dip, cheese ball (with crackers)
❖ Stuffed cherry tomatoes, stuffed mushrooms
❖ Mixed vegetable pickles

Sweet Treats

❖ Scones with Devonshire cream
❖ Fresh fruits and dip, raspberry trifle
❖ Quickbreads: lemon, cranberry, pumpkin, banana
❖ Mini muffins, sweet rolls, apricot danish
❖ Cream puffs, pecan tarts, brownie bites
❖ Little cookies: lemon crackers, pecan puffs, sugar cookies
❖ Chocolate truffles (orange or mint)

Serve with your favorite teas, (hot or cold) on your prettiest china, with a vase of flowers on the side, and surrounded by your friends. Take your time and enjoy the refreshments and the fellowship.

Come and share a pot of tea, my home is warm and my friendship free.

After Breakfast Prayer

Dear Lord, now that my family has gone to work and to school,
    a sudden quiet falls on this disordered house.

Help me to face the work for this day with a singing heart –
    the dishes to wash, the beds to make, the clothes to launder,
        and the picking up which sometimes seems as futile
            as sweeping the forest floor in autumn.

I thank Thee that I am needed;
    that my job in these busy years is to create a home
        that will be a place of warmth and comfort and love.

Help me to see each task, not as a dull chore,
    but as a strand woven into a pattern of living.

Grant, I pray, that it may be a pattern to remember,
    a pattern of order and beauty,
        and through it always may there gleam the
            golden thread of Christ's spirit.

– Amen.

Main Dishes
and
Meats

Cruelty of Cooks

If you itemize the terms of cooks,
You'll find we quite deceive our looks.
The things we do sound very cruel,
Like fighting a one-sided duel.

We beat the eggs, whip the cream,
Blow pudding up with hot steam,
We mash potatoes, slice the bread,
Tear apart the cabbage's head.

We chop the onion, grate the cheese,
Lemons and oranges get a squeeze,
We burn the sugar, gash the steak,
The celery's heart we often take.

We skin the tomato, peel the pear,
Scrape the carrots everywhere,
We scald the milk, freeze the salad,
Strain the tea that's really pallid.

We prick the unsuspecting pie,
And remove the baby potato's eye.
And then if that's not enough,
We smother chickens and other stuff.

Goodness knows what else we do,
I'm really quite abashed, aren't you?
We do all this and never cry—
'Til we get onions in our eye.

– Reprinted with permission
from the *MDS Cookbook*

Main Dishes and Meats

CRISPY FRIED TROUT

fresh trout – 1 per person
oil or margarine
flour and cornmeal
salt and pepper

Rinse freshly caught trout in cold water. If time allows, soak in
salt water. Roll in flour and cornmeal mixture. Fry in hot oil or
margarine over medium-high heat, turning once. Takes about 10
minutes, depending on thickness. Season with salt and pepper.
Serve at once.

GOLDEN FRIED FISH

Boneless fish fillets of your choice (flounder, catfish, perch, etc.)
1 egg, beaten with ½ cup milk
1 box Jiffy cornbread mix

Dip fish in egg mixture, coat with dry cornbread mix. Fry in just
enough hot oil to cover bottom of a heavy skillet. Season with salt
and pepper.

A fish in the frying pan is worth a dozen in the creek.

Shrimp Stuffed Flounder

½ cup chopped celery
½ cup chopped onion
¼ cup butter
1½ cups moistened bread cubes
1 lb chopped, cooked salad shrimp
2 Tbsp chopped parsley
1 egg, slightly beaten
salt and pepper
4 medium whole flounders or 8 fillets

Sauté celery and onion in butter over low heat. Add bread cubes, shrimp, parsley and egg. Sprinkle salt and pepper over stuffing and stir to combine flavors.

Split thick side of fish to make a pocket to stuff with bread mixture. (I use fillets, arranged in a single layer in a buttered sheet pan. Then spoon filling over fillets and bake at 350° until done). If using whole fish, brush top of fish with melted butter, salt and pepper. Bake whole fish at 375° for 30 minutes.

Scalloped Oysters

1 pint oysters
soda crackers
thin slices Velveeta cheese
salt
pepper
1 egg, beaten
½ cup milk
liquid from oysters

Grease a 1½ quart casserole dish. Layer unbroken crackers, then oysters, salt, pepper, and cheese. Repeat. Top with crackers. Combine egg and liquids. Pour over all. Let set 15 minutes or more. Bake at 350° about 30 minutes.

– Neva Horst

People forget how fast you did a job-
but they remember how well you did it.

-Howard Newton

PAN FRIED OYSTERS

1 gallon fresh, shucked oysters
4 eggs
1 tsp salt

Breading

1½ lbs crushed saltines
¾ cup cornmeal
3 Tbsp flour
2 tsp salt
1 tsp pepper

Drain oysters in a colander to remove liquid. Beat eggs and stir in 1 tsp salt. Combine breading ingredients and put in a shallow bowl.

Dip oysters, several at a time into eggs. Remove with a slotted spoon and drop them into the crumb mixture. Roll oysters to coat well, form cakes and let set several hours or overnight in fridge. Put wax paper or saran wrap between layers in container.

Fry until golden brown over medium heat. I use half Crisco shortening and half butter at a depth of about ⅛" of grease in the skillet. Keep oysters in warm oven until served.

Serve with cocktail sauce, mashed potatoes and your favorite salad. 1 gallon serves 16-20 oyster lovers.

OYSTER DRESSING

1 cup onion, chopped fine
1 cup celery, chopped fine
¾ cup butter
12 cups cubed stale bread
3 eggs, beaten
1½ cups milk
1½ tsp salt
1-1½ pints oysters, cut into pieces and save the liquid

Sauté onion and celery in butter. Combine eggs, milk, salt, and oyster liquid. Toss bread with onion mixture. Layer in 9x13 greased casserole dish with oysters hidden in the middle. Pour egg mixture over all. Bake at 350° until done, 45-55 minutes.

Smoked Salmon

Fillets of fresh salmon
1 quart water
¼ cup Morton's Tenderquick

Mix water and Tenderquick together. Add salmon and marinate in refrigerator for several hours. Fire up your wood or charcoal grill and smoke fish with your choice of woods, using indirect heat to cook fish. When meat flakes easily, remove to serving platter, drizzle with melted butter, and keep it hot until ready to serve. I serve it with a creamy dill sauce, or drizzle with frozen lemonade concentrate (thawed). (Scrub your grill rack with hot, soapy water to remove all traces of fish. If you don't, the flavor will ruin the next thing you grill.)

Creamy Dill Sauce

½ cup sour cream   2 tsp dill weed
½ cup mayonnaise   ¼ tsp of salt
4 tsp lemonade concentrate

Hot Pizza Dip

2 lbs sausage or hamburger
1 cup chopped peppers
1 cup chopped onions
8 oz cream cheese
1 pint pizza sauce
1 - 4 oz can sliced mushrooms
slices of pepperoni
2 cups shredded cheddar cheese

Brown meat in skillet and add peppers and onions when meat is almost done. Drain excess grease. Stir in pizza sauce. Spread cream cheese on bottom of 9x13 bake dish. Top with meat mixture, mushrooms and pepperoni. Last add cheese and bake at 350° for 30-40 minutes. Serve with crackers, corn chips, vegetables, etc. or Italian flat bread (see recipe page 18), and a frosty cold drink.
– *Jesse Rohrer*

Steamed Shrimp

1 lb shrimp in shell or peeled
1 pint water
1 cup vinegar
2 Tbsp Old Bay Seasoning
1 Tbsp salt

Rinse shrimp in cold water, drain. Heat rest of ingredients in sauce-pot to boiling. Stir in shrimp, cover, and cook until shrimp are pink. Do not overcook, it makes them tough. Serve with melted butter or cocktail sauce.

Barbecued Shrimp

5 lbs unpeeled shrimp
1½ cups butter
1 8-oz bottle Italian salad dressing
⅓ cup lemon juice
¼ cup olive (or cooking) oil
2-3 cloves garlic, peeled and minced
½ tsp hot pepper sauce
1 Tbsp black pepper, or to taste
1 Tbsp Worcestershire Sauce

Wash shrimp and drain well.

Melt butter in 3 quart casserole dish while you are preheating oven to 350º. Add salad dressing, lemon juice, oil, garlic, hot pepper sauce, pepper, and Worcestershire Sauce to butter. Stir to combine. Add shrimp.

Cover and bake 35-45 minutes, stirring occasionally so all shrimp cook evenly. Shrimp turn bright pink when done. Be sure all are completely cooked.

This is good reheated, but should not be frozen. Delicious served with melted butter and cocktail sauce. You will need to have plenty of napkins, and bowls for the shells on the table.

– Lorna (Good) Wenger

*Be not forgetful to entertain strangers: for thereby
some have entertained angels unawares. – Hebrews 13:2*

Favorite Pizza

1¾ cups warm water
1 Tbsp sugar
1 Tbsp yeast
2 tsp salt
¼ cup oil
5-6 cups flour (may use up to 1 cup of whole-wheat flour)

Mix as usual for yeast dough. (see page 23) Let rise. Divide dough. Roll out and put into 2 or 3 pizza pans. Let rise again. Pre-bake crust at 375° for 10-12 minutes. Freeze or use within a day. Cover with your choice of toppings:

❖ Pizza sauce (don't overdo it because too much makes a soggy pizza - ⅔ cup will cover a 12" crust)
❖ Browned, drained sausage, hamburger, or bacon; pepperoni; diced ham, etc.
❖ Basil or oregano flakes
❖ Chopped peppers, onions, mushrooms, or ripe olives
❖ Very thinly sliced summer squash or tomatoes
❖ Lots of Mozzarella, Colby, Provolone, etc.

Bake at 375° until pizza is piping hot and cheese is melted. I usually bake it until it is almost done before adding cheese.

Stovetop Spaghetti

2 lbs hamburger
1 cup chopped onion
1 quart tomato juice
2½ cups ketchup
½ cup brown sugar
1 tsp salt
2 Tbsp Kraft Barbecue sauce
1 Tbsp prepared mustard
1 lb uncooked spaghetti

Brown together hamburger and onion. Add rest of ingredients. Simmer 30 minutes. Cook and drain spaghetti. Combine with sauce and serve with grated cheese of your choice.

– Ethel Shank

PIZZA SHOP STYLE PIZZA CRUST

⅔ cup warm water
1 Tbsp sugar
2 Tbsp yeast
2 cups water
⅓ cup oil
2 Tbsp sugar
1 tsp salt
¼ tsp garlic salt
½ tsp oregano leaves
3 cups flour plus 3 cups flour

Combine first 3 ingredients and let set 10 minutes. Mix in the rest of the ingredients and gradually add 3 more cups of flour. Knead dough until smooth and elastic. Let rise. Makes 4-12 inch pizza crusts or 2-13x18 crusts. May be pre-baked at 375° for about 10 minutes and frozen until needed. (See Pizza Sauce recipes on page 296).

−Annette Wenger

ITALIAN SPAGHETTI

1½ lbs hamburger
1 cup chopped onions
1 lb spaghetti, cooked and drained
1 quart tomato juice
2 tsp parsley flakes
1½ tsp salt
1 Tbsp oregano flakes
1 Tbsp sugar
½ lb grated mozzarella cheese

Brown together hamburger and onions. Add rest of ingredients, except cheeses. Put in greased casserole dishes. Layer with cheese. Bake at 350° for 30-45 minutes until hot and bubbly.

−Ethel Shank

When a man has a "pet peeve" it's remarkable how often he pets it.

Mushroom Spaghetti

2 lbs hamburger
1 cup diced onion
1 lb spaghetti cooked and drained
1 quart tomato juice
½ cup brown sugar
2½ cups ketchup
1½ cups water
1 Tbsp prepared mustard
1 can Cream of Mushroom Soup

Brown hamburger and onion; drain excess fat. Combine with rest of ingredients. Stir into cooked spaghetti. Simmer 20-30 minutes over low heat on stovetop.

– Rosanna (Rhodes) Martin

Stuffed Manicotti

12 cooked manicotti shells*
2 Tbsp butter
¾ cup minced onion
1 pint tomato sauce
1 Tbsp flour
1 tsp (each) salt, basil, sugar
2 tsp oregano
¼ tsp pepper
2 cups water
1 can (4 oz) sliced mushrooms
1 lb ground beef
1 lb ricotta or cottage cheese
1 Tbsp parsley
1-2 cups shredded mozzarella cheese

Sauté onion in butter. Add tomato sauce. Combine flour and seasonings, stir into tomato mixture. Add water and mushrooms, simmer 20 – 25 minutes. Meanwhile brown beef, drain off excess fat. Stir in ricotta cheese and parsley. Sprinkle on salt to taste, stuff shells with meat mixture. Arrange in buttered 9 x 13 pan, pour sauce over all. Cover and bake at 350° for an hour. Remove cover, sprinkle mozzarella over all. Serves 6. *I use shell shaped pasta.

Spanish Rice

1½ lbs hamburger
1 large onion
1 green pepper
1 red pepper
1 small hot pepper (optional) or 1 tsp chili powder
2 cups uncooked rice
1 quart tomatoes (canned or frozen)
1 tsp salt
½ tsp garlic salt
¼ tsp pepper
few drops of Tabasco Sauce (optional)

Brown meat, onion and peppers while cooking rice. Mix together; add rest of ingredients. Cook until done. Enjoy!

–Sharon (Knicely) Horst

Juicy Hamburgers

1 lb hamburger
⅔ cup bread crumbs
⅔ cup milk
1 cup ketchup
2 Tbsp brown sugar
2 Tbsp white sugar
1 tsp salt
2 Tbsp Worcestershire Sauce
2 Tbsp vinegar
2 small onions, chopped

Combine hamburger, bread crumbs, and milk. Shape into patties and brown in a skillet. Place in a baking dish. Combine remaining ingredients in a saucepan and simmer for several minutes. Pour over the burgers and bake for 1 hour at 350º.

– Esther Burkholder

Don't use time or words carelessly—neither can be retrieved.

TOMATO CHEESEBURGER PIE

Crust

1 cup flour
¼ cup shortening
½ tsp salt
¼ cup cold water

Filling

1 lb hamburger
2 Tbsp chopped onion
½ cup ketchup
1 tsp salt
Sprinkle of basil and marjoram
1 egg, beaten
½ cup bread crumbs

1 large tomato
cheese of your choice

Brown burger and onion, add rest of ingredients. Make crust by cutting shortening into flour, add salt and water. Roll out and put dough in 10" pie plate. Fill with meat mixture and bake at 350° about 30-35 minutes. Top with 6 slices of tomato and sliced or grated cheese. I use cheddar. Cover until cheese melts. Serves 6

Four things a man must learn to do
If he would make his record true:
    To THINK without confusion clearly;
    To LOVE his fellowmen sincerely;
    To ACT from honest motives purely;
    To TRUST in God and heaven securely.
                – Henry van Dyke

SKILLET LASAGNA

¾ lb hamburger
1 large diced onion
3 cups uncooked ¼" noodles
1 lb cottage cheese
1 Tbsp oregano flakes
1 Tbsp basil flakes
1 tsp garlic powder
1 tsp salt
3½ cups tomatoes or juice
4 oz grated mozzarella cheese

Brown hamburger and onion in large skillet. Drain. Add rest of ingredients in order given (except mozzarella cheese). Cover and simmer on stovetop over medium heat for ½ hour until noodles are done. Don't stir. Sprinkle cheese on top. Cover and remove from heat. Serve in skillet. Delicious! Quick and easy and will become a family favorite.

– Esther Rohrer

GOLDEN LASAGNA

½ cup chopped onion
½ cup chopped pepper
3 Tbsp butter
4 oz mushrooms, drained
10½ oz can Cream of Chicken Soup
½ cup milk
½ tsp basil leaves
1½ cups cottage cheese
1 egg, beaten
3 cups cooked, cubed turkey (or chicken)
2 cups shredded cheddar cheese
½ cup grated Parmesan cheese, or mozzarella
8 oz lasagna noodles cooked and drained
    (I use 8 oz of ¼" wide noodles.)

Sauté onions and pepper in butter until tender. Stir in mushrooms, soup, milk, and basil. Heat well. Stir the egg into the cottage cheese. Arrange ½ of noodles in greased 9x13 baking dish, then half sauce, ½ cottage cheese, ½ turkey, and ½ cheddar and ½ Parmesan. Repeat layers. Bake at 350° for 45-50 minutes, until bubbling throughout. A good way to use leftover poultry.

– Esther Rohrer

SMOKEY BACON 'N BEEF LASAGNA

1 lb ground beef
12 oz chopped smoked bacon
¾ cup chopped onion
1 quart tomato sauce
2 tsp parsley flakes
2 Tbsp sugar
1½ tsp salt
1 tsp garlic salt
1 tsp basil leaves
1 lb lasagna noodles or ¼" noodles
3 cups cottage cheese
1 egg, beaten
½ cup Parmesan cheese (or cheddar cheese)
1 Tbsp parsley flakes
1 tsp oregano flakes
12 oz mozzarella cheese, shredded
½ cup Parmesan cheese (or cheddar cheese)

Cook and stir meat and onion in large skillet until meat is browned and onion is tender. Drain. Mix the tomato sauce, parsley flakes, sugar, salt, garlic salt, and basil together and combine with meat mixture. Cook and drain noodles. In a small bowl, combine cottage cheese, egg, Parmesan, parsley, and oregano. Line a greased 13x9x2 baking pan with a layer of noodles. Top with ½ meat sauce, ½ cottage cheese, ½ mozzarella. Repeat layers. Sprinkle final ½ cup Parmesan on top. (This dish may be covered and chilled or frozen at this point for later use.) Thaw before baking. Bake at 350° for 45 minutes until hot and bubbly.

Giving advice is like cooking—
we should try it before we feed it to others.

Chicken Chili Lasagna

8 oz cream cheese (softened)
1 small onion chopped
2 cups Mexican cheese (divided)
2 tsp garlic powder
½ tsp fresh parsley
3 cups cubed cooked chicken
¼ cup butter
¼ cup flour
1½ cups chicken broth
1 cup shredded Monterey Jack cheese
1 cup sour cream
1 4-oz can chopped green chilies (drained)
⅛ tsp thyme
⅛ tsp salt
⅛ tsp pepper
12 small flour tortillas (halved)

In a mixing bowl combine first 5 ingredients. Stir in the chicken. In a saucepan melt butter, stir in flour, and gradually add chicken broth. Bring to a boil. Cook until thickened. Remove from heat, and stir in Monterey Jack cheese, sour cream, chilies, thyme, salt, and pepper.

Spread ½ cup of sour cream mixture in a 9x13 pan. Top with 6 tortilla halves, a third of chicken mixture, and a fourth of cheese sauce. Repeat tortilla, chicken, and cheese layers twice. Top with remaining tortillas and cheese sauce. Sprinkle on remaining Mexican cheese. Cover and bake at 350° for 30 minutes. Uncover and bake 10 minutes more. Let stand 5 minutes before cutting.

– *Suetta (Rohrer) Horst*

The gift of a listening ear and an understanding heart is sometimes the greatest gift one Christian can give another.

R. Stedman

STROMBOLI

Dough

1½ cups warm water
1 Tbsp yeast
¼ cup oil
½ tsp salt
4 cups flour

Soften yeast in warm water. Add oil, salt, and four. Knead dough until smooth. Cover and let rise until doubled. Meanwhile, prepare filling ingredients:

Filling Ingredients

2-3 Tbsp prepared mustard
12-15 slices Velveeta cheese
1 lb thinly sliced ham
1½ lbs browned, drained sausage
4 cups shredded mozzarella cheese
4 thinly sliced hot dogs (optional)
Slices of pepperoni (optional)

Roll out dough in large rectangles on 2 cookie sheets. Spread filling ingredients in order given. Roll up and seal edges. Brush with oil and sprinkle with oregano. Let set 30 minutes or more to rise. Bake until nicely browned (about 25-30 minutes) at 350°. Slice into 1 inch portions. (May be refrigerated up to 24 hours before letting it rise to bake.)

– *Esther Rohrer and Zelda Rohrer*

*Come to the table
have a good look,
The first to complain
is the next meal's cook.*

TACO SQUARES

1 lb ground beef
2 Tbsp chopped onion
½ cup chopped green pepper
1 Tbsp taco seasoning
2 cups Bisquick mix
½ cup cold water
1 cup sour cream
⅓ cup salad dressing
1 cup shredded cheese
1½ cups pizza sauce
paprika

Cook ground beef, peppers, and onions until beef is browned. Drain and stir in taco seasoning. Mix Bisquick and water until dough forms. Pat into a 9x13 pan, and press ½ inch up sides. Bake at 350° for 8 minutes. Mix sour cream, salad dressing, cheese, and pizza sauce. Layer hamburger and sauce mixture on warm crust. Sprinkle on paprika. Bake at 350° for 25 minutes.
Fresh tomatoes and sliced peppers can be added for a change.

– Esther Burkholder

TACO DIP

1 lb hamburger
1 small onion, chopped
½ cup green peppers, chopped
1 pkg (or less) taco seasoning
1 cup refried beans (I use mashed kidney beans)
1 pt salsa
1 pt sour cream
2 cups grated cheddar cheese

Fry hamburger, onions and peppers. Drain. Stir in taco seasoning. In a 9x13 baking dish, layer ingredients in this order: beans, meat, salsa, sour cream, and cheese. Bake at 350° for ½ hour. You may top it with chopped tomatoes and lettuce just before serving. Eat with restaurant style tortilla chips. YUM!

– Benjamin Rohrer

Experience is a name we give to our mistakes.

Washday Dinner

1 lb hamburger
1 medium onion
5 medium potatoes
1 can mushroom soup
Enough milk to cover

Brown meat, put in bake dish. Slice onion and potatoes over meat. Sprinkle generously with salt and pepper. Pour soup on top and cover with milk. Bake at 350° for 1½ hours.

– Grandma Marie Rohrer

Quick and Easy Casserole

1 lb hamburger
1 medium onion, chopped
½ lb noodles
1 pint peas
1 can mushroom soup
1½ cups milk
salt and pepper

Fry hamburger and onion. Drain. Cook noodles. Mix mushroom soup and milk and combine with noodles, peas, and meat mixture. Bake in a greased casserole at 350° for about an hour. May be topped with buttered bread crumbs or cheese.

Tater Tot Casserole

2 lbs hamburger
1 onion diced
1 quart green beans (drained)
1 can Cream of Celery Soup + 1 can water
5-6 slices Velveeta cheese
1 lb Tater Tots

Brown hamburger and onions, drain. Put in shallow 2 qt bake dish. Top meat mixture with green beans. After adding soup, layer cheese and Tater Tots. Bake at 350° until Tater Tots are golden, about an hour.

–Ava (Eberly) Heatwole

Poor Man's Steak

3 lbs hamburger
½ cup minced onion
1 Tbsp salt
½ tsp pepper
1½ cups soda cracker crumbs
1½ cups milk

Combine all ingredients and mix well. Refrigerate 2-12 hours. Pat into a jelly roll pan. Cut into serving size pieces. Brown in oven at 400° (or broiler) turning pieces over once. If you want to make this meat taste extra special, grill it over a smokey wood fire instead of browning in in the oven. Layer pieces in a greased 9x13 pan. Top with mushroom sauce. Bake at 350° for 45-60 minutes. Serves 12-14

Mushroom sauce

¼ cup butter
4 cups rich milk
½ cup flour
2 tsp salt
pepper
1 cup sour cream
1 or 2 cans mushroom pieces, undrained

Melt butter in saucepan. Combine milk and flour. Pour into butter and stir over medium heat. Bring to a boil. Add rest of ingredients.

Savory Pot Roast

3-4 lb chuck roast
5 each: potatoes, carrots, onions

Sprinkle salt and pepper generously over roast. Dredge in flour and brown in Dutch oven in hot fat. When golden brown on all sides, add an inch or two of water to kettle and lower heat. Simmer, covered for 2-3 hours. When meat is tender, add vegetables that have been washed and cut into large chunks. Add more water if needed and salt, pepper and parsley to taste. When vegetables are done, arrange them around meat on a large, warm platter. Thicken broth to make gravy and serve with pot roast. (see page 83)

Pot Roast Meat Loaf

1 lb ground beef
⅔ cup canned milk
⅓ cup cracker crumbs
¼ cup ketchup
1 tsp salt
¼ tsp pepper
2 tsp Worcestershire Sauce

Mix all together in a bowl. Shape into a loaf. Place in center of a 9x13 pan.

Wash and chop into chunks

3 potatoes
3 onions
3 carrots

Place veggies around meat in pan. Sprinkle them with salt and pepper and parsley. Cover tightly with foil. Bake 1 hour at 375º. Uncover and bake 20 more minutes to brown meat.

– *Carolyn (Black) Shirkey*

Meat Loaf Supreme

1½ lbs hamburger
1½ cups thick tomato juice
½ cup minced onion
2 eggs
1 tsp salt
¼ tsp pepper
1 cup soda cracker crumbs or oatmeal

Mix all together. Place in pan. Frost it with a mixture of 1 cup ketchup, 2 tsp prepared mustard, and 2 Tbsp brown sugar before baking. Bake at 375º for 1 hour. Serves 8-10.

A man's worth consists not of what he has, but of what he is.

Wiener Meat Loaf

1 lb hamburger
½ lb ground hot dogs
1 cup cracker crumbs
1 egg
1 tsp salt
half of glaze mixture

Glaze
¾ cup brown sugar
½ cup water
½ tsp dry mustard
1 Tbsp vinegar
Mix and divide glaze

Combine all ingredients. Form into a loaf and spread the other half of glaze mixture on top of loaf. Bake 1 hour at 375°.

– Carolyn Landis

Oven Barbecued Hot Dogs

¼ cup chopped onion
1 Tbsp butter
2 Tbsp brown sugar
1 cup ketchup
½ cup water
2 Tbsp vinegar
1 Tbsp Worcestershire Sauce (or 1 tsp liquid smoke)
1 tsp prepared mustard

Sauté onion in butter. Add everything else. Cook a few minutes. Split 12-24 hot dogs. Lay in baking pan. Pour sauce over all. Bake at 350° for 45-50 minutes.

Barbecue for Buns

Brown together 2 lbs hamburger and ½ cup chopped onion. Add rest of ingredients.

½ cup brown sugar
3 Tbsp Worcestershire sauce
¾ cup ketchup
3 Tbsp lemon juice
3 Tbsp vinegar
2 tsp salt
½ tsp pepper
1 Tbsp prepared mustard
Simmer 20 minutes and serve on buns.

–Ethel Shank

CORN DOGS

1 cup cornmeal
1 cup flour
2 Tbsp sugar
2 tsp baking powder
½ tsp salt
1 egg, slightly beaten
1 cup milk
2 Tbsp melted shortening
1 lb hot dogs

Mix cornmeal with flour, sugar, baking powder and salt. Add egg and milk; stir in melted shortening. Mix well. Dip hot dogs in batter. Fry in deep fat at 350°-365° until golden brown.

WESTERN MEATBALLS

2 lbs hamburger
1½ cups milk
1 cup oatmeal
1 cup cracker crumbs
2 eggs
½ cup chopped onion
1 tsp garlic powder
1 tsp salt
1 tsp pepper
1 tsp chili powder
Mix together. Shape into little balls (1½"). Put into greased 9x13 pan or roaster. Spread sauce over balls. Cover and bake at 350° for 45 minutes. Uncover and bake 15 minutes longer.

Sauce

1 cup brown sugar
¼ cup onion
1 tsp garlic salt
½ tsp liquid smoke
1-2 cups ketchup

– Hazel (Rohrer) Horst and Lois Shank (Danny)

Chuckwagon Beans and Meat

1 lb smoked bacon
½ lb ground beef
1 medium onion, chopped
1 red pepper, diced

Cut bacon in ½" pieces, stir over med-high heat until done. Brown hamburger and onion, add pepper. Drain off grease. Meanwhile in a large bowl combine:

2 cans Bushes baked beans (28 oz. each)
2 cans kidney beans (16 oz. each)
½ cup ketchup
½ cup brown sugar
1 tsp salt

Add meat mixture and bake in 9" x 13" pan at 350°, uncovered for 45-50 minutes or until piping hot.
A great dish for a potluck meal or picnic.

Baked Bean Casserole

1 lb ground beef
½ cup chopped onion
16 oz. can baked beans
½ cup ketchup
⅓ cup brown sugar
1½ tsp mustard
¾ cup Bisquick
½ cup milk
1 egg

Brown beef with onion, drain. Add beans, ketchup, brown sugar, and mustard. Heat to a simmer. Pour into an 11" x 7" bake dish. Combine remaining ingredients and pour over meat. Bake at 375° for 25-35 minutes until lightly browned.

He who really wants to do something finds a way;
he who doesn't finds an excuse.

Baked Beans

8 oz bacon (or hot dogs)
½ cup chopped onion
28 oz can pork and beans
2 Tbsp brown sugar
1 Tbsp Worcestershire Sauce
1 tsp prepared mustard
¼ tsp chili powder

Fry bacon and break into pieces. If using hot dogs, slice them into bite-sized pieces. Combine all ingredients and pour into a greased bake dish. Cover and bake at 350° for 1½ hours.

– Sharon (Wenger) Good

Western Meal in One

1 lb ground beef
1 Tbsp salad oil
1 tsp salt
1 large onion, chopped
1 tsp chili powder
2½ cups tomatoes or juice
1 pint navy beans (cooked)
1 cup cooked rice or potatoes
¾ cup grated cheese

Brown meat in oil. Add salt, onions, and chili powder and simmer 5 minutes. Stir in tomatoes, beans and rice. Place in greased casserole dish and bake uncovered for 1 hour at 350°. Put cheese on top and bake 15 minutes longer or until cheese melts.

– Janice (Shank) Wenger

Good examples have twice the value of good advice.

Pizza Casserole

1 lb ground beef
1 pint pizza sauce
1 (7-oz) can sliced mushrooms
2 tsp garlic salt
1 tsp oregano flakes
4 cups cooked macaroni
⅔ cup milk
2 cups shredded mozzarella cheese
Pepperoni slices

Brown hamburger. Drain. Stir in pizza sauce, undrained mushrooms, garlic salt, and oregano. Bring to a boil. Remove from heat. Combine macaroni and milk. In a greased 2-quart bake dish, layer macaroni meat sauce, and cheese. Repeat layers. Bake uncovered at 350° for 30 minutes. Garnish with pepperoni.

– Carolyn (Black) Shirkey

Complete Skillet Meal

Fry any desired amount of hamburger. Layer with thinly sliced potatoes, carrots, and onions. Add any other vegetable available or in season (limas, green beans, corn, summer squash, asparagus, etc.) Make top layer sliced tomatoes. (Can be canned tomatoes.) Add ½ to 1 cup water. Put lid on. After it starts to cook, boil hard 10 minutes. Vegetables will be tender crisp. Sprinkle cheese on top. Cover until cheese is melted. Season vegetables on your plate. Healthy and very tasty!

– Neva Horst

If a task is once begun,
Never leave it till it's done.
Be the labor great or small;
Do it well, or not at all.

DELUXE GRILLED STEAKS

Choose good tender steaks such as: Rib Eyes, New York Strips, Top Sirloin, Porterhouse, T-Bones or Filet Mignon. Sauce will marinate 3 lbs of meat.

2 cups water
½ cup vinegar
2 tsp garlic salt
1 tsp salt
1 tsp coarse black pepper

Combine sauce ingredients and reserve ½ cup marinade. Cover meat with remaining sauce and marinate 4-6 hours. Grill steaks over hot coals until barely done. Remove from grill. Rub a stick of butter generously over steaks, sprinkle with salt and coarse pepper. Pile into a pan with reserved marinade; cover and keep piping hot until suppertime.

Serve with potatoes or sweet corn, fresh garden salad, and plenty of lemonade or iced tea.

MARINADE FOR STEAKS TO GRILL

½ cup margarine melted
½ cup oil
¾ cup Worcestershire Sauce
½ cup vinegar
1 Tbsp salt
2 tsp garlic salt
½ tsp pepper

Mix well and pour over steak. Soak at least 8 hours (up to 24 hours). Turn steaks several times. Grill as usual.

–Wilma (Rohrer) Shank

Enthusiasm is contagious—and so is the lack of it.

Easy Barbecued Pepper Steak

1 cup ketchup
½ cup water
¼ cup vinegar
¼ cup chopped green peppers
¼ cup chopped onions
1½ Tbsp Worcestershire Sauce
1 Tbsp prepared mustard
2 Tbsp brown sugar
½ tsp salt
½ tsp pepper
4 lbs steak

Combine all ingredients except steak in a saucepan, bring to a boil and simmer five minutes. Keep sauce hot.

Pound steak to tenderize if needed. Place in a roasting pan, pour hot sauce over each layer. Cover and bake at 350° for 1½ -2 hours.

Teriyaki Steak

½ cup soy sauce
3 Tbsp sugar
½ tsp ginger
½ tsp garlic salt
6 steaks

Pound steak to tenderize if needed. Mix marinade and pour over raw steaks. Marinate several hours. Bake at 350° until meat is done. Don't overbake.

– *Marilyn Eberly*

The best way to serve meals is with a smile.

Grilled Meat and Vegetable Kabobs

2 lbs beef tenderloin (or pork or chicken)
2 medium onions
2 red or green peppers
¾ lb fresh mushrooms
3 medium tomatoes (or 18 cherry tomatoes)
8 small new potatoes
1 summer squash

Cut meat into 1½" cubes. Quarter onions and separate into layers. Cut peppers into 1½" squares. Wash and cook potatoes until just done. Cut tomatoes into 6 wedges each.

Fill long skewers with meat, pepper, mushroom, squash, and onion pieces, alternating meat and veggies. Do not crowd pieces. Brush with oil or melted butter. Grill over hot coals until meat is done, turning to brown evenly on all sides. Thread tomatoes and potatoes on other skewers and begin grilling them when meat is half done. Baste with butter or oil.

Push food from skewers onto serving plates and season with salt and pepper. Be careful, cherry tomatoes get really hot when grilled. For extra flavor, meat can be marinated before grilling. Pretty and very tasty!

Roasting Meat (at low temperature)

Roasts of beef, poultry, or pork can be roasted very slowly in your oven—for the juiciest meat you'll ever eat. I've used this method for many years. Preheat oven to 250°. You may add ½" of water to your pan if you want to make gravy. Put meat in the oven and bake it uncovered until it reaches the correct internal temperature (145°-165°). Use a quick-read thermometer to test it after several hours. Let set 15 minutes before carving.
A whole turkey will need to reach 170° to ensure the joints are done. An 18 lb turkey will take 5 hours at this temperature. Brush butter over the surface for a golden brown glow. Do not stuff a turkey when roasting at low temperature.

Favorite Roast Beef

2 qts water
½ cup salt
½ cup sugar
1 beef roast

Combine water, salt, and sugar, and immerse roast in brine. Re-frigerate 24-48 hours. Remove meat from brine. Put a little water in roasting pan with meat. Bake uncovered in 250° oven until done. I use a quick-read thermometer to check it, and take it out at 150°-160°. The pan juices make good gravy. If you are short on time, roast at 350° and remove from oven when meat reaches 150°. Don't overbake. **To make gravy**, thicken broth with a batter of cornstarch and water. Add a dash of Kitchen Bouquet browning sauce for better color and flavor.

Prime Rib Roast

Marinate roast in brine of 1 gallon water, 1 cup salt and 1 cup sugar for up to 48 hours. Discard brine. Place roast on a rack in roaster, fat side down. Coat top and sides of meat thickly with honey mustard and sprinkle coarse pepper over top. Roast uncov-ered at 300°-350° until meat reaches 160°. Remove from oven, pour off grease and use pan juices to make gravy as described above. Slice beef and keep warm until serving time.

Peppery Brisket Roast

1½ tsp celery salt
1½ tsp onion powder
1½ tsp garlic salt
1½ tsp liquid smoke
2½ tsp Worcestershire Sauce
1½ tsp pepper
4 lb roast

Mix and pour over roast. Let stand overnight. Roast at 300° for 2½-3 hours.

– Annette (Eberly) Horst

STOVETOP ROAST BEEF

3-5 lb roast of beef
1 large onion, sliced thin
1 cup white vinegar
2 cups strong coffee
2 cups water

Cut 1" deep slashes over top of roast. Insert onion slices. Pour vinegar over beef and marinate 24-45 hours. Pour off vinegar. Brown meat in oil or margarine in a black iron skillet or heavy kettle. Pour coffee and water over roast. Cover and simmer <u>slowly</u> on stovetop 3-4 hours. Tender and tasty.

– Austin and Marie Eberly

HERB ROAST

3-4 lb beef roast
1 Tbsp salt
2 beef bouillon cubes
1½ cups hot water
2 bay leaves
⅛ tsp pepper
½ tsp marjoram
¼ tsp basil
½ tsp garlic
½ tsp parsley flakes

Dissolve bouillon and salt in hot water. Sprinkle seasonings all over roast. Add water. Cover roast and cook very slowly on stovetop until done and fork tender.

– Karen (Rohrer) Rohrer

The feeling of friendship
is like that of being completely filled with roast beef.
– D.R. Johnson

Roast Beef with Mushroom Gravy

3 to 3½ lb roast
1 Tbsp oil
1 tsp salt
1 tsp marjoram
1 tsp thyme
½ tsp oregano
½ tsp garlic powder
½ tsp pepper
1 (14½ oz) can beef broth
2 cups water
1-2 cups sliced mushrooms

Brown roast in oil. Sprinkle seasonings over meat. Add broth and water, bring to a boil. Cover and bake at 325° for 2 hours. Add mushrooms to broth before making gravy. Bring broth to a boil, thicken with a batter of cornstarch and cold water.

– Clarke and Marybeth Eberly

Rave-Bringing Beef Ribs

4-5 lb beef ribs
1 cup double-strength coffee
1 Tbsp liquid smoke
1 Tbsp brown sugar
1 Tbsp Worcestershire Sauce
salt to taste

Preheat oven to 350°.

Score ribs on both sides between bones. Lay ribs in bottom of roaster with tight-fitting lid.

Combine coffee, liquid smoke, sugar, and Worcestershire. Pour over ribs. Cover and bake in oven 2 hours or until ribs are almost tender. Remove cover and continue baking until ribs are browned and tender, another 20 minutes or so. Ribs may be turned over after 10 minutes to brown other side.

– Lorna (Good) Wenger

DRIED BEEF GRAVY

4 oz dried beef
2 Tbsp butter
3 cups milk
¼ cup flour
pepper to taste

Chop dried beef and sauté in butter over low heat. Make a batter of milk and flour, stir unto skillet and continue to stir over medium heat until gravy thickens. Add pepper.

BARBECUE SAUCE FOR BEEF SANDWICHES

1 cup Bull's Eye Hickory Barbecue Sauce
1 cup ketchup
¼ cup Worcestershire sauce
2 Tbsp brown sugar

Boil together a few minutes. Use 5 oz beef per bun. Top with sauce.

BEEF BURGUNDY

1 lb tender beef cubes
2 Tbsp butter
1 can Golden Mushroom Soup
⅛ tsp pepper
¼ cup burgundy or red wine
2 small onions chopped
2 Tbsp parsley

Toss beef cubes in flour and brown lightly in butter. Simmer with the rest of the ingredients for 1 hour or until tender. Serve over wide noodles or rice.

– *Beulah (Rhodes) Burkholder*

If you have to eat your words, try to eat them while they're hot.

Fajitas

1 lb sirloin steak strips
⅓ cup oil
5 Tbsp lime juice
4 Tbsp fajita seasoning
1 tsp salt
1 red bell pepper sliced
1 green bell pepper sliced
1 medium onion sliced
1 cup fresh mushrooms sliced
sour cream
1 pkg. warm corn tortillas

Mix oil, lime juice, seasonings and meat. Marinate for 4 hours.
Then drain meat and reserve marinade. In a heavy frying pan, heat
4 Tbsp of marinade and sauté vegetables 2½ minutes. Remove to
a platter. Add 2 Tbsp more of marinade. Add meat and toss until
cooked. Pour remaining marinade in frying pan and cook 1 minute
more. Toss in vegetables and serve in warm tortillas with generous
amounts of sour cream.

– Lydia (Eberly) Good

Golden Chicken Nuggets

4 deboned chicken breasts
½ cup melted butter
½ cup Parmesan cheese
¼ cup grated cheddar cheese
½ cup fine bread crumbs
¼ tsp basil
¼ tsp thyme
⅛ tsp pepper
½ tsp salt

Mix dry ingredients. Cut chicken into bite-sized pieces. Dip in
butter and roll in crumbs. Place on cookie sheet and bake at 350°
until golden, approximately 15-20 minutes.

–Wilma (Rohrer) Shank

These are good dipped in honey mustard dressing on page 143

CHICKEN CORDON BLEU

skinless, boneless chicken breasts (1 per serving)
thin slices of ham or Canadian bacon
thin slices of Swiss cheese
seasoned or plain bread crumbs
1 beaten egg + 1 Tbsp water

Pound breasts to ¼" thickness with a meat hammer. Lay a piece of ham and cheese on each breast, leaving ½" margin around edge of chicken. Roll up and secure with a toothpick if needed. Dip each breast into flour and then into the egg and water. Roll in bread crumbs to cover meat. These may be refrigerated for later use. Pan-fry or bake at 350° for 20-30 minutes or until they test done (165° inside).

My way of making Chicken Cordon Bleu

Use <u>chicken breast tenders*</u>. Roll them in seasoned flour or bread crumbs, lightly brown them in skillet, then wrap cheese and ham around each breast tender. Spoon sauce over chicken tenders, and bake in 250° oven for 30-35 minutes. Don't overbake.

   *Most people prefer these smaller servings.

Sauce for Chicken Cordon Bleu:

3 cups water
2 tsp chicken base
2 cups half and half milk
½ cup tapioca starch or cornstarch

Heat water, chicken base and 1 cup half and half in saucepan till almost boiling. Combine 1 cup half and half with tapioca starch and stir into hot liquid. Cook till it thickens. Let set 10-15 minutes. Spoon over meat. If you have extra sauce, use it to top the chicken after baking.

Deal with the faults of others as gently as with your own.
— Henrichs

CHICKEN CASSEROLE

3-5 cups cooked diced chicken
1 can Cream of Chicken Soup
8 oz sour cream

Mix and put into casserole dish. Top with cracker topping.
Bake at 350° for 45-60 minutes

Topping:

1½ cups crushed Ritz crackers
1 Tbsp poppy seeds
4 Tbsp melted butter

– Brenda (Shirk) Knicely

CHICKEN ENCHILADAS

1 cup chopped onions
½ cup chopped green pepper
2 Tbsp butter
2 cups chopped, cooked chicken
1 4-oz can green chilies, drained, rinsed, and seeded
3 Tbsp butter
¼ cup flour
1 tsp coriander
¾ tsp salt
2½ cups chicken broth
1 cup sour cream
1½ cups mozzarella cheese, divided
12 6-inch tortillas

Sauté onions and peppers in 2 Tbsp butter. Add chicken and
chilies. Mix. In another pan, brown the 3 Tbsp butter and the
flour. Add other ingredients (except for ¾ cup cheese) to make
sauce. Put enough sauce in chicken mixture to make it stick together. Spoon ⅓ cup mixture on each tortilla. Roll up and place
in casserole dish. Top with remaining sauce and cheese. Bake at
400° for 30 minutes.

Ina Sue (Showalter) Strite

Quick Chinese Chicken Wings

1 lb chicken wings
oil for browning wings
1 cup water
scant ⅓ cup soy sauce
pepper to taste
2 tsp Worcestershire sauce
sprinkling of sugar

Sprinkle garlic salt and onion salt on both sides of wings. Quickly brown chicken in oil in a large skillet. Add water to pan and simmer covered for 5 minutes. Remove lid and add remaining ingredients. Cook for 20 minutes, turning occasionally, or until pan juices are absorbed and chicken is quite crisp.

A family favorite.   – *Charlotte Rohrer*

Chicken-Macaroni Bake

2 cups uncooked macaroni
2 cups cooked, diced chicken
2 cans Cream of Chicken or Cream of Mushroom soup
1 cup Velveeta cheese melted in soup
½ medium onion
½ tsp salt
¼ tsp pepper
3 Tbsp butter

Cook macaroni and drain. Combine all ingredients. Place in greased casserole dish. Bake uncovered at 350° until hot and bubbly.

– *Barbara (Rohrer) Eberly*

No matter where I take my guests, it seems they like my kitchen best.
                                        – *Pennsylvania Dutch saying*

POULTRY AND STUFFING

12 oz seasoned stuffing mix
8 boneless skinless (4oz) breast pieces (chicken or turkey)
1 Tbsp vegetable oil
4 oz grated Swiss cheese
1 can of chicken soup
¼ cup water

Prepare stuffing by directions on package. Put in a greased 9x13 pan. Sauté breast pieces in oil, season with salt and pepper. Put meat on top of dressing, top with Swiss cheese. Blend soup and water, pour over all. Cover and bake at 350°for 50-55 minutes. Remove cover last 15 minutes of baking.

– Karen (Nolt) Martin

CREAMY BAKED CHICKEN BREASTS

4 whole chicken breasts
8 - 4x4 slices Swiss cheese
10¾ oz Cream of Chicken Soup (undiluted)
¼ cup white wine or water
1 cup herb stuffing mix (crushed)
¼ cup butter, melted

Split and debone breasts. Place chicken in greased 13x9x2 dish. Top with cheese. Combine soup and wine. Spoon over chicken and sprinkle with stuffing. Drizzle butter over crumbs. Bake at 350° for 45-50 minutes. Serves 8.

– Beulah (Rhodes) Burkholder

We should use every opportunity to give encouragement.
Encouragement is oxygen to the soul.

DEEP DISH CHICKEN POT PIE

Crust:

2 cups flour
½ tsp salt
⅔ cup butter
6-8 Tbsp water

Combine flour, salt, butter until crumbly. Add water. Roll out dough and line a 2 quart bake dish with pastry.

Filling:

3 Tbsp butter
3 Tbsp flour
1 cup cream
½ cup broth
½ tsp salt
½ tsp thyme
¼ tsp pepper
2½ cups cooked chicken
2 cups peas
3 cups cooked potatoes
1 cup cooked carrots
¼ cup chopped onion

Melt butter in saucepan, stir in flour, cream, and broth. Add seasonings, cook a minute or two. Stir in vegetables and chicken. Pour into pastry lined 2½ -3 qt dish. Cover with pastry, cut a few slits on top, brush with milk and sprinkle with poultry seasoning. Bake at 350° for 1 hour.

Mom used to serve a meat pie similar to this for Saturday's noon meal when we were young. She used leftover vegetables and meat from the previous week's meals. Her weekend deep dish meat pie was always a treat.

Nothing is so convincing as the silent influence of a good example.

Brine for Chicken or Turkey

2 quarts water
½ cup salt
½ cup sugar

Soak chicken pieces about 2 hours in brine in refrigerator. Remove skinless pieces after ½ hour. Use for a more delicious, moist result before frying, or baking chicken. You'll be amazed at the flavor. For a whole turkey, use 1 gallon of water, don't increase salt and sugar. Leave in brine several days. To roast a turkey see page 82.

Parmesan Chicken

16 pieces chicken
¾ cup cracker crumbs
¾ cup Parmesan cheese
1 tsp basil leaves
½ tsp oregano
½ tsp garlic powder
1 stick butter

Mix all dry ingredients. Melt butter in 9 x 13 pan. Dip chicken pieces in butter, then coat with crumbs. Bake at 350° for 1½ hrs or until done.

Poultry Seasoning

Mix 3 tsp sage with 1 tsp thyme or marjoram.

*Train up a child in the way he should go
and walk there yourself.*

– Josh Billings

SECRET HERBS AND SPICES RECIPE

1 Tbsp salt
1 Tbsp oregano
1 Tbsp sage
1 Tbsp rosemary
1 Tbsp onion powder
1 Tbsp garlic powder
1 Tbsp paprika
2 Tbsp chicken bouillon (or 4 cubes mashed)
3 Tbsp dried, minced parsley
3 Tbsp brown sugar
1 tsp black pepper
1 tsp marjoram
1 tsp ginger
1 tsp thyme

Combine all ingredients and mix well. Add 2 Tbsp of mix to 1 cup of flour for coating chicken before frying.

This is supposed to taste like a famous restaurant's chicken.

OVEN FRIED CHICKEN

Chicken pieces of your choice
1 cup butter
2 cups crushed cornflakes
2 cups flour
1 tsp thyme
1½ tsp coarse black pepper
2 tsp poultry seasoning
1 tsp salt

Marinate chicken pieces in Brine for chicken if you wish. (see page 93) Mix dry ingriedients. Melt butter in a 9x13 pan. Dip chicken in the butter, then coat with cornflake mixture. Turn pieces over to moisten crumbs. Bake at 350° for 1¼ hours or until done. (165°)

Jumping at the first opportunity
seldom leads to a happy landing.

CRISPY PECAN CHICKEN

2 frying chickens, cut into pieces
½ cup butter
1 cup buttermilk or milk
1 egg, slightly beaten
1 cup flour
1 cup ground pecans
1 tsp paprika
1 tsp salt
1 tsp pepper

Melt butter in 9x13 pan. Combine milk and egg. Mix rest of ingredients together. Dip chicken in milk, and coat with flour-nut mixture. Place skin-side down in pan. Turn over skin-side up. Bake at 350° for 1¼ hours or until done.

PAN FRIED CHICKEN

1¼ cups whole-wheat flour
1¼ cups white flour
1 cup cornmeal
1 tsp thyme
1 tsp black pepper
1 Tbsp poultry seasoning
1 tsp salt

Marinate chicken pieces in Brine for chicken if you wish. (see page 93) Drain and then dip chicken pieces in flour mix, then in milk, then in flour mix again. Fry in deep skillet in hot oil or shortening until done (about 25 - 30 minutes).

If you want to feel rich,
just count all the things you have that money can't buy.

"Old Lady on a Bus" Chicken

This recipe was overheard in conversation between two old ladies on a bus near Atlanta. It was a favorite of our helpers.

1 fryer chicken (cut up)
½ cup orange juice concentrate
⅓ cup Kraft barbecue sauce
⅓ cup ketchup
2 Tbsp Worcestershire sauce
2 Tbsp lemon juice
2 Tbsp brown sugar
½ tsp hickory smoke salt

Grease a 9x13 pan. Place chicken in pan. Combine sauce ingredients and pour over chicken. Bake for 1¼ hours at 350º, basting occasionally after first half hour.

– Ethel Shank

Barbecue Sauce and Marinade for Chicken

1 cup cider vinegar
1½ cups water
2 Tbsp salt
1 tsp pepper
2 tsp poultry seasoning
1 tsp garlic salt
1 Tbsp lemon juice
1 cup oil (optional)

Combine ingredients and use as a marinade or basting sauce for poultry. This recipe was intended for pit-barbecued chicken which is not apt to burn at 20-24" from the hot coals. When using a gas grill, I omit the oil, as it causes flare-ups when it drips onto the fire. Instead, brush finished meat with a stick of butter. Sauce makes enough for 10 halves chicken or an equivalent amount of boneless, skinless pieces, which are my favorite for gas grilling.

Good health and good sense are two of life's greatest blessings.

Barbecued Chicken

1 gallon water
2 cups Morton's Tenderquick
1 cup brown sugar
3 cups cider vinegar
3 bay leaves
25 lbs of chicken pieces

Combine marinade ingredients and pour over chicken. Refrigerate up to 24 hours. Drain meat and grill as usual.

I got this recipe from Indiana Amish friends who served it for their daughter's wedding supper. It was grilled over a wood fire and it was scrumptious.

Chicken Dressing Casserole

1 small loaf of bread, 12-16 slices, toasted
2 cups chicken broth
3 cups diced, cooked chicken
⅓ cup chopped onion
1¼ cups chopped celery
2 cups shredded potatoes
¼ cup shredded carrot
1 stick butter, browned
2 cans cream of mushroom soup
6 eggs, beaten
3 cups milk
poultry seasoning, salt and pepper to taste

Tear toast into pieces. Pour broth over toast. Saute potatoes, celery, and onion in butter until half done. Combine all ingredients, adding extra broth or milk if it seems dry. Bake in greased casserole dishes at 350° till puffy and golden brown. Serve with chicken gravy.

This casserole was served at an Amish couple's wedding that our family attended. It is their standard dish for the occasion, and is called "Roast".

CREAMY CHICKEN AND RICE

4 cups cooked rice
½ cup butter
¼ cup flour
2 cups milk
2 tsp chicken bouillon granules
½ to 1 tsp seasoned salt
½ tsp garlic powder
¼ tsp pepper
4 to 5 cups cooked, cubed chicken
12 oz American cheese cubed
2 cups sour cream
1¼ cups crushed butter-flavored crackers

Spread rice into a greased shallow 3 qt baking dish. Set aside. In a saucepan melt ¼ cup butter. Stir in flour until smooth. Gradually add milk, bouillon, seasoned salt, garlic powder, and pepper. Bring to a boil; cook until thickened. Add chicken, cheese, and sour cream. Stir until cheese is melted. Pour over rice. Melt remaining butter. Toss with cracker crumbs. Sprinkle over casserole. Bake uncovered at 350º for 30 minutes, or until heated throughout.

– Esther Burkholder

HERBED CORNISH GAME HENS

½ hen per person
oil
salt
pepper
herbs

Rub Cornish hens with oil, and sprinkle <u>lightly</u> all over with salt, pepper, and your favorite herbs. I use sage, poultry seasoning, marjoram, or thyme. Bake uncovered at 350º for an hour. Serve with seasoned wild rice or mashed potatoes and gravy.

This was a favorite birthday meal for the girls who worked in my home.

SCALLOPED CHICKEN

½ loaf white bread, cubed
1½ cups cracker crumbs
3 cups chicken broth
3 eggs lightly beaten
1 tsp salt
¾ cup diced celery
2 Tbsp chopped onion
3 cups cubed cooked chicken
8 oz sliced mushrooms, drained
1 Tbsp butter or margarine

In a mixing bowl, combine bread and 1 cup cracker crumbs. Stir in broth, eggs, salt, celery, onion, chicken, and mushrooms. Spoon into a greased 2 quart casserole dish. In a saucepan, melt butter; brown remaining cracker crumbs. Sprinkle over casserole. Bake at 350° for 1 hour.

– Dorothy (Shank) Wenger

SMOTHERED TURKEY OR CHICKEN

8 pieces of turkey or chicken breast
1 cup sour cream
1 can Cream of Mushroom Soup

Sprinkle both sides of meat with hickory smoke salt. Mix sour cream and mushroom soup together. Layer in baking dish. Cover and bake at 350° for 1 hour or 225° for 2½ hours.

– Hazel (Rohrer) Horst

If you aren't big enough for criticism,
you are too small for praise.

BAKED TURKEY BREAST

1 tsp liquid smoke
2 tsp salt
⅓ cup brown sugar
1½ cups water

Combine all and pour over raw turkey breast. Cover and bake at 250° until done. (165°)

OR:

Purchase a pre-cooked turkey breast. Combine marinade ingredients and pour over sliced turkey. Cover and heat in a low (225°) oven until ready to serve.

WESTERN RANCH DINNER

1 cup Bisquick
2 tsp salt
¼ tsp pepper
2 tsp paprika
½ cup shortening
1 cut up frying chicken
1 lb, 13 oz cling peach halves
Bisquick for making bisciuts

Heat oven to 375°. Mix first 4 ingredients in a paper bag. Place shortening in 9x13 pan. Set in oven to melt. Shake 3-4 pieces of chicken at a time in the bag to coat thoroughly. Place chicken, skin-side down, in 1 layer in hot shortening. Bake 45 minutes. Then turn.

Make biscuits using recipe on box. Roll out ¼" thick with cutter. Drain peaches. Push chicken to one side in the pan. Place biscuits on the other side. Put peach halves on top of chicken. Bake another 15 minutes until biscuits are lightly browned.

Put chicken and peaches on serving platter, arranging peaches around the outside and the chicken in the center. To make gravy add 2 Tbsp Bisquick from paper bag to pan drippings. Bring to a boil. Add 1½ cups water. Stir and boil one minute. Serve with biscuits.

– Anna Knicely (Amos)

Dried Beef Chicken Roll-Ups

12 skinless filleted chicken breasts
½ lb dried beef
4 strips bacon, cut into thirds
1 can Cream of Chicken Soup

Lay dried beef on chicken and roll up. Arrange meat snugly in roasting pan. Lay bacon on meat. Pour Cream of Chicken Soup over all. Bake at 300° for 2 hours or until done.
Pan drippings make tasty gravy to serve with mashed potatoes.
– Maria (Eberly) Horst

Baked Bacon

Place separated slices in a large shallow baking pan which has been lightly greased or sprayed with Pam. Bake at 350° - 400° about 20 minutes or until crisp. Remove and drain on paper towels. Baked bacon does not curl up.

Fried Tenderloin and Gravy

Slice fresh or frozen tenderloin and soak in a brine of 2 cups water and 2 Tbsp Tenderquick, for up to two hours. Dredge meat in flour and fry in skillet over medium heat using margarine, browning lightly on both sides. Sprinkle with a little pepper.

Brown a couple Tbsp flour in pan drippings and stir in cold water to make gravy. Season with salt or ham base seasoning. To enhance color, add a dash of Kitchen Bouquet sauce.

Tact is the art of making a point without making an enemy.

COUNTRY HAM

Soak sugar/salt-cured raw ham overnight in cold water, or bring it to a boil and pour off water. Cover ham with fresh water and heat to a boil. Reduce heat to just high enough to keep it slowly boiling. Cook to 160°. Remove from hot broth. As soon as you can handle it, debone and wrap ham tightly in foil or plastic wrap. Chill 24 hours or more. Slice and keep cold.

❖ To fry country ham, slice raw ham and soak in cold water for one hour. Dredge in flour and fry in margarine over medium-high heat, just until golden brown on both sides. Don't over-fry.

SMOKED SAUSAGE IN BROWN GRAVY

1 - 8" link smoked sausage
2 Tbsp shortening
2 Tbsp flour
1 cup cold water

Cut sausage in ½" pieces and brown in shortening. Remove meat from skillet, add flour and stir until brown. Add water and stir until smooth and bubbly. Add salt and pepper to taste, put sausage into gravy, and simmer about 5 minutes.

SUPER SAUSAGE GRAVY

1-2 lbs sausage
2 Tbsp minced onion
6 Tbsp flour
½ tsp poultry seasoning
½ tsp nutmeg
1 tsp salt and ¼ tsp pepper
1 qt milk
dash Worcestershire Sauce

Brown sausage and onion. Drain excess fat. Sprinkle flour over meat, and brown a little more. Add rest of seasonings, and pour in milk while stirring. Cook until thickened and bubbly. Try this with Potato Pancakes and applesauce. Good for breakfast, dinner, or supper.

BRUNCH ENCHILADAS

2 cups ground, cooked ham
½ cup sliced green onions
½ cup finely chopped green pepper
2 Tbsp cooking oil
8 flour tortillas (7-inch)
2½ cups shredded cheddar cheese
4 eggs
2 cups light cream
1 Tbsp all purpose flour
¼ tsp garlic powder
2-3 drops hot pepper sauce
salsa
sour cream

Sauté ham, onions, and green pepper in oil until tender. Put ⅓ cup down center of each tortilla and top with 3 Tbsp cheese. Roll up and place (seam side down) in a greased 9x13 baking dish.

In a bowl, beat eggs. Add cream, flour, garlic powder, and hot sauce; mix well. Pour over tortillas. Cover and chill 8 hours or overnight. Remove from fridge ½ hour before baking.

Bake uncovered at 350° for 40-45 minutes or until knife comes out clean. Sprinkle with remaining cheese. Let stand 5 minutes. Serve with salsa and sour cream.

– *Laura (Knicely) Horst*

Short Order Cook

When daddy cooks he doesn't read
The cookbooks mother seems to need;
He doesn't fuss with pies or cakes;
He never roasts or broils or bakes;
He doesn't use the rolling pin
Or measure level spoonfuls in;
He doesn't watch the oven clock;
He doesn't fill the cookie-crock;
We watch him with admiring eyes
While daddy fries and fries and fries!

SMOKED-SAUSAGE POTATO CASSEROLE

1 lb smoked sausage
2-4 Tbsp chopped onion
10 medium potatoes
1-2 cups grated cheddar cheese

Medium white sauce
Combine 2 cups milk and ¼ cup flour in batter shaker. Heat while stirring in saucepan over medium heat 'til thickened. Add 1 tsp salt.

Brown sausage and drain. Sauté onion. Peel, dice, or slice and cook potatoes, just until done. Make white sauce and combine with meat and vegetables. Season to your liking with salt and pepper. Pour into a greased casserole dish and top with cheese. Bake at 350° about 45 minutes or until hot and bubbly. The smoked sausage gives it a special flavor.

– Charlotte Rohrer

KRAUT-LOVERS CASSEROLE

1 pint sauerkraut
1 lb sausage, fried
6-8 potatoes, peeled

Partially drain sauerkraut and dump into 8x12 casserole dish. Pour undrained sausage over kraut. Cook and mash potatoes as usual with milk, salt, and butter. Spread over sausage. Bake at 350° for 15-20 minutes until lightly browned on top.

– Wilma (Rohrer) Shank

A conceited person has one good point.
He doesn't talk about other people.

Pork Chop Casserole

4-6 boneless pork chops
6 potatoes peeled and sliced thin
1 small onion, diced
1 cup grated cheddar cheese
½ cup milk
1 can cream of mushroom soup (see recipe on page 151)

Brown pork chops in hot fat in a skillet. Grease a 9x13 baking dish. Layer potatoes, then onion, salt, pepper, and cheese. Heat milk and soup together. Pour half of it over potatoes and onions. Lay meat on top of potatoes. Season with salt and pepper. Top with remaining soup. Bake at 350º for 1½ hours.

Pork Barbecue Sauce

1 quart oil
½ gal white vinegar
1 quart water
¾ cup salt
¼ cup pepper
⅓ cup garlic powder
1 cup lemon juice
¼ cup hot sauce
1 cup Zesty Italian salad dressing
1 cup Heinz 57 Barbecue sauce

This recipe will barbecue 6 pork loins. It is also delicious on poultry. For a less tart sauce you can leave out part of the vinegar and add that amount more of water.

– *Melinda (Wenger) Knicely*

Blessed are they which do hunger and thirst after righteousness: for they shall be filled. – Matthew 5:6

Smoked Whole Pork Loin

1 whole pork loin, halved
20 cups water
2-2½ cups Morton's Tender Quick

Marinate entire pork loin up to 48 hours. Prepare hickory wood chips by soaking in water an hour or more before starting your fire. When charcoal is hot, drain wood chips and sprinkle over coals. I use a water pan between the fire and the meat for moist, tender meat. Cook in smoker-grill over indirect heat and grill 4-6 hours until meat tests done (160°). Don't overcook. Add charcoal to fire as needed. If you're short on time, as I always am, pop it into the oven at 325° awhile before starting your fire. This will save you several hours of grilling time.

Sweet and Sour Pork

1½ pounds pork strips or chunks
1 cup water
20 oz can pineapple chunks, drained (reserve liquid)
¼ cup brown sugar
2 Tbsp cornstarch
¼ cup vinegar
1 Tbsp soy sauce
¾ cup green pepper strips
¼ cup thinly sliced onion
Cooked noodles or rice

Brown pork. Add water, cover, and simmer. In a saucepan, combine brown sugar and cornstarch. Add pineapple juice, vinegar, and soy sauce. Cook and stir over low heat until thick. Pour over hot pork. Let stand 10 minutes. Add pineapple, green pepper, and onion. Cook 2 or 3 minutes. Serve over noodles or rice. Serves 6 measly eaters or 3 hungry ones.

– Lois Y. Wenger

Never trust a skinny cook.

Baked Rice

1 cup white rice
2 cups water
1 tsp salt
1 tsp oil

Put ingredients in a greased 1½ qt bake dish. Cover and bake at 350° for 1 hour. Fluff with a fork and serve. Makes 3 cups.

Sausage Pie

1 medium onion, chopped
3 Tbsp butter
2 cups potatoes, grated
½ tsp salt
¼ tsp pepper
1½ lb sausage
2 cups water

Sauté onion in butter. Add potatoes, salt, and pepper. Cook until soft. Brown sausage. Drain. Add water. Bring to a boil, and stir in batter. Cook until thickened, add potatoes. Mix up dough. Divide into two pieces. Roll dough out and line the bottom of a 9x13 casserole dish. Put in sausage mixture. Top with 8 thin slices of Velveeta cheese and cover with remaining dough. Bake at 350° until golden brown, about 45-50 minutes.

Batter
½ cup water
¼ cup flour
⅓ cup half-and-half

Mix flour and water until smooth. Add half-and-half.

Dough
1¼ cups sour cream
¾ tsp soda
2 cups flour
3 Tbsp butter
½ tsp salt

Ina Sue (Showalter) Strite

Sausage Stuffing

1 small loaf of white bread
1 lb sausage
1 medium onion, chopped
2 Tbsp sage
3 eggs, beaten
2 cups milk

Tear bread into pieces into a large bowl as much as a day ahead. Brown sausage and onion. Drain excess fat. Add sage and sausage to the bread and toss all together. Pour beaten eggs and milk over all. Stir to moisten. May bake in greased casserole dish or use to stuff a turkey. Bake at 300° until done.

Variation: For stuffing without meat, add 1 cup chopped celery and leaves, 1 cup broth, and salt and pepper to taste.

– Lois Y. Wenger

German Pizza

1 lb ground sausage or hamburger
2 Tbsp margarine
6 medium potatoes (peeled and grated)
¼ cup diced green peppers
¼ cup diced red peppers
½ cup diced onion
3 eggs
⅓ cup milk
salt and pepper to taste
grated sharp cheddar

Brown and drain meat. Melt margarine and grease 12 or 14 inch skillet. Layer potatoes to form crust. Add onions, peppers, and meat in layers. Mix eggs, milk, and seasonings and pour over potatoes and meat. Simmer covered until potatoes are soft. Sprinkle cheddar over all. You can also place ingredients in a 9x13 baking dish and bake at 350° for 35-45 minutes.

– Dorothy (Shank) Wenger

RED BEANS AND RICE

1½ lbs sausage
½ large onion, diced
6 cups red cooked kidney beans (3 15-oz cans)
½ tsp coarse black pepper
1 tsp salt
½ tsp red pepper
½ tsp oregano
2 Tbsp molasses <u>or</u> ¼ cup brown sugar
2 Tbsp vinegar

1 tsp butter
2¼ cups uncooked rice
½ tsp salt
4½ cups water

Brown sausage and onion in skillet. Drain excess fat. Add beans and seasonings. Simmer about an hour on low heat. Stir occasionally.

About ½ hour before serving, combine butter, rice, salt, and water in a saucepan. Bring to a rolling boil. Stir, then reduce heat to a low simmer. Cover and cook 20 minutes. Serve with bean mixture.

SAVORY HERB RICE

2 cups water
1 cup rice, white or brown
2 beef bouillon cubes
½ tsp salt
½ tsp marjoram
½ tsp rosemary
½ tsp thyme
1 tsp onion flakes
1 Tbsp butter

Combine all ingredients in a heavy saucepan. Bring to a boil, stir once, cover and reduce heat to low. Simmer 12-14 minutes until rice is fluffy. Serves 4-6. If using brown rice, you will need to add ½ cup water and cook about one hour.

HAM LOAF

2 lbs ground ham
½ lb sausage or hamburger
1½ cups soft bread crumbs
⅓ cup finely chopped onion
1 cup milk
2 eggs
dash of pepper

Combine and press into a large loaf pan. Cover with pineapple glaze (recipe below). Bake in 350° oven 60-70 minutes or until done.

PINEAPPLE GLAZE FOR HAM

¾ cup brown sugar
1 cup pineapple juice
2 Tbsp vinegar
¼ cup water
2 Tbsp cornstarch
1½ tsp dry mustard

Cook over medium heat until thickened and pour over ham loaf before baking. This is also a nice sauce to serve over warm sliced western ham.

A Lunch Prayer from Former School Days:

To God who gives us daily bread,
a thankful song we raise,
And pray that He who sends us food
will fill our hearts with praise.

– Amen

HOMEMADE NOODLES

6 egg yolks, beaten
6 Tbsp water
1 tsp salt
3 cups flour

Combine and mix well. Make 4 balls of dough. (If you have a pasta maker, shape dough to fit into it and cut in desired width.) Roll out large rectangles as thinly as possible. Lay on a cloth to dry awhile. Cut into narrow strips the width you like. Air dry several hours. Store in fridge until used. Cook in chicken or beef broth. Use 6 cups broth to cook ½ lb noodles. Season to your liking and add fresh minced parsley before serving. For a special treat, pour browned butter over cooked noodles.

We had turkeys on the range (living outdoors on pasture) when I was young. With our large turkey eggs, my mother made fluffy angel food cakes and used the yolks to make homemade noodles. I always liked to watch her fold the dough and cut the noodles with a long knife. We girls would then spread them out to dry. How nice they looked stored in gallon jars on our open kitchen shelves.

CREAMY PARMESAN NOODLES

3 qts water
1½ Tbsp salt
8 oz noodles or pasta
1 cup heavy cream
½ cup butter
1 cup Parmesan cheese
Fresh ground black pepper

Cook noodles in salted water. Drain. Put cream in a heavy sauce-pan over low heat. Stir in soft butter and cheese. When hot and bubbly add noodles and stir gently, until noodles are evenly coated. Serve with pepper.

*For a low-fat version make these changes: Combine 1 cup whole milk with two teaspoons flour in a batter shaker. Melt 1 Tbsp butter in heavy saucepan and stir in milk mixture. Add a pinch of salt and cook while stirring until sauce thickens. Stir in cheese and hot noodles.

Beans and Ham

1 lb navy beans
2 qts water
1 or 2 meaty ham bones
1 medium onion, chopped
1½ tsp salt
¼ tsp pepper

Soak beans overnight in 2 qts water to soften them, and shorten cooking time. Drain, then cover beans with fresh water and simmer with ham bone for 30 minutes. Turn off heat, let set with lid on for an hour. Add rest of ingredients and either simmer; or bake in 300° oven until beans are tender. Cooking takes an hour or two; oven time is 2-3 hours. Serve with ketchup.

Macaroni and Cheese

2 cups macaroni
2 Tbsp butter
2 Tbsp flour
2½ cups milk
1 tsp salt
1 tsp dry mustard
2 cups shredded cheese
½ cup buttered cracker crumbs

Cook macaroni in water, drain. In saucepan, melt butter. Make a batter of flour and milk, pour into saucepan, add salt and mustard, stir over medium heat until mixture thickens. Add cheese. Pour over macaroni and top with crumbs. Bake at 350° until hot and bubbly. Serves 8-10. I use both cheddar and Velveeta cheese. You may cover the top with cheese after baking instead of the crumb topping.

A good spirit attracts friends.

Sunday Morning Macaroni and Cheese

2 cups uncooked macaroni
1½ tsp salt
1½ tsp dry mustard
⅛ tsp pepper
3-4 cups grated cheddar cheese
6 cups milk

Generously grease a large casserole or 9x13 dish with soft butter or margarine. Layer macaroni and cheese in dish. Stir salt, mustard, and pepper into milk, and pour over all. Bake at 225° for about 3 hours. Stick a ham loaf in the oven, too, and dinner will be ready when you get home from church. For a creamier dish, use Velveeta cheese. If you are home, stir it when half done baking. Serves 10-12.

Macaroni for Six to Eight

1½ cups uncooked macaroni
1 tsp salt
1 tsp dry mustard
Dash of pepper
2-3 cups grated cheese*
4½ cups milk

*My macaroni dish is a melting pot of whatever cheese I can find in the fridge. Sometimes I use 4 kinds. Bake in a 2 qt. casserole dish, use same procedure as in the recipe above.

*Money is the universal provider of everything but happiness
and a passport to everywhere but heaven.*

DEER BOLOGNA

70 lbs meat (deer and pork)
1 qt sorghum molasses
1 pt honey
3 lbs brown sugar
1⅓ cups salt
5 Tbsp black pepper
1½ Tbsp mace
1 Tbsp coriander
¼ tsp red pepper
½ Tbsp cloves
2½ cups Morton's Tender Quick

We use 20 lbs sausage and 50 lbs of deer burger. Mix meats and spread out on large surface. Drizzle molasses and honey over all. Combine brown sugar, salt, spices and Tender Quick and sprinkle evenly over meat. Mix seasonings into meat and regrind. Stuff into 6½" diameter bags, and keep in a cool place for 48 hours.

Put bologna bags in cold water in large kettles for cooking. Bring to a boil and cook for 1¼ hours or until bags float. Hang until cool. Smoke for 4-6 hours. Makes about 8 bags (6½"x24"). Slice and freeze.

– Sharon (Wenger) Good

Let this kitchen be a place
  Where those who hunger can be fed
As much with understanding
  And affection, as with bread.

A place where those who thirst
  Can drink of peace and kindness, too...
A place where everyone is served
  With love in everything we do.
– Selected

Vegetables

You Can Do It

One seed at a time and the garden grows;
One drop at a time and the river flows.
One word at a time and the book is read;
One stroke at a time and the paint is spread.
One chip at a time and the statue's unveiled,
One step at a time and the mountain is scaled.
One thing at a time and that done well,
Is the only sure way to succeed and excel.
You can write, you can paint, you can sculpt,
    you can climb,
You can do it by taking one step at a time.

– Author Unknown

Vegetables

How Much Shall I Prepare?

One way to determine how much you need to feed a crowd is this: If you're serving two or more vegetables in one meal, figure ⅔ cup per person for potato dishes, macaroni and cheese, etc. For fresh or frozen vegetables, prepare about ½ cup per person (one quart feeds 8 people). These amounts may vary somewhat, according to the age and appetites of your guests.

CREAMED PEAS OR LIMAS

Cook 3-4 cups vegetables in a small amount of water. Add butter, salt, and a pinch of soda and sugar. Cook just until tender. Make a batter of 1 cup half and half and ¼ cup flour. Stir into cooking water, and simmer until it thickens. If too thick, add more cream. Remove from heat, and serve. (The soda keeps vegetables bright green). I sometimes cook a bay leaf or two with my limas. Remove bay leaf before serving.

CREAMED ASPARAGUS

Prepare like peas or limas in previous recipe. Add cubed Velveeta cheese just before serving. Delicious when served over toast and an egg, or as is.

BAKED ASPARAGUS

2 Tbsp butter
6-8 slices white bread, cubed
1 quart asparagus, cooked until tender crisp
3 or 4 hard boiled eggs diced
½ cup milk
4 Tbsp flour
3 cups milk
1 tsp salt
dash of pepper
½ lb Velveeta cheese, cubed

Melt butter in large skillet and toss bread to toast. Layer bread cubes in bottom of greased 8x12 dish. Then layer asparagus and hard boiled eggs. Make a batter of flour and ½ cup milk. Heat remaining 3 cups milk, salt and pepper to a simmer over medium heat. Stir in batter and cook until mixture boils. Stir in cheese. Pour over casserole. Top with a few bread crumbs and a sprinkle of black pepper. Bake at 350° for 45-50 minutes.

BARBECUED GREEN BEANS

3 quarts green beans, drained
6 strips bacon, fried and crumbled
1 onion, chopped
1 cup ketchup
¾ cup brown sugar

Sauté onion in bacon grease. Mix in remaining ingredients. Bake in oven at 250° or cook in crock-pot slowly for several hours.
– *Ina Sue (Showalter) Strite*

GLAZED BUTTERED CARROTS

Peel and slice 3-4 carrots. Cook in salted water. Drain. Add 1½ Tbsp butter and 3 Tbsp brown sugar.   Heat slowly for 10-15 minutes until nicely glazed, stirring occasionally. Serves 4.

Fresh Green Beans

4-6 slices bacon (or chipped dried beef, or ham scraps)
1 onion, chopped
green beans

Fry bacon in kettle used to cook beans, preferably pressure cooker or heavy kettle. Turn when crisp on one side and add onion, continuing to fry bacon. When bacon is crisp and onions are hot, remove from pan and add beans with desired amount of salt, a pinch of sugar, and enough water to cover bottom one inch deep. Put bacon and onion on top of beans. If using a pressure cooker, time for 3 minutes after pressure is up. If a kettle is used, cook just until tender – about 30 minutes. Don't let them scorch.

Harvard Beets

3 cups cooked beets
1 Tbsp butter
2 Tbsp sugar
½ tsp salt
1 Tbsp vinegar
1 Tbsp cornstarch

Combine vinegar and cornstarch. Add butter, sugar and salt to beets. Stir all together with beets and beet juice. Cook until thickened.

Bread Dressing

10 slices of bread, cubed
⅔ cup hot chicken broth or bouillon
¼ cup melted butter
4 eggs
2 cups milk
1½ tsp salt and pepper
fresh parsley
Layer bread in 2-quart bake dish. Moisten each layer with broth and butter, until dish is full. Beat eggs. Add salt, pepper, and milk. Pour over bread and sprinkle with parsley. Bake at 350° for 1 hour or 250° while at church. Lay foil on top but don't seal for church time.

– Mary Rohrer (Raymond)

SAVORY CORN DRESSING

½ cup butter
1 cup chopped celery
½ cup chopped onion
1 Tbsp fresh parsley
8-10 cups dry bread cubes*
3 cups chicken broth
3 cups fresh or frozen corn
3 beaten eggs
½ tsp pepper
2 tsp salt

Sauté celery and onion in butter, add parsley. Stir into bread cubes, add broth, corn, eggs, salt and pepper. Mixture will be soupy. Dip into a greased 9x13 bake dish. Bake at 350° about 1¼ hours until golden brown. Serves 12-16. *I use homemade white bread or purchased Italian bread, or other firm textured white bread.

SAVORY BREAD DRESSING

Omit corn in above recipe.

BAKED CORN

3 Tbsp flour
1 tsp salt
⅛ tsp pepper
2 tsp sugar
2 cups milk
1 pint corn
3 Tbsp butter, melted
3 eggs

Combine flour, salt, pepper, and sugar. Add milk gradually. Stir in corn, melted butter, and beaten eggs. Pour into 2½ quart buttered bake dish. Bake at 350° for 45 minutes.

CREAMED CORN

6 ears fresh sweet corn
½ cup water
1 tsp salt
1 tsp sugar
¼ cup butter
½ cup cream, optional

Cut corn from cobs, by first cutting down through kernels, then scraping the pulp from the cob with the back of knife. Combine corn, water, salt, and sugar. Melt butter in saucepan, add corn and stir until hot. Turn heat very low and cook about 15 minutes, stir occasionally. Add cream and cook until piping hot. For creamier corn, split the kernels with a knife before slicing off the cob, or use a corn creamer. (A handy gadget found in kitchenware shops.)

SWEET CORN TO FREEZE

4 qts corn
¼ cup sugar
4 tsp salt
3 cups water

Wash fresh-picked sweet corn and cut off the cob. Combine corn, sugar, salt, and water in heavy kettle over medium heat and stir continuously to a boil. Cook 10-15 minutes. Cool, put in containers, and freeze. "Tastes like the day you shucked it."

Variation: Wash fresh - picked sweet corn, drop into boiling water. Boil 8-10 minutes, cool completely in cold water.
Cut corn off cobs as described in Creamed Corn (above) and freeze immediately. Season with salt and butter before serving
– *Zelda Rohrer and Melissa (Rohrer) Wenger*

CORN PUDDING

1 qt corn – whole kernel or creamed
1 cup sour cream
1 stick of butter, melted
1 egg, beaten
1 pkg Jiffy Corn Muffin Mix (8 ½ oz)

Mix all together and pour into greased 2 qt baking dish. Bake at 350° until done, about 50 minutes.

FRIED CORN

4 ears fresh sweet corn
2 strips crisp bacon and drippings
1 small minced onion
Salt and pepper

Cut corn from cob and add to bacon drippings. Add onion, salt and pepper. Cook over medium heat, stirring occasionally, until corn is tender, about 15 minutes. Crumble bacon over top.

SCALLOPED CAULIFLOWER

1 large head of cauliflower, chopped and boiled until tender crisp
1 cup grated cheese
3 hard boiled eggs, chopped
2 cups buttered bread crumbs or Ritz cracker crumbs

White Sauce

2 cups milk
¼ cup flour
1 tsp salt
¼ cup butter

Mix milk and flour in batter shaker – add salt and stir while heating until it thickens. Add butter.

Layer cauliflower, cheese, and eggs in greased 9x13 dish. Pour white sauce over all. Top with crumbs. Bake at 350° until hot and bubbly (30-40 minutes). This dish can be made using other vegetables, also. It is real good with a mixture of cauliflower, broccoli, and carrots. The eggs can be left out.

It is a good thing to give thanks unto the Lord. – Psalm 92:1a

Broccoli Rice Casserole

1 small onion chopped
½ cup chopped celery
10 oz frozen chopped broccoli
1 Tbsp butter
8 oz Velveeta cheese
1 can Cream of Mushroom Soup
5 oz can evaporated milk
3 cups cooked rice

Sauté onion, celery, and broccoli in butter for 3-5 minutes. Sir in cheese, soup, and milk until smooth. Place rice in a greased 8-in square dish. Pour cheese mixture over rice. Do not stir. Bake uncovered at 325° for 25-30 minutes.

– *Wanda (Rohrer) Good*

Carolyn's Cabbage Casserole

2 cups crushed corn flakes
½ cup melted butter
4 cups raw chopped cabbage
1 onion, diced
1 can cream of celery soup
½ cup milk
½ cup mayonnaise
1 cup grated cheese

Mix corn flakes with melted butter. Spread half in a greased 8x12 casserole dish. Layer cabbage and onion on top of corn flakes. Combine soup, milk, and mayonnaise, and pour over all. Top with remaining corn flakes and cheese. Cover with foil. Bake at 350° for 45 minutes.

– *Carolyn (Black) Shirkey*

Happiness is a habit—cultivate it.

CABBAGE CASSEROLE

1 12 oz box Stove Top Stuffing mix
3 lbs cabbage, cooked and drained
1 can mushroom soup
8 oz sour cream
1 cup cheese, cubed

Prepare Stove Top Stuffing mix according to box. Place ½ of mix in a greased 9x13 casserole dish. Blend soup, sour cream, and cheese with cabbage. Spread on the stuffing. Top with remaining stuffing. Bake at 350° for 45 minutes.

– Ina Sue (Showalter) Strite

CHEDDAR BAKED POTATO SLICES

1 can Cream of Mushroom Soup
½ tsp paprika
½ tsp pepper
½ tsp salt
4 medium potatoes cut in ¼ inch slices
1 cup shredded cheddar cheese

Combine soup and seasonings. In greased 2 quart casserole, arrange potatoes in overlapping rows. Sprinkle with cheese. Spoon soup mixture over cheese. Cover with foil. Bake approximately 1 hour at 375°.

– Karen (Rohrer) Rohrer

SIMPLE SCALLOPED POTATOES

Generously butter casserole dish(es). Wash potatoes. Whether or not you peel them is up to you. Layer into the dish(es) as follows: potatoes sliced to ⅛ inch thickness, a sprinkling of flour, a sprinkling of pepper, a sprinkling of garlic salt, grated onion, grated cheese. Continue layering until your dish(es) are nearly full. Pour enough milk into each dish so that the milk barely covers the potatoes when they are squished down with your hand. Cover and bake at 350° for 1¼ - 1½ hours.

– Lois Y. Wenger

CREAMY RANCH POTATOES

¼ cup butter
⅓ cup chopped onion
¼ cup flour
1½ tsp salt
¼ tsp pepper
2 cups milk
1 cup Velveeta cheese, cubed
½ cup sour cream
⅓ cup (liquid) ranch dressing
4 cups cubed, cooked potatoes
¼ lb fried, crumbled bacon
1 cup bread cubes
1 Tbsp butter

Sauté onion in butter; add flour, salt, and pepper. Stir in milk and cook until thickened. Add cheese, sour cream, and ranch dressing, stirring until cheese is melted. Mix sauce with potatoes. Put in greased 1½ qt bake dish. Top with bacon and buttered bread crumbs. Bake at 350° for 30 minutes. Double recipe for a 9x13 dish.

– Janice (Shank) Wenger

RANCH POTATOES

6-8 medium potatoes
¾ cup sour cream
½ cup Ranch style dressing
½ cup bacon crumbled
1 cup shredded cheese
1 tsp dry parsley
1 tsp salt

Topping:
½ cup grated cheese
¼ cup melted butter
1½ cups Ritz cracker crumbs
½ cup bacon crumbled

Dice potatoes and cook. Mix other ingredients and pour over potatoes. Toss gently. Place in 9x13 baking dish. Sprinkle on topping. Bake at 350° for 45 minutes or until bubbly.

– Lydia (Eberly) Good

STUFFED BAKED POTATOES

4 baking potatoes
8 oz. Velveeta cheese
4 tsp milk
4 tsp butter
4 Tbsp sour cream
1-2 pints hot cooked broccoli
Salt and pepper to taste

Bake potatoes in 375° oven until done. Meanwhile, melt cheese in milk until smooth. Split potatoes lengthwise and put into individual soup bowls. Fluff with fork, then put butter and sour cream on potatoes. Top with broccoli, salt and pepper, and pour cheese sauce over all. Serve while hot.

SOUR CREAM SCALLOPED POTATOES

8 large baking potatoes
1 medium size onion, diced
4 Tbsp butter
2 cups sour cream
4 hard cooked eggs, sliced (optional)
salt, pepper, and paprika

Pare and slice potatoes ⅛ inch thick. Cook in salt water until almost tender. Drain. Set aside. Sauté onion in butter until glossy but not brown. Stir in sour cream and let heat thoroughly, but not boiling. In greased casserole, layer ½ of potatoes, egg slices, and sour cream mixture. Repeat layers with rest of ingredients. Bake, uncovered at 350° for approximately 40 minutes or until potatoes are tender. (I never add the eggs.)

– *Mary Ethel Wenger*

Never speak loudly to one another unless the house is on fire.

Gourmet Cheese Potatoes

¼ cup butter
⅓ cup chopped onion
¼ cup flour
1 tsp salt
¼ tsp pepper
1½ cups milk
2 cups Velveeta cheese
4 cups cooked cubed potatoes
¼ cup dry bread crumbs
1 tsp butter

Sauté onion in butter until soft. Add flour, salt, and pepper. Gradually add milk and cook until thickened. Add cheese. Arrange potatoes and cheese sauce in layers in casserole dish. Top with buttered bread crumbs and bake at 350° for 25 minutes.

– Barbara (Rohrer) Eberly

Make and Bake Mashed Potatoes

10 lbs potatoes
1 lb cream cheese
1 pint sour cream
½ cup minced fresh onion
1½ Tbsp salt
½ cup butter
Pepper
Milk

Peel, cook, drain, and thoroughly mash potatoes. Add rest of ingredients and enough potato water or milk to make soft consistency. Put into greased casserole dishes. Bake at 350° or chill (or freeze) until needed. This amount serves 25.

Tip for cooking potatoes:
When cooking potatoes, put a little butter in kettle to prevent boiling over.

CREAMY MASHED POTATOES

potatoes, peeled and chunked
rich milk, heated
butter, melted in milk
salt and pepper

Figure on 2½ servings per pound of potatoes (unpeeled). Five pounds serves 12-13; 6 pounds serves 15; 8 pounds serves 20, etc. Peel potatoes and cook until tender. Drain off water. Mash thoroughly to remove lumps. Add hot milk a little at a time, butter, salt, and pepper. Use <u>plenty</u> of milk to make potatoes soft and creamy. Whip until fluffy. Serve piping hot with some good gravy.

COTTAGE POTATOES

10 large potatoes (or 6 lbs)
1 large onion
¼ cup butter
½ lb sharp cheddar cheese
1 Tbsp fresh, minced parsley
3 cups milk
1 Tbsp salt
1 tsp pepper

2 cups crushed cornflakes
¼ cup butter, melted

You may peel potatoes first or cook potatoes in skins. Cool, peel, and cube, or grate into large mixing bowl. Chop onion fine and sauté in ¼ cup of butter. Grate cheese. Add parsley. Combine all and mix with potatoes. Stir in milk. Pour into greased 9x13 pan . Combine butter and cornflakes and sprinkle over potatoes. Bake at 350° for about 40 minutes. Serves 15.
Variation: fry and crumble some bacon and sprinkle on potatoes beneath cornflakes. Red and green peppers may be added.

How richly blessed we are
because of God's great and precious promises.

CREAMY COMPANY POTATOES

2 cans cream of celery soup
2 cans cream of chicken soup
1 lb Velveeta cheese, cubed
2 cups sour cream
⅔ cup butter divided
2 tsp seasoned salt
½ tsp garlic salt
1 tsp pepper
10 lbs potatoes peeled, cubed, cooked, and drained
1-2 cups crushed Ritz crackers

Combine soups, cheese, sour cream, half of butter, seasoned salt, garlic salt, and pepper. Cook until cheese is melted and smooth. Add potatoes. Mix well and pour into greased casserole dishes.

Bake at 350° for 40 to 60 minutes. Melt rest of butter and mix with crackers. Sprinkle onto potatoes when half done baking. Serves 25-30 Really handy for company dinners!

– Charlotte Rohrer

EASY GOURMET POTATOES

6 cups potatoes
2 cups Velveeta cheese
1-2 Tbsp grated onion or onion flakes
¼ cup butter
½ - 1 cup milk
1 tsp salt
pepper to taste

Grate cooked, cooled potatoes, cheese, and onion. Mix in butter and seasonings and milk to desired consistency. Bake at 350° for 45-50 minutes.

Brenda (Shirk) Knicely

Good cooks never lack friends.

ZESTY HERB POTATOES

½ cup mayonnaise
1 Tbsp oregano
1½ tsp garlic powder
1½ tsp onion powder
1 tsp seasoned salt
1 Tbsp water
2 lbs potatoes cut into 1" cubes

Mix mayonnaise, seasonings, and water in a bowl. Toss in potatoes. Place potatoes on greased cookie sheet. Bake at 400° for 30 to 40 minutes. Stir after 15 minutes.

— Ina Sue (Showalter) Strite

ONION PIE

2 cups chopped onions
2 Tbsp butter
2 beaten eggs
¾ cup milk
¾ tsp salt
¼ cup grated white cheese

Sauté onions in butter. Add remaining ingredients. Bake at 350° in greased casserole until partially set, about 30 minutes. Remove from oven. Sprinkle this crumb mixture on top:

1 cup Ritz cracker crumbs
4 Tbsp melted butter
1 cup grated yellow cheese
½ tsp garlic salt
½ tsp ground mustard
½ tsp Season-All

Bake for 15 minutes or until top is golden brown.

— Marilyn Eberly

The best antique is an old friend.

Tomato Dumplings

½ cup finely chopped onion
¼ cup finely chopped green pepper
¼ cup finely chopped celery
¼ cup butter or margarine
1 bay leaf
1 can (28 ounces) tomatoes with liquid, cut up
1 Tbsp brown sugar
½ tsp dried basil
½ tsp salt
¼ tsp pepper

In a medium skillet, sauté onion, green pepper and celery in butter until tender. Add bay leaf, tomatoes, brown sugar, basil, salt, and pepper. Cover and simmer for 5-10 minutes. Meanwhile, make dumplings:

Dumplings

1 cup flour
1½ tsp baking powder
½ tsp salt
1 Tbsp cold butter or margarine
1 Tbsp snipped fresh parsley
⅔ cup milk

Combine dry ingredients in a bowl. Cut in butter. Add parsley and milk; stir just until mixed. Drop by tablespoonfuls into six mounds onto bubbling tomato mixture; cover tightly and simmer for 12-15 minutes or until a toothpick inserted into dumpling comes out clean. Remove and discard bay leaf. Serve immediately. Serves 6.

– Martha Rohrer (David)

*Three essential ingredients in the recipe for a happier life
are prayer, patience and understanding.*

SQUASH CASSEROLE

2½ cups diced squash
1 cup diced onion
1 cup diced celery (optional)
⅔ cup margarine
1½ cups water
2 cups cracker crumbs
1 cup grated cheese
2 eggs, beaten
1½ tsp salt
½ tsp pepper

Cook first five ingredients together for 5 minutes. Add remaining ingredients. Bake in a large bake dish at 350° for 30-35 minutes.
— *Melissa (Rohrer) Wenger*

SUMMER SQUASH SKILLET

4 cups thinly sliced summer squash
½ small onion, chopped
1½ Tbsp butter
½ tsp salt
½ tsp sugar
coarse black pepper
2 oz grated cheese or Velveeta slices

Melt butter in large skillet. Wash and slice small summer squash. Sauté squash and onion in skillet. Sprinkle seasonings over all. Cover and simmer on low heat until squash is tender. Turn off heat. Top with cheese. Cover until serving time. Serves 4.

*All that is necessary for the triumph of evil
is that good men sit back and do nothing.*
— *Edmund Burke*

Poor Man's Zucchini Cakes

2 cups grated zucchini, squeezed dry
2 Tbsp chopped onion
1 Tbsp mayonnaise
¾ Tbsp Old Bay seasoning
2 eggs, beaten
2 cups cracker or bread crumbs

Mix the zucchini with the other ingredients. Make patties, dust with flour and fry until golden brown. These taste like crab cakes.
— *Wanda (Rohrer) Good*

Delicious Crab Cakes: If you have a hankering for the real thing, use 1 lb of flaked crabmeat instead of zucchini in above recipe.

Stuffed Zucchini

2 medium zucchini (8" long)
½ lb ground beef or sausage
¼ cup chopped onion
⅔ cup seasoned bread crumbs
⅓ cup milk
⅛ tsp dillweed
1 cup spaghetti sauce
1 cup shredded cheese

Cut zucchini in half lengthwise. Scoop out pulp, leaving ¼" shell. Chop pulp and set aside. Brown meat and onion. Drain. Add pulp, bread crumbs, milk, and dillweed. Spoon into zucchini shells. Place in greased 2-quart dish and top with spaghetti sauce and cheese. Cover and bake at 325° for 30 minutes. Serves 2.
— *Beulah (Rhodes) Burkholder*

A wise man thinks twice, before he speaks once.

TEXAS SWEET POTATO BALLS

2 cups mashed sweet potatoes
½ tsp salt
2 Tbsp melted butter or margarine
3 Tbsp brown sugar

Mix all ingredients well in a bowl. Wrap a tablespoon of the mixture around a large marshmallow. Roll balls in grated coconut or crushed corn flakes or chopped pecans. Place balls into a greased casserole dish. Bake at 350° for 10-15 minutes. Be careful not to melt marshmallows.
These freeze well. Take from freezer and pop into oven.
Very pretty.

– Martha Rohrer (David)

SWEET POTATO CASSEROLE

4 cups mashed sweet potatoes
   (2¾ lbs before peeling)
5 Tbsp butter, melted
2 beaten eggs
3 Tbsp brown sugar
2 Tbsp. flour
1 tsp salt
½ cup milk

Combine all ingredients and put in shallow 2-qt bake dish. Make topping and sprinkle over casserole. Bake at 350° for 25-30 minutes. Serves 10-12.

Topping
½ cup brown sugar
¼ cup flour
2½ Tbsp butter
½ cup chopped pecans

Combine sugar, flour, and butter to make crumbs. Add pecans.

Most of the friction in our everyday life
is caused by someone using the wrong tone of voice.

STUFFED MUSHROOMS

- ❖ Fresh mushrooms
- ❖ Browned sausage or bacon crumbles
- ❖ Sautéed minced onions or peppers
- ❖ Grated cheddar cheese
- ❖ Sour cream or mayonnaise
- ❖ Salt and pepper

Wash mushrooms, remove stems. Combine your choice of filling ingredients.
Stuff mushrooms with meat mixture and bake at 350° until piping hot, about 15 – 20 minutes.
(slice and saute stems for a casserole, soup, omelet, pizza, etc.)

SIMPLE STUFFED MUSHROOMS

1 lb fresh mushrooms
5.2 oz pkg Boursin cheese
Bacon bits
Grated Monterey Jack cheese

Remove stems from mushrooms. Put Boursin cheese in caps. Pack tightly in a 9 x 13 pan. Sprinkle bacon bits and cheese over all. Bake at 350° for 20 minutes.

Boursin is a creamy cheese from France. I use the herb and garlic flavored Boursin. You'll find it in the deli at larger grocery stores. Baby portobella mushrooms are my favorite, but any kind will do.

A rose can say I love you... orchids can enthrall...
but a weed bouquet in a chubby fist,
oh my, that says it all.

Vegetable Pizza

Crust

¼ cup scalded milk
¼ cup margarine
2½ Tbsp sugar
¼ tsp salt
1 beaten egg
½ Tbsp yeast
¼ cup warm water
2 cups all purpose flour

Pour hot milk over margarine, sugar, and salt. Put yeast in warm water to dissolve. Mix all ingredients together with 1 cup of the flour. Mix 3 minutes. Add rest of flour and knead a bit. Grease top of dough and let rest for 1 hour. Roll out ¼ inch thick on greased cookie sheet or large baking pan. Let raise about 15 minutes. Prick dough with fork and bake at 350° for 10-12 minutes. Cool.

Creamy Filling:

16 oz cream cheese
⅔ cup mayonnaise
½ tsp salt

Mix until smooth. You may season with Italian or Ranch Seasoning or leave plain. Spread over the dough. Top with 6 cups chopped, fresh, raw vegetables of your choice: carrots, cucumbers, cauliflower, broccoli, peppers, tomatoes, onion, etc. Sprinkle black pepper on top of vegetables.

Variation: If you'd like, substitute 2 cans of refrigerated crescent roll dough for the crust, and save 1½ hours of time!
The addition of grated cheddar and crumbled bacon will turn a vegetable pizza into a main dish.

Do for others with no expectation of return favors.
We should all plant some trees we'll never sit under.

Garden Salads

Our Garden's Bounty

Ah, summer is here, and the gardeners cheer,
    For there's food in the old garden patch;
Where the killdeer will stalk, and put up a squawk
    While they're waiting their young'uns to hatch.

Oh, the bounty galore we can lay up in store,
    For the days when winter is nigh…
There are corn and tomatoes, white, and red taters,
    The squash in their yellow garb lie.

There are cabbage and beets, and carrots so sweet;
    What more could we ask for than this?
Yet there's onions and beans, ripe melons supreme,
    To add to our summertime bliss.

Though we gardeners seed, and hoe many a weed,
    And water and tend it with care;
Without God to supply sun and rain from the sky,
    We'd have no garden bounty to share.

                – Hazel Horst

What fun to page through new seed books
    And dream of how our plants will look…
But oh, alas! It is a dream—
    For when we view the summer scene
We find it's hot, our plants are dry,
    The bugs molest, the weeds grow high!
Each year I plan the perfect plot—
    Then find the one I grow is not.

                – Barbara Eberly

Garden Salads

SPINACH & FRUIT SALAD

2 quarts fresh spinach, torn
¼ small sweet onion, diced
1 quart strawberries, sliced <u>or</u>
 2-3 cans mandarin oranges, drained
½ cup toasted, sliced almonds or pecans
½ cup feta cheese, crumbled

Dressing:
½ cup sugar
⅓ cup vinegar*
2 Tbsp honey
½ cup oil

Mix together and pour over salad ingredients just before serving. Looks pretty and is delicious! *I use red wine or rasp-berry vinegar. Purchased raspberry vinegarette dressing is very good too. 1 Tbsp poppy seeds may be added to the dressing for variety.

Serving food is not about impressing people,
it's about making them feel comfortable.

Spring Salad With Warm Bacon Dressing

8 slices bacon
3 Tbsp flour
1½ cups cold water
¼ cup sugar
3 Tbsp cider vinegar
1 tsp salt
2-3 hard-cooked eggs
Spinach, dandelion greens, or watercress, washed and chopped

Fry bacon until crisp. Remove to drain. Stir flour into bacon grease remaining in skillet and gradually add water, stirring briskly to blend until smooth. Cook and stir over medium heat until thick like gravy. Add sugar, vinegar, and salt. Allow to cool a few minutes before tossing over greens and diced eggs. Top with crumbled bacon.

Spinach Salad

2 qts fresh spinach, torn
4 hard boiled eggs, chopped
8 strips bacon, fried and crumbled
1 small red onion, diced
½ cup fresh mushrooms, sliced

Toss with your favorite dressing. Serves 12.

Egg Salad and Tomatoes

Cook, peel, and mash 4 eggs. Combine eggs with mayonnaise or salad dressing, and salt and pepper to taste. A bit of vinegar and sugar will give it a little zip. Refrigerate.

Top fresh tomato slices with egg salad for a satisfying cool summer lunch. Garnish with bacon crumbles. It tastes even better on a slice of toasted bread.

MARINATED VEGETABLES

1 small head cauliflower, cut into small pieces
3 cups sliced carrots, (half-cooked)
1 onion, sliced thin
1 green pepper, sliced thin
6 ribs celery, cut in pieces
1 cup green beans, cooked
2 cucumbers, sliced thin
4 tomatoes, cut up

Dressing:
1 cup salad oil
¼ cup white vinegar
¾ cup sugar
½ cup dill pickle juice
1 tsp salt
½ tsp pepper
1 tsp prepared mustard
1 Tbsp Worcestershire Sauce
1 tsp celery seed
½ tsp celery salt

Combine dressing ingredients and mix well. Pour over vegetables and mix. Marinate at least 24 hours in your refrigerator. A potluck favorite.

– Esther Rohrer

CREAMY SLICED TOMATOES

1 cup Miracle Whip
½ cup light cream
2 tsp sugar
1 tsp fresh chopped dillweed or fresh basil
salt and pepper to taste

Combine all ingredients. Serve over sliced or chopped fresh tomatoes and red onion. It's especially pretty served on lettuce leaves.

STUFFED CHERRY TOMATOES

24-30 cherry tomatoes
4 oz cream cheese
⅓ cup mayonnaise
1½ Tbsp grated Parmesan
¼ cup bacon, fried and crumbled
⅓ cup grated cheddar
1 tsp minced onion
1 tsp minced parsley
pinch of salt

Mix ingredients for filling and refrigerate until needed.   Slice a thin slice off the tops of cherry tomatoes. Carefully scoop out pulp using your ¼ tsp measure . Invert on paper towels to drain. Fill with cheese mixture. Garnish with extra bacon crumbles.Arrange on a platter of parsley to keep tomatoes from rolling, or cut a sliver off the bottom of each tomato.

– Melissa (Rohrer) Wenger

BROCCOLI AND CAULIFLOWER SALAD

4 cups cauliflower florets
4 cups broccoli florets
½ cup minced red onion
8 strips bacon, fried and crumbled
½ cup golden raisins or dried cranberries
¼ cup chopped peanuts or sliced almonds
1 cup cheddar cheese, grated

Wash vegetables and cut into small pieces. When ready to eat, combine all ingredients, and toss with dressing.

Dressing
1 cup mayonnaise
⅓ cup sugar
1-2 Tbsp vinegar
pinch of salt

This salad is especially good when topped with Crunchy Salad Topping. Recipe on following page.

MACARONI SALAD

Salad Ingredients

2 cups raw macaroni, cooked and cooled
4 hardboiled eggs, diced
diced celery, sweet peppers, minced onion

Dressing

¾ cup sugar
3 Tbsp flour
1 tsp salt
¼ cup vinegar
¾ cup water
1 egg, beaten
¾ cup cream
2 tsp mustard
½ cup Miracle Whip

Heat all except Miracle Whip, while stirring over medium heat. Bring to a boil. Remove from heat. Stir in Miracle Whip. Cool awhile. Pour over salad ingredients, and mix well. Refrigerate. This works well for potato salad, too.

– *Rosanna (Rhodes) Martin*

CRUNCHY SALAD TOPPING

Melt 2 Tbsp butter in a skillet over low heat. Add one cup sliced almonds and stir for a few minutes while nuts are browning <u>lightly</u>. Remove from heat. Crumble a pack of uncooked instant ramen noodles (without seasoning) into nuts and stir to blend. Good on any green salad. I especially like it on broccoli salad.

You give but little when you give of your possessions.
It is when you give of your time and effort that you truly give.

MAKE-AHEAD LETTUCE SALAD

12 slices bacon
1 head chopped lettuce
½ cup chopped celery
½ cup chopped onion
1-2 cups frozen peas
4 hard-boiled eggs, sliced
1-2 cups grated cheddar cheese
2 cups Miracle Whip or mayonnaise
2 Tbsp sugar

Fry, drain, and crumble bacon. Layer vegetables in a 9x13 pan or shallow dishes. Top with sliced eggs. Mix sugar and Miracle Whip and spread over eggs. (Do <u>not</u> add milk or extra sugar; it causes dressing to soak into salad.) Top with bacon and cheese. Refrigerate 4-24 hours before serving.

SEASONED WELL POTATO SALAD

9 cups cubed potatoes
2 Tbsp salt

Dressing
4½ Tbsp flour
1c sugar
1½ tsp salt
1¼ cups water
¼ cup vinegar
1⅛ cups cream
2 eggs, beaten
1 Tbsp prepared mustard
scant ½ tsp celery seed
scant ½ tsp celery salt

6 hard boiled eggs, chopped
1 cup mayonnaise

Place first two ingredients in kettle. Cover with water and cook until tender. Drain immediately.
Cook the dressing ingredients until thickened. Cool. Stir into potatoes and hard boiled eggs. Add mayonnaise and any of the following to suit your own taste: onion, celery, peppers.

– *Wilma (Rohrer) Shank*

ZELDA'S POTATO SALAD

4 quarts diced, cooked potatoes
2½ cups potato water
½ cup vinegar
1 cup sugar
⅓ cup flour
2 tsp salt
2 egg yolks, beaten
1 cup salad dressing
1 tsp prepared mustard
Celery
Peppers
Paprika
Celery seed
Minced fresh onion
6-8 hard boiled eggs

Combine sugar, flour, and salt. Stir into potato water and vinegar and bring to a boil while stirring. Last add egg yolks. Remove from heat. Stir in salad dressing and mustard. Pour over potatoes; add any amount you like of diced celery, peppers, onions, etc. When mixture is cool, stir in the chopped hard boiled eggs. Refrigerate. Yields over 1 gallon.

– *Zelda Rohrer*

These are the things I prize
And hold of dearest worth;
Light of the sapphire skies,
Peace of the silent hills,
Shelter of the forests, comfort of the grass,
Music of birds, murmur of little rills,
Shadow of clouds that swiftly pass
And after showers the smell of flowers
And of the good brown earth.
And best of all, along the way,
Friendship and mirth.

– *Henry van Dyke*

Taco Salad

1 lb hamburger
1 small onion
1-2 Tbsp taco seasoning
1 can kidney beans

Fry meat and onion together, add seasoning and beans, keep warm.

Cut a green salad of
1 head lettuce
3 tomatoes

Have ready
8 oz grated cheddar cheese
1 bag taco or corn chips
Your favorite dressing (see recipes on following pages)

Layer ingredients in each plate in the order you like, topping with dressing and cheese. Eat with chips.

Cole Slaw

1 head cabbage, grated
1 small carrot, grated
1 medium cucumber, chopped fine, (optional)

Combine vegetables and dress with Favorite Salad Dressing (made without milk). Recipe on page 143. Garnish with tomato wedges.

Cucumber, Tomato, and Onion Salad

Peel and chop the above veggies in any amount or combination you like. Dress with Favorite Salad Dressing (page 143, made without milk). Top with fresh ground black pepper. This salad is especially good to serve with fresh green beans.

*FAVORITE SALAD DRESSING

2 cups Miracle Whip
½ cup sugar
½ tsp salt
¼ tsp coarse pepper
1½ cups milk

Combine first four ingredients and add milk to thin dressing. Good on lettuce salads. For coleslaw or for cucumber, tomato, and onion salad, don't add milk. Store in fridge.

*I use this simple dressing on most of the salads I serve.

COOKED SALAD DRESSING

3 eggs, beaten
1½ cups sugar
3 Tbsp flour
1½ tsp salt
dash pepper
1 cup vinegar
¼ cup water
¼ cup butter
1½ tsp celery seed
2 cups mayonnaise
¾ cup Italian dressing or French dressing
1 cup sugar

Mix the first three ingredients together in a saucepan. Then add the salt, pepper, vinegar, water, butter, and celery seed, and bring just to a boil. Remove from heat. Cool. Finally add mayonnaise, dressing, and sugar. This keeps well in the fridge and is especially good on Taco Salad.

HONEY MUSTARD DRESSING

1 cup mayonnaise
¼ cup prepared mustard
¼ cup honey
1 Tbsp lemon juice

Mix and chill. I use Gulden's spicy brown mustard. This is also a good dipping sauce for chicken nuggets, fondue, etc.

Buttermilk Salad Dressing

1 cup buttermilk
¾ cup mayonnaise
2 Tbsp grated onion
2 tsp fresh dill weed
⅛ tsp coarse black pepper
¼ tsp salt
½ tsp hickory smoke salt

Mix and store in fridge.

– Neva Horst

Vinegar and Oil Dressing

½ cup white vinegar
½ cup water
½ cup sugar
½ cup oil

Put vinegar, sugar, and water in a jar and shake well to dissolve sugar. Add oil and salt and pepper if desired. Shake well before using. Use a flavored vinegar if you like.

Celery Seed Dressing

1 cup sugar
1½ tsp dry mustard
1½ tsp salt
½ medium onion, grated
½ cup vinegar
1¼ cups salad oil
1 tsp celery seed

Combine in a jar and shake to blend. Refrigerate.

– Beulah (Rhodes) Burkholder

Hope is the beacon that lights our path into the future.
– Sidney Sheldon

CREAMY ITALIAN DRESSING

1 cup mayonnaise
½ small minced onion
2 Tbsp vinegar
⅛ tsp coarse black pepper
½ tsp garlic salt
¾ tsp Italian Seasoning
sugar (to your liking)
pinch of salt
Mix and store in fridge.

BLUE CHEESE DRESSING

2 cups mayonnaise
1 cup sour cream
¼ cup vinegar
¼ cup fresh parsley
2 tsp sugar
½ tsp salt
¼ tsp pepper
½ tsp ground mustard
4-6 oz blue cheese crumbles
Mix well. Store in fridge.

SUMMER DAY LETTUCE DRESSING

2 cups mayonnaise
1 cup sour cream
¾ cup sugar
¾ tsp salt
2 Tbsp vinegar

Blend mayonnaise and sour cream. Add remaining ingredients.
Refrigerate. Makes 1 quart.

– *Maria (Eberly) Horst*

Triumph is is umph added to try.

STUFFED SALAD EGGS

6 eggs
¼ cup Miracle Whip
1 Tbsp sugar
1 tsp vinegar
1 tsp prepared mustard
¼ tsp salt

Let eggs set at room temperature for a day before cooking for easier shelling. Cook eggs for 10-14 minutes. Cool under running water. Remove shells and cut in half lengthwise. Mash yolks and add rest of ingredients. Stuff egg whites with yolk filling. May garnish eggs with grated cheese, bacon crumbles, pickles, olives, etc. Keep refrigerated until served.

SALAD PEARS

8 oz softened cream cheese
½ cup powdered sugar
½ cup drained crushed pineapple
16-20 pear halves

Combine cream cheese and sugar, stir until smooth, add crushed pineapple. Spoon filling into pear halves, garnish with a cinnamon heart or a sprinkle of Tang. May be served on a leaf of lettuce.

– *Marilyn Eberly*

TWELVE LAYER JELLO SALAD

6 3 oz pkgs Jello (scant ½ cup each)
    cherry, lime, lemon, orange, pineapple, strawberry, etc.
16 oz sour cream

Pour 1 cup boiling water over cherry jello, take out half and slowly combine with ⅓ cup sour cream. Pour into 9x13 pan. Chill 20 minutes until firm. Add ¼ cup cold water to remaining cherry jello and pour on top of first layer. Repeat the same with all the flavors of jello, in order given. Cut into squares for serving. Very pretty.

You can live without music, you can live without books,
but show me the one who can live without cooks.

Soups
and
Sandwiches

A Cook's Advice

While chatting with a friend one day
　　As friends are known to do;
She offered me some sound advice
　　I'm passing on to you.

She said when going through a spell
　　That cooking seems a bore,
And even thinking what to fix
　　Becomes a dreadful chore....

Then do not sigh and force yourself
　　To cook and stir and bake–
Just open up a jar of soup
　　And take a little break!

Of course your family has to eat;
　　But for a day or two,
Just serve up what is close at hand,
　　'Most anything will do.

Go out and raid your freezer
　　To find some handy food;
Just throw quick meals together,
　　Don't worry if they're crude.

Then soon you'll grab those cookbooks
　　And cook a meal worthwhile;
You'll find it's fun to cook again,
　　Your family will smile.

– Barbara Eberly

Soups and Sandwiches

CHEDDAR CHOWDER

2 cups water
2 cups diced potatoes
½ cup diced carrots
½ cup diced celery
¼ cup chopped onion
1 tsp salt
¼ tsp pepper

Combine all ingredients in large kettle. Boil 10-12 minutes. Meanwhile make white sauce. Stir white sauce into undrained vegetable mixture. Heat throughout. Makes 6 servings.

White Sauce

¼ cup butter
¼ cup flour
2 cups milk
2 cups cheddar cheese, grated
1 cup cubed ham or fried bacon crumbles

In a small saucepan melt butter. Add flour and stir until smooth (about 1 minute). Slowly add milk while stirring. Cook until thickened. Add grated cheese, and stir until melted. Toss in ham.
Variation: Use chicken broth instead of water, and 2 cups diced, cooked chicken instead of ham, or use smoked sausage for a change.

CHEESEBURGER CHOWDER

1 lb ground beef
½ cup chopped celery
¼ cup chopped onion
2 Tbsp chopped green pepper
3 Tbsp flour
½ tsp salt
4 cups milk
1 Tbsp beef flavored gravy base
1 cup sharp cheddar cheese, grated

Brown meat in skillet. Add celery, onion, and peppers. Cook until vegetables are tender. Blend in flour and salt. Add milk and gravy base. Cook and stir over low heat until thickened. Add cheese. Cook and stir just until cheese melts.

— Rebecca (Shank) Shank

CHICKEN NOODLE SOUP

One 3 lb chicken
3 quarts water
1 cup diced carrots
1 cup diced celery
¼ cup diced onion
2 tsp salt
1 Tbsp chicken base
pinch of marjoram, thyme, pepper
1 bay leaf
2-3 cups raw noodles

In a large pot, put all except noodles. Bring to a boil. Reduce heat and simmer covered for one hour. Remove chicken from broth; cool, debone and dice chicken. Skim fat from broth. Add noodles, and stir in diced chicken. Cook until noodles are done, adding more water if needed.

*When nobody around you seems to measure up,
it's time to check your yardstick.*

CHEESEBURGER SOUP

½ lb ground beef
¾ cup chopped onion
¾ cup chopped carrots
¾ cup chopped celery
1 tsp dried basil
1 tsp dried parsley flakes
1 Tbsp butter
¼ cup water
3 cups chicken broth
4 cups diced potatoes
1½ cups milk
¼ cup flour
½ lb Velveeta cheese, cubed
1 tsp salt
¼ to ½ tsp pepper
¼ cup sour cream

Brown beef. Sauté onions, carrots, , celery, basil, and parsley in 1 Tbsp butter and ¼ cup water until veggies are tender. Add broth, potatoes, and beef. Bring to a boil. Reduce heat. Cover and simmer for 10-12 minutes or until potatoes are tender.

Combine milk and flour to make a smooth batter, and stir into soup. Cook and stir for 3-5 minutes or until bubbly. Reduce heat to low. Add cheese, salt, and pepper and stir until cheese melts. Remove from heat. Stir in sour cream.

– Laura (Knicely) Horst, Melinda (Wenger) Knicely,
and Dorthy (Eberly) Good

There's so much good in the worst of us,
And so much bad in the best of us,
That it's hard to tell which one of us
Ought to reform the rest of us.

CORN CHOWDER

2 cups water
2 cups diced potatoes
½ cup sliced carrots
½ cup diced celery
¼ cup chopped onion
1 tsp salt
¼ tsp pepper
¼ cup butter
¼ cup flour
2 cups milk
3 cups (12 oz) shredded cheddar cheese
1 qt creamed corn

Cook veggies in water, salt, and pepper until they are tender-crisp. Don't drain. Melt butter in a 3 or 4 qt saucepan. Make a batter with flour and milk. Stir into butter. Bring to a boil while stirring. Add the cheese. Stir in corn and vegetable mixture, including the cooking liquid. Season to taste. Serve piping hot. Makes 2 ½ quarts.

CREAMY BROCCOLI SOUP

2 Tbsp minced fresh onion
3 Tbsp butter
2½ cups water
1 qt (1 lb) chopped broccoli
1 large carrot, grated
5 cups milk
½ cup (scant) flour
1 Tbsp chicken base or 3 chicken bouillon
1-2 tsp Worcestershire Sauce
½ lb Velveeta Cheese, cubed
salt and pepper

Sauté onion in butter. Add water, broccoli, and carrot. Cook until veggies are tender. Add 3 cups milk and bring to a boil. Shake a batter of 2 cups milk and flour, add to the pot, and stir in seasonings. Bring to a boil while stirring. Last, add cubed cheese. Remove from heat, and stir to melt cheese. Serve hot. May garnish with bacon crumbles.

CREAM OF MUSHROOM, CHICKEN, OR CELERY SOUP

Homemade cream soups are quick and easy, and taste much better than canned soup. I hope you will agree after trying these.

Mushroom Soup

3 Tbsp butter
1 Tbsp minced onion (optional)
1 cup diced fresh mushrooms or 4 oz can mushroom pieces
2 cups rich milk
⅓ cup flour
½ tsp salt

Sauté mushrooms and onion in butter. Combine milk and flour in batter shaker. (If using canned mushrooms, use the liquid for part of the milk.) Stir into mushrooms. Add salt and heat while stirring until soup thickens. Dilute soup with milk to suit your recipe.

Chicken Soup

Use 1 cup chicken broth or bouillon for part of the milk. Omit mushrooms. Add diced, cooked chicken if you have it on hand.

Celery Soup

Sauté 1 cup diced celery and 1 Tbsp minced onion. Omit mushrooms.

We can all do more than we have done,
And not be one whit the worse;
It never was loving that emptied the heart
Nor giving that emptied the purse.

CREAMY ONION POTATO SOUP

7 Tbsp butter
1½ cups bread cubes
3 large onions, quartered and sliced
2 cups diced potatoes
1½ cups water
4½ tsp chicken bouillon granules
¼ cup flour
1¾ cups milk
1½ cups Swiss cheese
pepper to taste
fresh minced chives or parsley

Melt 3 Tbsp butter; toss bread cubes in it. Place on a lightly greased baking sheet. Bake at 350° for 7 minutes. Turn and bake 7 minutes longer until toasted.

In a large saucepan, sauté onions in 4 Tbsp butter until lightly browned. Stir in potatoes, water, and bouillon. Bring to a boil. Reduce heat and simmer for 15 minutes. Combine flour and ½ cup milk until smooth, gradually stir into remaining milk. Stir into the soup and heat to boiling. Add cheese, pepper, and chives. Serve with toasted bread cubes.

– Esther Burkholder

GREAT POTATO SOUP

4 cups diced potatoes
4 cups water
1 cup sliced carrots
1 cup celery
½ cup chopped onions
1-1½ tsp salt
½ cup flour
2 cups milk
2 cups fried, diced tenderloin or ham
½-1 cup Velveeta or other cheese

Simmer vegetables together in water and salt until tender. Don't drain. Combine flour and milk, and stir into simmering vegetables. Add the meat and cheese.

– Melissa (Rohrer) Wenger

Gone-All-Day Stew

1 can tomato soup
1 cup water or cooking wine
¼ cup flour
2 beef bouillon cubes
1 tsp each of oregano, thyme, and rosemary
1 bay leaf
pepper to taste
2 lb beef roast, cut into 1 inch cubes
3 medium carrots, cut in 1 inch slices
6 quartered medium onions
4 medium potatoes, cut in 1½ inch chunks
½ cup celery, cut in 1 inch chunks
12 whole large mushrooms, (canned may be used)

Mix together tomato soup, water, and flour until smooth. Combine with remaining seasonings, and pour over meat and veggies in roasting pan. Cover and bake at 275° for 4-5 hours. Remove bay leaf and adjust seasoning if desired. Serve with warmed French bread or noodles or rice.

– Lois Shank (Danny) and Mary Ethel Wenger

Chili Soup

2 lbs ground beef
¾ cup chopped onion
1½ tsp salt
2 Tbsp chili powder
½ cup brown sugar
2 Tbsp Worcestershire sauce
1 cup ketchup
3 Tbsp vinegar
2 qts canned tomatoes or juice
1 (40 oz) can kidney beans

Brown beef and onions together. Add rest of ingredients and simmer over low heat for 20-30 minutes. Serve hot with cornbread or corn chips, sour cream and shredded cheddar cheese.

TACO SOUP

1½ lbs ground beef
½ cup chopped onion
½ pkg taco seasoning
1 pint kidney beans
1 pint corn
2 quarts tomato juice
⅓ cup brown sugar
1½ tsp salt
¼ tsp pepper
Sour cream
Grated cheddar cheese
Corn chips

Brown beef in large kettle. Add onion last five minutes of cooking meat. Drain off excess fat. Stir in rest of soup ingredients and simmer about 15 minutes. Serve with garnishes of sour cream, cheddar cheese and corn chips on the side.

– *Melinda (Wenger) Knicely*

HEARTY HAMBURGER SOUP

2 Tbsp butter
1 lb hamburger
1 cup chopped onion
2 cups tomato juice
1 cup sliced carrots
½ cup chopped green pepper
1 cup diced potatoes
1½ tsp salt
¼ tsp pepper
1 tsp seasoned salt
¼ cup (or more) flour
4 cups milk

Melt butter in saucepan; brown meat and add onion. Cook until transparent. Stir in remaining ingredients except flour and milk. Cover and cook over low heat until vegetables are tender, about 20-25 minutes. Combine flour with one cup milk and stir into soup. Bring to a boil, add remaining milk.

– *Janice (Shank) Wenger*

MEXICAN BEEF AND BARLEY SOUP

1 lb ground beef
1 small onion (chopped)
3 cups beef broth
2 cups chunky salsa
½ cup quick cooking barley
2 15-oz cans red kidney beans (rinsed and drained)

Brown beef and onion in a skillet. Add broth, salsa, and barley, and cook until barley is tender. Add beans and cook until fully heated.

This is good served with cornbread.

Miriam (Rohrer) Martin

SALMON SOUP

1 can (15 oz) salmon
1 Tbsp butter
2 - 3 cups milk
½ tsp salt
coarse black pepper

Drain salmon, and reserve liquid. Melt butter in saucepan over low heat. Remove skin from salmon pieces. Put in saucepan and fry over low heat a few minutes in the butter. Add milk, liquid from fish, salt, and pepper. Heat until almost boiling. Serve hot with crackers or toast. A great lunch on a cold winter day.

All the fine compliments, all the good wishes,
will never replace help with the dishes.

Louisiana Gumbo

1 broiler/fryer chicken (3-3½ lbs), cut up
2 qts water
¾ cup all purpose flour
½ cup cooking oil
½ cup sliced green onions
½ cup chopped onions
½ cup chopped green pepper
½ cup chopped sweet red pepper
½ cup chopped celery
2 garlic cloves, minced
½ lb fully cooked smoked sausage, cut into 1" cubes
½ lb fully cooked ham, cut into ¾" cubes
½ lb fresh or frozen uncooked shrimp, peeled and deveined
1 cup fresh or frozen okra
½ tsp salt
¼ tsp pepper
¼ tsp hot pepper sauce

Place the chicken and water in a Dutch oven. Bring to a boil. Skim fat. Reduce heat; cover and simmer 30-45 minutes or until chicken is tender. Remove chicken; cool. Reserve 6 cups broth. Remove chicken from bones. Cut into bite-sized pieces. In a 4 qt kettle, mix flour and oil until smooth; cook and stir over medium-low heat until browned (2-3 minutes). Stir in onions, peppers, celery, and garlic; cook for 5 minutes or until vegetables are tender. Stir in the sausage, ham, reserved broth, and chicken; cover and simmer for 45 minutes. Add the shrimp, okra, salt, pepper, and hot pepper sauce; cover and simmer 10 minutes longer or until shrimp is cooked. Serves 12.

– Ina Sue (Showalter) Strite

Gratitude to God should be as regular as your heartbeat.

FROGMORE STEW

This stew has an interesting history, and one story shared with me by a 94-year-old friend is this. The Creole folks, shrimpers by trade, who settled in a little community near Beaufort, South Carolina named Frogmore created this recipe. They boil it outdoors in an iron kettle over an open flame. It is also tasty cooked indoors in your soup kettle.

5 quarts water
2 tsp salt
2 Tbsp Old Bay seasoning
4 lbs small red potatoes
Vidalia onions, cut in chunks
2 lbs sausage links cut into 1½" pieces
    (Kielbasa is good, but smoked sausage is tops)
8-12 ears fresh corn, halved
3 - 5 lbs raw shrimp

In large kettle boil potatoes and seasonings in water for 10 minutes. Add onions and sausage. Cover and cook 10 more minutes. Add corn and boil 5-7 minutes longer. Last add shrimp. Stir stew and sprinkle in some more seasoning if you like. Cook a few more minutes until shrimp is pink. Serves 15.

Dip heaping portions into soup bowls and provide napkins and a frosty, cold drink for a delicious meal. Pass cocktail sauce for the shrimp and butter, salt and pepper for the potatoes.

SHRIMP CHOWDER

1 lb small, cooked salad shrimp
2 medium potatoes, finely diced
1 cup fresh or frozen peas
1 small onion chopped
1½ cups boiling water
3 Tbsp butter
2 cups milk (or more)
¼ cup flour

Cook potatoes, onion, and peas until tender. Add shrimp, butter, and milk mixed with flour. Add salt and pepper to taste. (A little Old Bay seasoning or basil is good too.) Simmer 3-5 minutes. A family favorite.

– Esther Rohrer

MILD TOMATO SOUP

2 gallons chunked tomatoes
4 large onions, diced
3 stems celery, diced
2 red peppers
2 cups sugar
¼ cup salt
1 cup cornstarch

Simmer vegetables together 45 minutes. Sieve. Combine remaining ingredients and stir into soup. Seal in canning jars and cook 45 minutes in boiling water.

– Wilma (Rohrer) Shank

VEGETABLE CHILI

1 cup chopped onions
½ cup chopped peppers
½ cup chopped celery
¼ cup butter
1 qt canned tomatoes
3-4 cups tomato juice
2 cups sliced carrots
1 qt kidney beans
1 Tbsp chili powder
dash red pepper
1-2 Tbsp sorghum molasses
salt to taste

Sauté chopped veggies in butter. Add tomatoes, juice and carrots. Cook until tender. Add beans and seasonings. Good with crusty bread or cornbread.

The woman who helps her neighbor, does herself a good turn.
– Brendan Francis

Wiener Chowder

4 medium potatoes, diced
1 onion, chopped
4 wieners, sliced thin
1 Tbsp butter
2 cups cooked corn
2 cups whole milk
8 oz cream cheese, cubed

Cook potatoes in 2 cups water until tender. Do not drain. Fry wieners and onion in butter. Add to potato kettle, stir in corn and milk, and heat until piping hot. Season with salt and pepper. Remove from heat and stir in cubed cream cheese. Garnish with fresh parsley.

– Esther Rohrer

Cabbage Soup

2 lbs hamburger or sausage
2 qts canned tomatoes
1 medium head cabbage, shredded
5 stems celery, chopped
3 medium onions, chopped
2 Tbsp brown sugar
1-2 tsp salt
½ tsp pepper

Brown meat in a large kettle. Add all other ingredients and bring to a boil, adding water as needed. Simmer until vegetables are tender, about 25 minutes.

*A little bit of love is the only bit
that will bridle the human tongue.*

Thanksgiving Turkey Soup

1 leftover turkey carcass from a 12-15 lb turkey
2 medium onions, chopped
2 stems celery, diced
½ stick butter
2 large carrots, grated
1 tsp salt
½ tsp pepper
½ tsp marjoram
1 Tbsp chicken base
1 cup uncooked long grain rice
1 cup flour
2 cups half and half cream

Put turkey bones in a large kettle and cover with water. Simmer over medium heat for an hour. Remove carcass and set aside to cool. Boil down broth to about 3 quarts. Sauté onions and celery in butter. Pour broth over onions in large kettle and bring to a boil, add carrots, seasonings, and rice. Let soup simmer while you remove bits of meat from turkey bones. Shake a batter of cream and flour, stir into soup when rice is tender, cook several more minutes. Add turkey meat and adjust seasonings to suit your taste. Makes 1 gallon of creamy turkey soup.

White Bean 'N' Ham Soup

2 cups dried white beans
1 meaty ham bone
7 cups water
1 cup sliced carrots
1 cup diced celery
½ cup chopped onion
1 Tbsp brown sugar
2 tsp salt
¼ tsp pepper
2 cups diced ham

Soak beans overnight in water. Drain excess water, then put beans, ham bone and 7 cups water in a large kettle. Cook for 1½ hours. Add veggies and cook until tender. Add seasonings and ham.

– Ethel Shank

GRILLED LASAGNA SANDWICHES

Butter or margarine, softened
8 slices bread
4 slices mozzarella cheese
⅓ cup sour cream
2 Tbsp chopped onion
pinch of dried oregano
2 medium tomatoes, sliced
8 strips bacon, fried and drained

Spread butter on both sides of each slice of bread. On four of the slices, layer cheese, sour cream, onion, oregano, tomato, and bacon. Top with remaining bread. Place sandwiches, cheese side down, in a skillet. Cook until bread is golden brown, and cheese is melted. Turn and brown other side.

– Lorna (Good) Wenger

PIMENTO CHEESE SPREAD

2 lbs Velveeta cheese, grated
½ lb sharp cheddar cheese, grated
1 cup pimentos (recipe on page 291)
2 cups Miracle Whip

Blend ingredients together. Good on sandwiches or crackers.

Converse in mind with God, thy spirit heavenward raise;
Acknowledge every good bestowed, and offer grateful praise.

Reuben Sandwich

❖ Whole-wheat or rye bread buttered on the outside
❖ Miracle Whip spread inside the bread (or Thousand Island
    dressing)
❖ Sliced corned beef (I use peppered corned beef from the deli.)
❖ Swiss cheeses slices
❖ Lettuce
❖ Tomato, sliced thin
❖ Sautéed onion
❖ Sauerkraut (if desired, instead of veggies)

Layer corned beef, kraut or veggies, and cheese. Top with
bread. Toast or grill in skillet until browned and cheese melts.
Delicious and quite filling!

Subs (Hoagies)

❖ Sub or round sandwich buns (made from your favorite bread
    dough)
❖ Miracle Whip or mayonnaise
❖ Sandwich meats: ham, turkey, bologna, bacon, etc.
❖ Thinly sliced tomatoes, lettuce, and onions
❖ Oregano flakes or Italian dressing
❖ Slices of cheese (any kind you like)

Spread insides of bun with dressing. Layer ingredients in
order given. Top with bun. Wrap each sub in saran wrap and
let flavors blend several hours or overnight if time allows.
Enjoy with a cold drink and potato chips.

Chicken Salad/Turkey Salad/Ham Salad

Dice any desired amount of cooked chicken, turkey, or ham. Add
chopped crisp pickles, celery or onion (optional) and enough
Miracle Whip to make it spreadable. You may even add some
sweet pickle juice. Season to your liking with salt and pepper. Refrigerate. Good on sandwiches or snack crackers.

Desserts

Rules for Daily Living

To talk with God each morning before
    I walk and talk with men.
To do my daily duties with sunshine on my face,
To be strong in the presence of temptation,
    awake in the presence of opportunity,
        open-hearted to my neighbors,
            obedient to the calls of good conscience,
                open-minded to views of truth.
To make duty a joy and work a duty.
To work and not worry; to be energetic without being fussy.
To be true to myself, false to no one,
    and earnest to make a real life while trying to make a living.
To cherish friendships and guard my confidences.
To be loyal to principle even at the loss of popularity.
To make no promises I do not mean to keep, and few of them.
To be faithful to every honest obligation.
To be sweet-tempered under criticism
    and charitable in my judgments.
To honor no one because he is rich,
    to despise no one because he is poor.
To be respectful to the great; gentle to the weak;
    helpful to the fallen; courteous to all.
To remain simple in tastes, pure in speech, temperate in pleasures,
    and to companion with a few great books, particularly the Bible.
To fear nothing but sin, hate nothing by hypocrisy.
At last to leave the world a little better for my brief stay in it;
    to face death without fear, with firm faith in Christ.

— Anonymous

Desserts

Baked Apples

10 tart apples*
⅔ cup sugar
¼ cup clearjel
1¾ cups water
2 Tbsp cinnamon heart candy

Peel and halve apples. Place core side up in a greased shallow baking dish. Combine rest of ingredients and bring to a boil while stirring over medium heat. Pour over apples. Bake at 375° until apples are cooked. Serve warm, or chilled with whipped cream.

*See list of good cooking apples on page 197.

Fried Apples

5 tart apples*
2 Tbsp butter
⅓ cup brown sugar
pinch of salt
½ tsp cinnamon

Peel and slice apples into 12 pieces. Melt butter in iron skillet. Add apples, sugar, salt, and cinnamon. Stir 5 minutes while frying. Cover and fry about 10 more minutes. Serve hot. These are especially good served with pork.

SNITZ AND DUMPLINGS

2 cups dried apple slices (snitz)
Water to cover apples
2 Tbsp brown sugar

Soak snitz overnight and then add 2 Tbsp brown sugar. Cook until apples are tender in a large diameter pan. Meanwhile mix dumplings.

1 cup flour
1½ tsp baking powder
¼ tsp salt
½ cup milk

Mix all together. Drop dough by soup-spoonfuls onto gently boiling fruit, and cover tightly. Boil 20 minutes without peeking. Serve with rich milk and sugar, or ice cream. Another good topping is sweetened whipped cream which melts down over the hot fruit.

Snitz is the Pennsylvania Dutch word for one fourth of an apple.

– Esther Rohrer

FRUIT AND DUMPLINGS

1 - 1½ quarts cherries, berries, etc.
water to cover
sugar to taste

Follow the dumpling recipe above.

The things that count the most cannot be counted.
The most important things in life are not things.

DELUXE APPLE CRUNCH

6 large apples, sliced
½ cup sugar
cinnamon or nutmeg
½ cup butter
1 cup brown sugar
½ cup flour
1 cup oatmeal
½ cup chopped pecans

Spread apples in a buttered bake dish. Cover with sugar. Sprinkle with spices. Blend rest of ingredients until crumbly and spread over apples. Bake at 325° for 50-60 minutes. Serve warm with ice cream.

APPLE DANISH CHEESECAKE

1 cup flour
½ cup butter
¼ tsp almond extract
½ cup finely chopped pecans
¼ cup sugar

8 oz cream cheese
¼ cup sugar
¼ tsp cream of tartar
2 eggs
2 tsp lemon juice

⅓ cup brown sugar
1 Tbsp flour
1 tsp cinnamon
⅓ cup chopped pecans
5 cups thinly sliced apples

Make a crumbly dough of the flour, butter, flavoring, pecans, and sugar. Roll into a 10" circle or press into the bottom of a springform pan and up the sides (or in an 8x12 baking dish). Refrigerate crust for 30 minutes. Meanwhile beat cream cheese, sugar, and cream of tartar until smooth. Add eggs and lemon juice. Beat until combined. Pour over crust. Combine remaining ingredients and toss over apples. Top filling with apple mixture. Bake at 350° for 40-45 minutes. Serve warm or cold.

APPLE GINGERBREAD COBBLER

4 cups apples, sliced
½ cup brown sugar
1 Tbsp lemon juice
¼ tsp cinnamon
1 cup water
2 tsp cornstarch

Combine first 5 ingredients in sauce pan. Cover and cook until almost tender. Mix cornstarch with a few drops of water and stir into apples. Pour into buttered 1½ quart baking dish. Note: You can use apple pie filling if preferred.

Gingerbread

¼ cup sugar
2 Tbsp oil
1 cup flour
1 egg
½ tsp ginger
½ tsp baking powder
½ cup buttermilk
¼ tsp nutmeg
½ tsp soda
¼ cup molasses

Combine all ingredients and beat together. Spoon over apples. Bake at 350° for 35 minutes. Great with ice cream.

– Lydia (Eberly) Good

God make my life a little flower that giveth joy to all,
Content to bloom in native bower, although its place be small.
– Matilda B. Edward

Spiced Baked Fruit

4 cups sliced peaches
4 cups cooked apple slices
2 cups pineapple tidbits
1 cup sugar
2 Tbsp cornstarch
1 tsp cinnamon
½ tsp nutmeg
¼ tsp curry powder
2 tsp lemon juice
2 Tbsp cinnamon hearts

Lightly drain fruits. Combine sugar, spices, and cornstarch, and mix with fruit, lemon juice and cinnamon hearts. Pour into a 2½-3 quart glass baking dish. Bake at 350° about an hour. Stir occasionally while baking. Serve warm or cold. Good as a side dish with hot foods, or as a dessert. Pears are good in this dish too.

Pear Custard Bars

¾ cup butter
⅓ cup sugar
1 ½ cups flour
½ tsp vanilla
1⅓ cups finely chopped nuts
8 oz cream cheese
¼ cup sugar
½ tsp vanilla
2 eggs, beaten
2 qts canned pears, drained and sliced
1 tsp cinnamon
1 tsp sugar

Cream butter and sugar; add flour, vanilla, and nuts. Press into agreased 9x13 pan and bake at 350° for 20 minutes.
Blend cream cheese and sugar, vanilla, and eggs. Pour over crust. Arrange pears over filling and sprinkle with the cinnamon and sugar. Bake for 35 minutes. Cool and refrigerate. Serve with whipped cream. Luscious!

– *Wilma (Rohrer) Shank*

CARAMEL PUDDING

½ cup brown sugar
¼ cup water
1 Tbsp butter
½ tsp salt
¼ tsp soda
¼ cup sugar
⅓ cup cornstarch*
4 cups Half and Half milk
1 tsp vanilla
few drops of black walnut flavoring (optional)

Combine brown sugar, water, and butter in a saucepan over medium heat. Bring to a boil, add soda and salt, and simmer 3 to 5 more minutes until thick and syrupy to create caramel flavor. Combine sugar, cornstarch, and milk. Add to hot mixture. Stir and cook until thickened. Add flavorings. Cover surface of pudding with waxed paper or saran wrap and chill. Stir a bit before serving. You may garnish with whipped cream and walnuts if you like.

– Mary Rohrer (Raymond)

Puddings made with cornstarch will begin to break down and liquefy after being chilled and stirred. If you like a creamy, stirred pudding use 2 Tbsp extra cornstarch.

COCONUT ALMOND CRUNCH PUDDING

Crumbs

½ cup butter or margarine
¼ cup brown sugar
1 cup flour
1 cup slivered almonds
1 cup coconut

Mix together and bake at 325° until golden. Stir often.

Pudding

3 cups cold pasteurized milk
2 small boxes instant vanilla pudding
2 cups whipped cream or Cool Whip

Beat milk and pudding together. Fold in cream. Alternate layers of crumbs and pudding in dessert dish. Top with crumbs.

– Neva Horst

Deluxe Tapioca Pudding

2 qts whole milk
½ cup minute tapioca
1 cup brown sugar
scant 1 tsp salt
3 egg yolks
1 Tbsp cornstarch
2 Tbsp browned butter
1½ tsp vanilla
Bananas
2 Snickers bars

Heat milk in a heavy saucepan over medium heat. Stir in tapioca, brown sugar and salt. Cook until tapioca is clear. Meanwhile, beat egg yolks and 1 Tbsp cornstarch. Stir in a little hot milk mixture, then add eggs to saucepan and bring to a simmer, stirring constantly. Remove from heat, add butter and vanilla. Cover with plastic wrap, chill thoroughly. Garnish with sliced bananas and chopped Snickers candy bars.

– Wilma (Rohrer) Shank

Vanilla Pudding

4 cups milk
1 cup sugar
⅓ cup cornstarch
⅛ tsp salt
2 beaten eggs
1½ tsp vanilla

Heat 3 cups milk in top of double boiler over simmering water. Mix sugar, cornstarch, salt and eggs with 1 cup milk. Stir into hot milk and cook until thickened and bubbly, stirring continuously. Remove from heat and add vanilla. Cover with saran wrap and chill. May be served plain, or with the addition of sliced bananas, broken vanilla wafers, graham crackers etc.

One way to break a habit is to drop it.

Favorite Fruit Cobbler

1 cup sugar
½ cup soft butter
⅔ cup milk
1 tsp vanilla
1 cup flour
1½ tsp baking powder
½ tsp salt

Use cherries, peaches, or berries, thickened as shown in recipe below. Cream butter and sugar. Add rest of ingredients and stir well. Pour over thickened fruit and bake at 350° until done. Your fruit cobbler will bake much faster if you heat the fruit before topping with dough. Test for doneness with a toothpick. (Double recipe for a 9x13 dish)

Peach Cobbler

Fruit Layer
1 quart sliced peaches (drained)
½ cup sugar
¼ cup butter
½ cup water
3 Tbsp clearjel

Dough
2 cups flour
1½ cups sugar
4 tsp baking powder
½ tsp salt
1½ cups milk
1 tsp vanilla

Combine peach juice, water, sugar, and clear jell and bring to a boil over medium heat. Stir in butter. Add peaches and pour into 9x13 baking dish. Combine dough ingredients. Spread over fruit. Sprinkle ¼ cup sugar and 1 tsp cinnamon over top. Last pour ½ cup melted butter over all. Bake at 375° for 30 minutes.

– Rosanna (Rhodes) Martin

PEACHES-N-CREAM DESSERT

1 quart peaches (drained; reserve ½ cup juice)
¾ cup flour
1 small box regular vanilla pudding
1 tsp baking powder
1 egg, beaten
½ cup milk
3 Tbsp butter
8 oz cream cheese
½ cup sugar
1 Tbsp sugar
½ tsp cinnamon

Mix together flour, pudding mix, baking powder, egg, milk, and butter. Pour into greased and floured 8" x 12" baking dish. Arrange peaches over batter. Beat together cream cheese, ½ cup sugar, and peach juice. Pour over peaches and sprinkle with sugar and cinnamon. Bake at 350° for 45 minutes.

– *Lorna (Good) Wenger*

PEACH DESSERT TO CAN

1 pound, 14 oz can pineapple juice
enough water to make 20 cups liquid
8 cups sugar
2½ cups tapioca starch
1½ cups Tang (orange powdered drink mix)
½ tsp salt
½ bushel peaches peeled, and sliced

Cook all except peaches until thick. Cool. To mix, layer filling and sliced peaches alternately in a large container. This prevents crushing fruit, as the filling is very stiff. Ladle into jars, being sure to save at least 2 inches headspace. Process in boiling water 7 minutes. Turn heat off and let set 7 minutes before slowly removing from canner. This helps prevent spewing. Use as a base for mixed fruit, or a topping for fruit pizza, or cream cheese dessert. Yields approximately 14 quarts.

– *Wilma (Rohrer) Shank*

CREAM PUFFS

1 cup water
½ cup butter
1 cup flour
4 eggs

Boil water and butter. Add flour and stir over medium heat until it forms a gummy ball (1-2 minutes). Remove from heat, let set for 10 minutes. Stir in eggs, one at a time, beating with a spoon after each addition. Put dough into a pastry bag and pipe onto a lightly greased baking sheet (or drop dough by teaspoons). Leave plenty of room for puffs to expand while baking. A cookie dipper works well for making mini cream puffs. Bake at 350° for 30-45 minutes (depending on size).

Fill with one of the following:

❖ vanilla cream filling, topped with chocolate glaze
    (see recipes on pages 241 and 243)
❖ strawberry – cream cheese – whipped cream mixture
❖ chicken or ham salad (see recipes on page 162)

MOM'S CUP CUSTARD

2 cups milk
2 eggs
⅓ cup sugar
pinch of salt
1½ tsp vanilla
nutmeg

Pour milk into a bowl. Add eggs and beat lightly. Stir in sugar, salt and vanilla. Pour into 4 custard cups or mugs. Sprinkle generously with nutmeg. Put into a pan with 1½" or so of cold water. Cover with lid. Bring to a boil over medium heat. You'll hear the cups rattling when the water boils. Leave lid on and remove from heat. Let set 45 minutes.

This was our "comfort food" when we were young and just getting over a tummy ache. It's delicious warm or cold.

Homemade Ice Cream

6 cups milk
6 eggs, beaten
1½ cups sugar
½ tsp salt
3 cups heavy cream
1 – 2 Tbsp vanilla

Combine eggs and 1 cup milk, set aside. Heat 5 cups milk, sugar and salt in a kettle over medium heat. When it begins to boil, stir in egg mixture. Cook over low heat, stirring constantly, until mixture coats spoon. (160°) Add vanilla and cream. Cool thoroughly. Freeze in 1 gallon freezer, using ice and salt as directed.

Strawberry Ice Cream

Add 3 – 4 cups crushed sweetened fresh strawberries. Leave out 3 cups milk.

Peach Ice Cream

Stir in 3 – 4 cups mashed sweetened fresh peaches (frozen fruit can be substituted for fresh). Leave out 3 cups milk.

I grew up on a dairy farm and we made ice cream from our cows' milk. We small children had our own little 2 quart freezer to crank, while Mom and Daddy made 1½ gallons in the big freezer. We got to choose any flavor we wanted, and I remember picking a fruit flavor or chocolate-peanut butter most often. After the ice cream was frozen, we had the fun of licking two dashers! ☺

Good intentions are like babies crying in church—
They should be carried out immediately.

Frozen Lemon Pudding

3 eggs, separated
½ cup sugar
4 Tbsp lemon juice
1 tsp grated lemon rind
1 pint whipping cream
3 cups graham cracker crumbs
¼ cup sugar
⅔ cup melted butter

Make crust with last three ingredients. Press into a 9 x 13 pan.
Bake at 350° for 10 minutes. Cool. Cook yolks, sugar, and lemon
juice in double boiler until thick. Cool. Beat egg whites and whipping cream. Add to egg yolk mixture. Pour over crust and freeze.

– Annette (Eberly) Horst

Quick and Easy Lemon Cheesecake

Crust:

32 graham crackers (squares)
½ cup melted butter
2 Tbsp powdered sugar

Filling:

3 oz lemon jello
1 cup boiling water
3 Tbsp lemon juice
12 oz chilled evaporated milk or 1½ cups whipping cream
1 cup sugar
8 oz cream cheese
2 tsp vanilla

Crush graham crackers. Add butter and powdered sugar. Press
crumbs in 9x13 baking dish. Bake 10 minutes at 350°. Cool.

Dissolve jello in boiling water. Cool. Add lemon juice.
Whip evaporated milk until stiff. Set aside. Cream sugar, cream
cheese and vanilla. Add ¼ cup jello mixture. Slowly add rest
of jello to whipped milk. Blend cream cheese and whipped milk
mixture together. Pour over crust and chill until set.

Orange Cheesecake: Using recipe above, substitute orange jello
and orange juice. Garnish with mandarin orange slices.

Lush Dessert (Coconut, Banana, Lemon, Chocolate, Fruit)

Crust:

1 cup flour
½ cup butter
½ cup chopped pecans

Cheese Layer:
8 oz cream cheese
1 cup powdered sugar
1 cup Cool Whip

Pudding Layer:

2 (3.4 oz) pkgs instant pudding
3 cups cold pasteurized milk

Topping:
2-3 cups Cool Whip

Mix flour, butter, and pecans until crumbly. Press into a 9x13 pan or 2 pie plates. Bake 10-15 minutes at 350º. Meanwhile blend cream cheese, sugar, and Cool Whip until creamy. Spread over cooled crumb layer. Beat pudding and milk for 2 minutes. Pour over all. Chill. When pudding sets up, top it with rest of Cool Whip and garnish as you wish.

Variations:

❖ Use 2 of your favorite flavor puddings or combine 1 vanilla with 1 chocolate, (I do this for a milder chocolate flavor).
❖ This crust and cheese layer makes a wonderful base for a fruit dessert. Spoon thickened fruit over all and chill until served.
❖ Also can be used as a base for fruit pizza, recipe on page 194

Instant Pudding Tip:

Use pasteurized milk when making instant pudding. Heat raw milk to 160º (scalding) and cool. Raw milk and uncooked pudding develop a soapy taste after a period of time.

Pumpkin Cobbler

½ cup butter

Batter
1 cup flour
1 cup sugar
4 tsp baking powder
½ tsp salt
1 cup milk
1 tsp vanilla

Filling
2 eggs, beaten
1 cup milk
3 cups mashed pumpkin
1 cup sugar
½ cup brown sugar
1 Tbsp flour
1 tsp cinnamon
¼ tsp ginger
¼ tsp ground cloves
¼ tsp nutmeg
½ tsp salt

Melt butter in 9x13 baking pan. Mix batter and pour over melted butter. Mix the filling ingredients together and slowly pour mixture over batter. Bake at 350° for 1 hour or until set.

– Mary Ethel Wenger

Hershey Bar Pudding

40 large marshmallows (10 oz)
1 cup milk
6 Hershey almond bars (or 1 - 8 oz bar)
2 cups whipped cream
2 cups graham cracker or vanilla wafer crumbs

Melt marshmallows and milk in saucepan, stirring constantly. Cool. Grate (coarsely) chocolate almond bars and fold into whipped cream. Combine both mixtures and pour into a large dessert dish you have lined with crumbs. You may save some crumbs for the top. Chill 12-24 hours. My favorite dessert!

– Jesse Rohrer

HAZEL'S SOUR CHERRY TORTE

Batter

1 cup sugar
2 Tbsp butter
1 egg, beaten
1 cup flour
¼ tsp salt
1 tsp soda
2 cups sour cherries, drained (reserve juice)

Cream butter and sugar. Add egg and dry ingredients. Stir in cherries. Bake in greased 9x13 pan at 350° for 30 minutes. When ready to serve, top with 1½ cups Cool Whip and drizzle with the following sauce.

Sauce

1 Tbsp cornstarch
1 cup cherry juice
½ cup sugar
2 Tbsp butter

Cook and stir over medium heat until thickened.

– Hazel (Rohrer) Horst

DANISH DESSERT FRUIT SAUCE

1¾ cups fruit juice or water
¼ cup jello (any flavor)
⅓ cup sugar
1½ Tbsp cornstarch or clearjel

Heat 1 cup liquid to boiling. Combine jello, sugar, and cornstarch and stir in ¾ cup reserved liquid. Add jello mixture to boiling liquid. Cook about 1 minute. Pour over 1 quart drained, canned fruit, or crushed strawberries, etc. Stir to blend well and chill until served.

Blessed are the flexible,
for they shall not be bent out of shape.

SIMPLY DELICIOUS CHEESECAKE

Crust:

1¼ cups graham cracker crumbs
3 Tbsp sugar
½ cup melted butter
Combine and press crumbs into a 10" pie plate or line an 8" spring-form pan.

Filling:

1 lb softened cream cheese
⅔ cup sugar
½ tsp salt
1 tsp vanilla
3 eggs
Combine and beat until smooth. Pour over crust. Bake at 350° for 25-30 minutes. Cool 15 minutes and top with a sour cream topping for a special occasion. (It is quite yummy even without the added topping.) Serve plain, or with fruit of your choice.

Topping:

1 cup sour cream
2 tsp sugar
½ tsp vanilla
Return to oven and bake 5 more minutes.

Use what talents you possess.
The woods would be very silent if no birds sang there
except those that sang the best.

- Henry van Dyke

Meringue Crust Fruit Pizza

Meringue Crust:
4 egg whites at room temperature
1 cup sugar
1 tsp cornstarch
1 tsp vinegar
1 tsp vanilla

Cream Layer:
1 cup whipping cream
2 Tbsp sugar
1 tsp vanilla
1 pint fresh strawberries
2 kiwi fruits
You may substitute any fruit you choose.

Glaze:
¼ cup sugar
¼ cup water
1½ tsp cornstarch
dash of almond extract

Beat egg whites until soft peaks form. Gradually add sugar and cornstarch, beating until stiff and glossy. Beat in vinegar and vanilla. (Test meringue by rubbing between thumb and finger; it should not be grainy.) Spread meringue on a foil or parchment paper lined 12 inch pizza pan or form in any desired shape. Bake at 275° for 50-60 minutes. Turn oven off and leave in 1 hour.

Meanwhile make cream layer. Whip cream until stiff. Fold in vanilla and sugar. Spread over cooled meringue. Arrange fruit in attractive pattern over cream layer. Set aside.

Make glaze by combining ingredients. Cook and cool. Brush glaze over fruit to seal until served. Chill thoroughly.

– *Mary Ethel Wenger*

Life is like a shower. One wrong turn and you end up in hot water.

GRAPE SALAD

2 lbs seedless grapes
4 oz. cream cheese, softened
1 cup sour cream
⅔ cup powdered sugar
1½ tsp lemon juice

Wash and stem grapes. Combine other ingredients and fold in grapes.

ANGEL SALAD

20 oz can pineapple chunks
2 Tbsp corn starch
½ cup sugar
pinch of salt
2 beaten eggs
2 cups whipped cream
3 chopped oranges
2 cups halved grapes
2 cups mini marshmallows

Drain juice from pineapple. To the juice, add cornstarch, sugar, salt, and eggs. Stir while heating until it thickens. Cool and add whipped cream. Stir in the three fruits and marshmallows. May be garnished with pecans or walnuts.

This has been a favorite dessert for special occasions in Mennonite homes for many years.

God give me sympathy and sense and help me keep my courage high.
God, give me calm and confidence—
And please—a twinkle in my eye.
– Margaret Bailey

Raspberry Trifle

1 angel food cake cut into slices
2 pkg (3.4 oz each) instant vanilla pudding mix or
    1 qt vanilla pudding (recipe on page 169)
1½ pints fresh red raspberries or your choice of fresh fruit

Arrange one third of sliced cake on the bottom of large serving dish. If using the instant pudding, prepare according to package directions. Place one-third more cake slices around sides of dish, using half of pudding to hold them in place. Layer on half the raspberries. Cover with remaining cake pieces. Layer remaining pudding and raspberries. Chill before serving.

– Clarke and Marybeth Eberly

Strawberry Cheesecake Trifle

16 oz cream cheese
2 cups powdered sugar
1 cup sour cream
1½ tsp vanilla
¼ tsp almond extract
1 cup whipping cream
1 Tbsp sugar
1 angel food cake torn into bite-size pieces
2 quarts fresh strawberries thinly sliced
3 Tbsp sugar
½ tsp almond extract

In large bowl, cream together cream cheese and powdered sugar. Add sour cream, ½ tsp vanilla, and almond extract. Set aside.

In a small, deep bowl, whip the cream, 1 tsp vanilla, and sugar. Fold whipped cream into cream cheese mixture. Add cake pieces; set aside. Combine strawberries, sugar, and almond extract. Layer together in a large, clear glass dish starting with strawberries and then adding cake mixture. Continue layering, finishing with strawberries. Cover with plastic wrap and chill. Serves 24

– Mary Ethel Wenger

STRAWBERRY CUSTARD TORTE

Cake

1 yellow cake mix, prepared and baked in two 9" pans and cooled

Custard

⅓ cup sugar
1 Tbsp cornstarch
⅛ tsp salt
1 cup milk
2 egg yolks, lightly beaten
1 Tbsp butter
1 tsp vanilla

Combine all in saucepan, and stir over low heat until custard thickens. Cool.
1 - 8 oz Cool Whip
3-4 cups strawberries, fresh or frozen
Split cake layers in half. Put half of cool whip on first layer, top with half of berries, then a layer of cake. Put custard on top of next layer, then repeat cake, cool whip, and berry layer. Garnish top of torte with more cool whip and a few berries. Chill until served.

– *Karen (Nolt) Martin*

FRUIT CRISP

1 qt fruit pie filling or 1 qt canned fruit, drained
     (apple, peach, blueberry, cherry, etc.)
¾ cup flour
¾ cup brown sugar
¾ cup quick oats
½ cup butter
½ tsp salt
1 tsp cinnamon

Place fruit in greased 8x11 or similar size bake dish. Mix other ingredients until crumbly, and sprinkle over fruit. Bake at 350° for 25-30 minutes. Serve warm, with milk or ice cream.

Keep conscience clear, then never fear.

SUMMERTIME FRESH FRUIT COBBLER

4 cups fresh fruit (raspberries, peaches, blackberries, etc)
½ cup soft butter
1½ cups flour
2 tsp baking powder
1 tsp salt
1 cup milk
1-1¼ cups sugar
2 Tbsp cornstarch
½ tsp cinnamon
1 cup boiling water

Spread fruit in a greased 8x11 or similar size bake dish. Combine butter, flour, baking powder, salt, and milk. Pour over fruit. Mix sugar, cornstarch, and cinnamon, and sprinkle over dough. Pour water over all and bake at 350° for about an hour. Serves 8-10.

– *Janice (Martin) Schmucker*

BERRY SURPRISE

½ cup soft butter
1 cup sugar
1 cup flour
1 ½ tsp baking powder
¼ tsp salt
⅔ cup milk
½ tsp vanilla
1 qt berries (fresh or canned)

Cream butter and sugar. Add other ingredients, and stir to blend. Spread in a greased 8x11 or similar size pan. Top with fruit. Bake at 350° for 1 hour or until done. Dough will come to the top as it bakes. Serves 8-10.

– *Marilyn Eberly*

Conscience is the still small voice that makes you feel still smaller.

MY FAVORITE FRESH FRUIT DESSERT

6-8 cups assorted fruits
1 can pineapple tidbits or chunks
¼ cup clearjel
½ cup sugar
pinch of salt

Choose from apples, oranges, grapes, kiwi, blueberries, strawberries, peaches, pears, raspberries, bananas, etc. Cut fruit into bite-sized pieces. Drain pineapple and reserve juice. Mix bananas and apples with pineapple to keep them light; then combine with rest of fruit in a large bowl. Chill.

Mix clearjel in water and pineapple juice (1 pint of liquid). Cook over medium heat until it thickens. Add sugar and salt. I add a Tbsp of orange juice concentrate for extra flavor. Cool and combine with fruit.

Thickening Equivalents:
1 Tbsp clearjel = 1 Tbsp cornstarch = 1 Tbsp tapioca starch or 2 Tbsp flour
Clearjel and tapioca starch are available at bulk food stores.

FAVORITE APPLE SALAD

2 crisp apples (Fuji or Red Delicious)
2 bananas
1 cup seedless grapes
Chop apples and bananas. Add grapes.

Dressing
½ cup crunchy peanut butter
1 Tbsp sugar
¼ tsp salt
1 tsp vinegar
¼ cup light cream
Stir all together until creamy and combine with fruit. Serve within ½ hour.

The best thing to spend on children is time.

Sawdust Salad

Bottom

1 large box (scant cup) strawberry/banana or other jello
2 cups boiling water
2 cups cold water
¾ bag mini marshmallows
4 diced bananas (optional)
1 large can <u>drained</u>, crushed pineapple

Middle

1¼ cups liquid (pineapple juice and water)
¾ cup sugar
1 beaten egg
3 Tbsp flour

Top

8 oz cream cheese (may use fat free)
a little milk
8 oz Cool Whip (lite is fine)

Dissolve jello in boiling water. Combine remaining ingredients for "Bottom." Pour into a 3-quart oblong dish. Cool until set. Cook "Middle" over medium heat until thick, stirring constantly. Cool. Spread over congealed salad. Combine "Top" and spread over "Middle." Garnish with some grated Cheddar or Colby cheese.

– Beulah (Rhodes) Burkholder

Autumn Apple Salad

20 oz undrained, crushed pineapple
⅔ cup sugar
3 oz lemon jello
8 oz cream cheese, softened
2 cups diced, unpeeled apples
½ -1 cup chopped nuts
1 cup whipped topping

In saucepan combine pineapple and sugar. Bring to a boil. Boil for 3 minutes. Add jello. Stir until dissolved. Add cream cheese. Stir until thoroughly combined. Cool. Fold in apples, nuts, and whipped topping.

– Karen (Rohrer) Rohrer

APRICOT DELIGHT

1 quart water
¼ cup tapioca
1 cup sugar
½ tsp salt
1 6-oz pkg orange jello (scant 1 cup)
1 cup boiling water
½ lb dried apricots

Cook tapioca in 1 quart water until soft. Cook apricots until tender and put through sieve. Dissolve jello in hot water. Combine all ingredients. Chill until set.

Martha Rohrer (David)

CRANBERRY SALAD

3 oz orange jello (½ cup)
3 oz cranberry jello (½ cup)
1½ cups boiling water
½ cup sugar
¼ tsp salt
2 cups ice water
12 oz fresh cranberries
4 oranges
6 apples
20 oz can crushed pineapple

Dissolve jello in hot water. Add sugar and salt. Stir in ice water. Wash and finely chop or grind raw cranberries. Grate the rind of two oranges and add to jello. Peel and dice oranges. Peel apples and grate on coarse side of grater. Add fruits to jello and stir in pineapple. Chill. Garnish with nuts or mandarin oranges or chopped celery. Delicious with hot foods or served with cheese and crackers. Keeps in fridge for several weeks. This recipe makes about a gallon.

Note: If your apples or oranges are large, you'll need to use an extra ½ cup jello. If using red apples, I leave several unpeeled for extra fiber and color.

MANDARIN ORANGE SALAD

6 oz box orange jello (scant 1 cup)
2 cups boiling water
15 oz can mandarin oranges, drained
6 oz can frozen orange juice
1 small can crushed pineapple
1 box lemon instant pudding (3.4 oz)
2 cups pasteurized milk
1½ cups Cool Whip (or whipped cream)
4 oz cream cheese, softened

Dissolve jello in boiling water. Cool, and add oranges, juice, and pineapple. Pour into serving dish, and chill until set. Beat pudding and milk. Add cream cheese and Cool Whip. Spread on congealed salad.

– *Ethel Shank*

CARROT SALAD

⅔ cup orange jello
2 cups boiling water
½ cup sugar
pinch of salt
2 Tbsp orange drink powder or orange juice concentrate
2 cups cold water
15½ oz can crushed pineapple
1 can mandarin oranges or apricots chopped
3 or 4 carrots, shredded

Dissolve jello in boiling water. Stir in sugar, salt, and orange powder or juice. Add cold water. Cool until beginning to thicken. Stir in fruit and carrots. Pour into dish. Chill until firm.

– *Zelda Rohrer*

Jello Tips:

Don't add pineapple to hot jello, wait until jello cools as it can prevent it from setting.

When using bulk jello:
  6 oz. jello is 1 cup minus 1 Tbsp • 3 oz jello is a scant ½ cup

LAYERED PINEAPPLE SALAD

First Layer

3 oz lemon jello
3 oz lime jello
2 cups boiling water
2 cups cold water
20 oz can crushed pineapple (drained)

Second Layer

1 cup whipping cream
 8 oz cream cheese
sugar to taste
vanilla to taste

Third Layer

3 eggs, slightly beaten
⅔ cup sugar
1 cup pineapple juice
3 Tbsp flour

Dissolve jello in boiling water. Add remaining ingredients for "First Layer." (Save out a few Tbsp of pineapple for the "Third Layer.") Pour into 9x13 dish and allow to jell. Blend "Second Layer" together and spread on "First Layer." Combine eggs, sugar, juice, and flour. Cook over medium heat until thickened. Cool and add a few Tbsp of pineapple. Top the "Second Layer."

– Rosanna (Rhodes) Martin

PINEAPPLE CHEESE SALAD

3 oz orange jello
¾ cup hot water
¾ cup pineapple juice
1 Tbsp lemon juice
1 cup crushed pineapple (drained)
1 cup whipping cream, whipped
1 cup grated cheese

Dissolve jello in hot water. Cool. Then add juices and chill until partially set. Add remaining ingredients and top with grated cheese.

– Frances Martin

CHRISTMAS RIBBON SALAD

First layer

2 – 3 oz. pkg. lime jello
2½ cups boiling water
1¼ cups cold water
Dissolve jello in boiling water. Add cold water. Pour into lightly oiled
9 x 13 or larger dish. Chill

Second layer

1½ cups pineapple juice
20 large marshmallows, cut into pieces
1 (3 oz.) pkg. lemon jello
1½ cups boiling water
1 8 oz. pkg. cream cheese

Heat juice and marshmallows until melted. Dissolve lemon jello in
water, stir in cream cheese. Combine with pineapple mixture and
pour over firm first layer. Chill.

Third layer

2 – 3 oz.. pkg. jello (strawberry, raspberry, or cherry)
2½ cups boiling water
1¼ cups cold water
Prepare like first layer. Pour over firm second layer. Chill until set.
A very pretty dessert to finish your holiday meal.

FIVE CUP SALAD

1 cup mandarin oranges
1 cup pineapple chunks
1 cup coconut
1 cup sour cream
1 cup grapes

Drain fruits, combine all ingredients. Chill until served. (You may
use miniature marshmallows instead of grapes.)

Every day may not be good,
but there's something good in every day.

COTTAGE PEAR SALAD

15½ oz can crushed pineapple
1 qt diced pears
6 oz (1 cup) lime jello (or part lemon)
1 qt cottage cheese
1 cup whipping cream

Drain pineapple and pears. To pineapple juice, add enough pear syrup to make 3 cups liquid. Heat 2 cups to boiling and dissolve jello in it. Add other cup liquid and set aside to cool. Mash pears with potato masher until soft and chunky. Whip cream. When jello begins to thicken, stir in pears, pineapple, cheese, and whipped cream. Pour into a pretty dish. Cover and refrigerate. Light and refreshing.

COTTAGE PEACH SALAD

Use peaches and orange jello in above recipe.

FOUR MINUTE DESSERT

16 oz cottage cheese
3 oz pkg lime jello (or any other flavor)
15½ oz can crushed pineapple, drained
8 oz Cool Whip

Mix cottage cheese and dry jello. Add the rest of the ingredients. Chill and serve.

FIVE MINUTE FRUIT SALAD

2 lbs cottage cheese
1 3-oz pkg orange jello (½ cup)
15½ oz can fruit cocktail (drained)
15½ oz can crushed pineapple (drained)
2 cups cool whip

Mix cottage cheese and dry jello together. Add fruit and cool whip.

Cottage Cheese Salad

1 lb marshmallows
½ cup milk
1 pint cottage cheese
8 oz cream cheese, softened
20 oz crushed pineapple, drained
2 cups whipped cream

Melt marshmallows in milk. Cool. Add both cheeses. Fold in pineapple and whipped cream. Pour in serving bowl and refrigerate.

– Esther Rohrer

Old Timey "Sunday Dessert"

Prepare several small boxes of jello in varied flavors and pour each
into a shallow pan. Chill until set.

Just before serving, cut jello into bite-sized cubes, and layer with
the following in a pretty crystal bowl:
❖ Broken graham crackers
❖ Whipped cream, sweetened
❖ Jello cubes
❖ Sliced bananas
❖ Mini marshmallows

*Quick, pretty, and delicious! When I was a child, we children
used to put this dessert together while Daddy mashed the potatoes and
Mom dished up our Sunday dinner.*

*A kitchen is a friendly place,
full of living's daily grace.*

RHUBARB DESSERT

4 cups sliced rhubarb
1 cup sugar
3 oz strawberry jello (½ cup)
1 yellow cake mix
½ cup butter, melted
1 cup water

Put rhubarb in greased 9x13 dish. Sprinkle sugar and jello over rhubarb. Spread dry cake mix over top and drizzle butter over all. Pour water on top and stir lightly with a fork in a swirling motion. Bake at 350° about 45-50 minutes. Serve with milk or ice cream.

– Neva Horst

GRAHAM CRACKER FLUFF

2 egg yokes
½ cup sugar
⅔ cup milk
1 Tbsp gelatin
½ cup cold water
2 egg whites
1 cup whipping cream
1 tsp vanilla
3 Tbsp melted butter
3 Tbsp sugar
12 graham crackers, crushed

Beat egg yolks, add sugar and milk. Cook over medium heat while stirring until mixture starts to thicken. Soak gelatin in cold water, stir into milk mixture. Chill until it begins to thicken. Whip egg whites until stiff. Whip cream to soft peaks. Combine egg whites, cream, and vanilla, stir into chilled milk mixture. Combine butter, sugar, and graham cracker crumbs. Put half of crumbs in a large dessert dish. Pour fluff over crumbs, top with remaining crumbs. Chill.

An effort made for the happiness of others lifts us above ourselves.
– Lydia M. Child

PINEAPPLE TAPIOCA

1 qt water
¾ cup sugar
½ tsp salt
⅓ cup minute tapioca
20 oz can crushed pineapple
½ tsp orange flavor
1 Tbsp lemon juice

Put first four ingredients in top of double boiler over simmering water. Cook until clear, about 15 minutes. Remove from heat and pour over crushed pineapple in a large bowl. Add flavorings, stir all together. Cool and refrigerate.

– Ethel Shank

FROSTY PUMPKIN DESSERT

Gingersnap Crust (see recipe page 206)

1 qt vanilla ice cream
2 Tbsp brown sugar
1½ tsp pumpkin pie spice
½ tsp salt
15 oz can pumpkin (1¾ cups)
2 cups sweetened whipped cream

Prepare gingersnap crust in a 10" pie plate or similar sized bake dish. Soften ice cream in fridge for 30 minutes. Combine brown sugar, spice, salt, and pumpkin and fold into ice cream. Pour over crust and freeze until firm, 4-48 hours. Thaw in fridge for an hour before serving. Top with whipped cream and a sprinkle of cinnamon.

Remember the three R's—
Respect for self,
Respect for others,
Responsibility for your actions.

FRUIT PIZZA

Crust

½ cup butter
½ cup sugar
1 egg
1⅓ cups flour
1 tsp baking powder
¼ tsp salt

Mix and pat onto a 12" greased pizza pan. Bake at 350° for about 12-15 minutes. Cool.

Cream Filling

8 oz cream cheese
¼ cup powdered sugar
1-2 cups Cool Whip

Mix and spread over crust. Arrange fruits of your choice in a pretty design over filling. You may use: grapes, strawberries, kiwi, peaches, blueberries, bananas, mandarin oranges, pineapple, apples, apricots, plums, raspberries etc.

Glaze

2 cups pineapple or other fruit juice
½ cup sugar
2 Tbsp clearjel

Combine sugar and clearjel. Add juice and cook until thickened. When cool, spread over fruit.

Prayer will cause a man to
cease from sin,
or sin will entice a man to cease from prayer.

– John Bunyan

Pies

Food Talk

When was the last time you said somebody didn't know beans about something or said the fog was as thick as pea soup?

We really take the cake when it comes to using foods as a figure of speech. For example, when things go right, they are in apple pie order, and life is a bowl of cherries. But when they go wrong, we're in a pickle.

If a man is important, he's top banana. If he's clumsy, he's butterfingered. If he's cowardly, he's chicken livered. If he's poised, he's cool as a cucumber. If he talks too much, he spills the beans, and if he doesn't talk, he clams up.

Moreover, he doesn't earn money, he earns dough, or he brings home the bacon. If he's working for peanuts, his wife may egg him on to butter up the boss.

If something is good; it's a peach. If it's bad, it's a lemon, or some will say it's just sour grapes.

If you're not worth your salt, you may wind up eating humble pie... and that would be getting your just desserts.

And now, just to ice the cake, I want to say that you may take most of these claims with a grain of salt.

— *Selected*

Pies

Never Fail Pie Crust

4 cups pastry flour
1½ cups cold shortening
1 egg, beaten
1½ tsp salt
2 tsp vinegar
7-8 Tbsp ice cold water

Blend butter and flour with pastry blender until crumbs are pea-sized. Combine ice water, beaten egg, salt, and vinegar. Pour over crumb mixture and mix quickly to form a ball. Divide into 4 pieces and roll to fit pie pans. Makes 4 single or 2 double crusts.
– Maria (Eberly) Horst

Flaky Pie Crust

1½ lbs pastry flour (5 cups)
2 Tbsp sugar
1 tsp salt
½ tsp baking powder
2 cups Crisco shortening
1 cup cold water (approximately)
Mix dry ingredients. Cut in shortening. Gradually add water, and mix well. Roll out crusts. These freeze well in foil pans with deli paper or saran wrap between each crust for easy separation. Makes six to seven 9-inch crusts.
Pie Crust Tip: Empty pie crusts shrink less while baking if you let them set ½ hour before you bake them. Bake at 375º for 12-15 minutes, until light, golden brown.

Chocolate Wafer Crust

2⅔ cups fine chocolate wafer cookie crumbs
6 Tbsp soft butter

Mix together until blended. Press into two 9-inch pie pans. Bake at 350° for 10 minutes.

Graham Cracker Crust

1½ cups graham cracker crumbs
2 Tbsp sugar
6 Tbsp melted butter

Mix and press into a 9 or 10 inch pie plate. Bake at 350° for 10 minutes.

Pie or Cobbler Crumb Topping

2 cups brown sugar
3 cups flour
3 cups oatmeal
1 tsp soda
1 tsp salt
1 tsp baking powder
4 tsp cinnamon
1½ cups butter

Combine dry ingredients. Cut in butter until you have a fine, crumbly mixture. Store in fridge and use as needed for a quick dessert topping. For crumb topping without oatmeal, see pages 201, 202, or 208.

A rotten apple spoils his companions.

Dad's Favorite Apple Pie

4-6 baking apples
1 Tbsp. lemon juice
½ - ¾ cup sugar
3 Tbsp flour
2 tsp cinnamon
pinch of salt
2 Tbsp butter

Peel and slice apples and stir in lemon juice. Combine sugar, flour, cinnamon, and salt. Stir into apples. Pile into an unbaked 9"-10" pie crust. Dot with butter. Top with a crust or crumbs. Bake at 350° until done, about an hour.

Apple Pie

4-6 baking apples
1 tsp lemon juice
¾ cup water
½ cup sugar
2 Tbsp clearjel or cornstarch
pinch of salt
2 tsp cinnamon
2 Tbsp butter

Peel and slice apples. Stir in lemon juice. Combine dry ingredients and water and bring to a boil while stirring in a saucepan. Add butter to thickened mixture and stir over apples. Pile into an unbaked 9" or 10" pie crust and cover with crumb topping or a top crust. Bake at 350° about one hour.

Good Baking Apples

Golden Delicious, Jonagold, Gingergold, Cortland, York, Jonathan, Winesap, Stayman, Granny Smith, McIntosh or Rome. They may be used for good results in almost any recipe that uses apples and is cooked or baked. Tart apples make the best pies.

APPLE PIE IN A JAR

8 lbs baking apples (page 197)
4 cups sugar
4 tsp cinnamon
½ tsp nutmeg
1 tsp salt
4 cups water
1 cup clearjel or cornstarch
3 Tbsp lemon juice

Peel and slice apples   Combine dry ingredients in kettle. Add 2 cups hot water. Stir to dissolve sugar and heat to a boil. Mix clearjel and 2 cups cold water. Stir into hot syrup and cook until thick and bubbly. Add lemon juice.

Fold in apples and spoon mixture into quart jars, allowing 2" head space. It is very important to allow enough space for apples to expand in jar while cooking. If the jars are too full, the sauce will seep out and your jar won't stay sealed. Boil 20 minutes in a hot water bath. Turn off heat and remove jars after 5 minutes. Makes 7-8 quarts. Handy for making pie or cobbler.

APPLE DUMPLINGS

prepared pie dough (enough for 3 pie crusts)
8-10 whole baking apples, peeled and cored

Grease 9x13 baking dish. Roll pie dough out in a large rectangle. Cut into 6" squares and place an apple on each. Fill cores with a cinnamon sugar mixture. Fold dough corners to top of apples and press dough around apples to seal edges. Brush dumplings with water and sprinkle generously with sugar. Bake at 350° until done (50-60 minutes). Serve warm with milk or ice cream.

The two hardest things to handle in life are failure and success.

CARAMEL CRUNCH APPLE PIE

Topping

¼ cup flour
⅓ cup brown sugar, packed
2 Tbsp butter softened
½ tsp cinnamon

Pie

6 cups sliced, peeled baking apples
1 Tbsp lemon juice
½ cup sugar
3 Tbsp flour
½ tsp cinnamon
28 caramels
5 oz evaporated milk

Combine topping ingredients; spread in ungreased 8" pan. Bake at 400º for 6-8 minutes or until golden brown. Cool; crumble and set aside. Sprinkle apples with lemon juice. Combine sugar, flour, and cinnamon; toss with apples. Place in an unbaked 9" pie shell. Cut a circle of foil to cover apples but not edge of crust. Place over pie. Bake at 425º for 10 minutes. Reduce heat to 375º; bake for 35 minutes or until apples are tender. Meanwhile in saucepan over low heat, melt caramels with milk, stirring frequently. Remove foil from pie. Pour caramel mixture over apples. Sprinkle with topping; return to oven for 5 minutes. Serve warm.

– Lorna (Good) Wenger

PEACH CUSTARD PIE
BERRY CUSTARD PIE

4-5 cups sliced fresh peaches or
4 cups fresh berries (blackberries, raspberries, blueberries)
⅔ cup sugar
⅓ cup flour
¼ tsp salt
½ tsp cinnamon or nutmeg
1 cup cream

Put fruit in a 10 inch pastry-lined pie pan. Mix remaining ingredients together and pour over fruit. May bake uncovered or with a lattice top. Bake at 375º until custard is set around fruit. (45-50 min)

Famous Country Inn Cream Pie

2½ cups milk
½ cup sugar
⅓ cup cornstarch
3 egg yolks
1 Tbsp butter
¼ tsp salt
1 tsp vanilla

Combine 2 cups milk, sugar, cornstarch, and salt in top of double boiler. Heat until thickened. Combine ½ cup milk and egg yolks. Stir into milk and heat until bubbly. Add butter, salt and vanilla. Cool. Beat until creamy. Pour into baked 9" pie shell. Top with whipped cream, or topping, or meringue (pg 215)

Peanut Butter Cream Pie

❖ Combine ½ cup peanut butter, ½ cup powdered sugar. Make crumbs and put on crust before adding pudding.

Banana Cream Pie

❖ Slice 2 bananas into crust. Top with pudding and whipped cream.

Coconut Cream Pie

❖ Stir ⅔ cup coconut into pudding.

Chocolate Cream Pie

❖ Stir ½ cup chocolate chips into hot pudding.

If you have something to say, to do or to write, do it today;
for in life there is not always a second chance.

Virginia Beach Blueberry Pie

1 large graham cracker crust
2 bananas
lemon juice
8 oz cream cheese
1 cup sugar
12 oz Cool Whip
1 can blueberry pie filling
1 cup fresh blueberries

Slice bananas in bottom of crust. Sprinkle with a little lemon juice. Cream together cream cheese and sugar. Mix with Cool Whip. Spread over bananas. Mix canned and fresh blueberries together and pour over cream cheese filling. Chill 4 hours before serving.

– Wilma (Rohrer) Shank

Pear Pie

3-4 cups pears, peeled and sliced
½ cup sugar
2 Tbsp flour
½ tsp salt
1 egg, beaten
1 cup sour cream
½ tsp vanilla

Mix everything except pears. Place pears in unbaked pie crust and pour mixture over them. Sprinkle nutmeg on top. Bake at 400° for 15 minutes. Remove from oven and top with crumb topping:

Crumb Topping

½ cup brown sugar
⅔ cup flour
½ tsp nutmeg or cinnamon
⅓ cup butter

Mix brown sugar, flour, and spice. Cut in butter. Sprinkle crumbs on pie and bake at 350° for 45 minutes or until pears are done. Serve cold.

– Janice (Shank) Wenger

The time is always right to do what is right.

CREAMY PEAR PIE

9-inch unbaked pie shell
4 cups sliced, peeled pears
⅓ cup sugar
pinch of salt
2 Tbsp flour
1 cup sour cream
½ tsp each of vanilla, lemon, and almond extract

Topping
¼ cup flour
2 Tbsp butter, melted
2 Tbsp brown sugar

In large bowl, toss pears with sugar, salt and flour. Combine sour cream and extracts; add to pear mixture and mix well. Pour into pie shell.

In small bowl, mix topping ingredients until crumbly. Sprinkle over pears. Bake at 400° for 10 minutes. Reduce heat to 350° and bake 40 minutes or more until pears are tender. Pie is best served chilled.

– *Lorna (Good) Wenger*

GRAPE PIE

5 ½ cups Concord grapes
1 cup sugar
¼ cup flour
1¼ tsp lemon juice
pinch of salt
1-2 Tbsp butter, melted

Pop grapes from skins and cook pulp in a pan (no water). Stir to a rolling boil. Mash through a strainer or sieve to remove seeds. Combine strained pulp with grape skins and add rest of ingredients. Pour into pastry lined 9" pie pan. Cover with pie crumb topping, or a top crust or lattice. Bake at 350° about an hour.

Key Lime Pie I

6 limes, juiced (1 cup)
1 lb cream cheese
2 - 14 oz cans low fat sweetened condensed milk

Beat all together. Pour into baked 9" crust. Garnish with lime zest.
Rich and tangy. Serves 10-12.

Key Lime Pie II

1 graham cracker crust, baked
2- 14 oz cans sweetened condensed milk
1¼ cups fresh lime juice
2 large eggs, lightly beaten
½ cup sour cream
2 Tbsp powdered sugar

Whisk together milk, lime juice, and eggs until well blended. Pour
into crust and bake at 325° for 18 minutes. Stir sugar into sour
cream and spread over pie. Chill at least 4 hours. Serves 10-12.
You may also top pie with meringue when it comes out of the oven,
and leave off the sour cream topping.

Fresh Strawberry Pie

½ cup sugar
pinch of salt
3 Tbsp cornstarch or clearjel
1¼ cups water
3 Tbsp strawberry jello
few drops red food coloring
1 quart fresh strawberries, whole, sliced, or halved

Bring sugar, salt, cornstarch, and water to a boil and cook until
clear and thick. Remove from heat and add jello and coloring.
Cool and pour over strawberries. Put into a baked pie shell. Chill.
Top with whipped cream.

Rhubarb Strawberry Pie

1½ cups diced rhubarb
2 cups sliced strawberries
3 eggs, separated
¼ cup water
1 cup sugar
2 Tbsp flour
pinch of salt
1 Tbsp melted butter

Put berries and rhubarb in an unbaked 9" or 10" pie shell. Beat egg whites and set aside. Mix yolks and water; stir in sugar, flour, salt, and butter. Last, fold in egg whites. Pour over all. Bake at 350° for 45-55 minutes.

Peppermint Pie

1 graham cracker crust <u>or</u> chocolate wafer crust (page 196)
24 large marshmallows
½ cup milk
1 tsp vanilla
⅛ tsp salt
6 drops peppermint extract
6 drops red food color
1 cup whipping cream, chilled
2 Tbsp crushed peppermint candy

Heat marshmallows and milk over low heat, stirring constantly until marshmallows are melted. Remove from heat, and stir in next 4 ingredients. Refrigerate. Stir occasionally until mixture mounds slightly when dropped from a spoon. Beat cream in a chilled bowl until stiff. Fold into marshmallow mixture. Pour into crust. Garnish with crushed peppermint. Chill until served. Light and refreshing and pretty, too!

– Carolyn Landis

*The most comfortable sleeping position
is the one you find after turning off the alarm.*

Rhubarb Pineapple Pie

3 Tbsp flour
1½ cups sugar
1 egg
¾ cup crushed pineapple
2 Tbsp lemon juice
¼ cup melted butter
3 cups diced rhubarb

Mix flour and sugar. Add egg and beat well. Add remaining ingredients except rhubarb. Spread rhubarb over unbaked pie crust. Pour filling over all. Top with lattice and bake at 350° until done (about 1 hour).

Cherry Pie

4 cups red tart cherries, seeds removed
¾ cup sugar
⅛ tsp salt
1¼ cups water
¼ cup clearjel
½ tsp almond flavoring (optional)
9" or 10" unbaked pastry crust

Combine sugar, salt, water and clearjel in a saucepan. Bring to a boil, while stirring. Add a few drops red color and stir in cherries. Pour into unbaked pie crust and top with pastry or pie crumb topping. Bake at 350° until golden brown, 35-40 minutes.

Early to bed and early to rise...
gives us time to bake those pies.

SOUR CREAM LEMON PIE
WITH GINGERSNAP CRUST

1 cup sugar
3½ Tbsp cornstarch
1 Tbsp grated lemon peel
½ cup fresh lemon juice
3 egg yolks, slightly beaten
1 cup milk
¼ cup butter
1 cup sour cream

Combine all except butter and sour cream in a heavy saucepan; cook over medium heat until thick. Stir in butter and cool to room temperature. Stir in sour cream and pour into pre-baked pie shell. Cover with whipped cream and garnish with lemon twists. (a thin slice of lemon twisted in an "s" shape). Store in refrigerator.

– Ethel Shank

GINGERSNAP CRUST

1½ cups gingersnap cookie crumbs
¼ cup butter

Mix until crumbly. Press into 9" pie pan and bake at 350° for 8 minutes.

The greater part of our happiness or misery
depends on our disposition
and not on our circumstances.
– Martha Washington

Lemon Supreme Pie

9 inch pie crust, baked

Filling

1½ cups sugar
6 Tbsp cornstarch
½ tsp salt
1¼ cups water
2 Tbsp butter
2 tsp grated lemon peel
4-5 drops yellow food coloring
⅔ cup fresh lemon juice

Bottom and Top

8 oz cream cheese
¾ cup powdered sugar
1½ cups whipped topping
1 Tbsp fresh lemon juice

Combine sugar, cornstarch, and salt in saucepan. Stir in water and bring to a boil. Reduce heat and cook and stir until thick and bubbly. Remove from heat. Add butter, lemon peel, and coloring (if desired). Gently stir in juice. Cool to room temperature.

In a mixing bowl beat cream cheese and powdered sugar. Fold in topping and juice. Save ½ cup of mixture for garnish. Spread remaining mixture in crust. Top with lemon filling and garnish. Chill overnight.

– *Wanda (Rohrer) Good*

Labor to keep alive in your breast
that little spark of celestial fire, called Conscience.
– *George Washington*

COLORADO PEACH PIE

3½-4 cups peaches sliced
¾ cup sugar
2 ½ Tbsp flour
1 egg beaten
¼ tsp salt
½ tsp vanilla
1 cup sour cream

Topping

⅓ cup sugar
⅓ cup flour
¼ cup butter
1 tsp cinnamon

Mix all ingredients, adding peaches last. Pour into unbaked pie crust. Bake at 350°-375° for 45-50 min. Add crumb topping about 20 minutes before pie is done. Note: ¼ cup sugar sprinkled over drained, canned peaches may be used in place of the first two ingredients.

– Ava (Eberly) Heatwole

RAISIN PIE

3 eggs
¾ cup brown sugar
¼ cup melted butter
1 cup dark corn syrup
¼ cup walnuts or pecans
1 cup raisins
1 tsp vanilla
¼ cup water

Beat eggs until light. Add other ingredients. Pour into a 9" or 10" pie shell. Bake at 350° for 35-40 minutes.

– Grandma Marie Rohrer

It isn't hard to make a mountain out of a mole hill.
Just add a little dirt.

New Orleans Pecan Pie

2 eggs, separated
1 cup sour cream
1 cup sugar
¼ cup flour
½ tsp vanilla
9 inch pie crust, baked
1 cup brown sugar
1 cup chopped pecans

In saucepan mix egg yolks, sour cream, sugar, flour, and vanilla. Cook and stir over medium heat until thickened. Pour into pie shell; set aside. In large bowl, beat egg whites until soft peaks form. Gradually add brown sugar. Continue to beat until stiff. While filling is still warm, spread egg white topping over filling. Sprinkle with pecans. Bake at 375° for 12-15 minutes.

– *Lydia (Eberly) Good*

Shoofly Pie

1¼ cups flour
¾ cup brown sugar
3 Tbsp butter
¾ cup dark corn syrup
¼ cup sorghum molasses
1 egg
¼ tsp salt
1 cup hot water
½ tsp soda

Mix first three ingredients until crumbly. Reserve 1 cup crumbs. Dissolve soda in hot water. Add rest of ingredients to remaining crumbs. Stir in soda and water. Pour into unbaked pie crust and top with reserved crumbs. Bake at 350°-375° until set in center (30-45 minutes).

You will not make yourself clean by soiling others.

SOUTHERN PECAN PIE

3 large eggs, beaten
½ tsp salt
1 tsp vanilla
1½ cups light corn syrup
1 Tbsp flour mixed with 1 Tbsp water
2 Tbsp melted butter
1½ cups pecan pieces

Prepare an unbaked 9 inch pie crust. Spread pecans in bottom. Mix remaining ingredients and pour over pecans. Bake at 350° for 50-55 minutes. This pie is not as sweet as most pecan pies.

CHOCOLATE PECAN PIE

Same as Southern Pecan Pie. Use only 1¼ cups pecan pieces and put ½ cup chocolate chips in pie crust before filling. Then sprinkle another ¼ cup chocolate chips on top after filling is added. Serve warm with vanilla ice cream.

OATMEAL PECAN PIE

Same as Southern Pecan Pie. Add ¾ cup oatmeal to filling and stir in only 1 cup pecans.

PECAN TARTS

Use Southern Pecan Pie filling. Make Tart shells with the following:

3 cups flour
8 oz cream cheese
¼ tsp salt
1 cup margarine

Mix together well. Divide into 4 portions. Shape into a rectangle and cut each into 12 equal pieces. Shape into balls and form into tart pans. Put a rounded half teaspoon of pecans in each shell. Fill with pie filling. Don't overfill. Bake at 325° for 25 minutes. Makes 4 dozen.

PUMPKIN PIE

(Makes 2)

4 eggs
¾ cup sugar
¾ cup brown sugar
1½ tsp salt
1 Tbsp flour
1 Tbsp cinnamon
1½ tsp ginger
1 tsp cloves
½ tsp nutmeg
4 cups canned pumpkin or 1(29 oz.) can
1 qt. half and half

Combine sugars, salt, flour and spices. Beat eggs in large bowl and add sugar mixture. Add pumpkin and gradually stir in half and half. Pour into two 9" unbaked pie shells. Bake at 350° about an hour or until set.

Before I married Maggie dear,
I was her pumpkin pie,
Then precious peach, her honey lamb,
The apple of her eye.

But after years of married life
This thought I pause to utter;
Those fancy names are gone, and now
I'm just her bread and butter.

ICE CREAM PEANUT BUTTER PIE

Two Chocolate Wafer Crusts, baked and cooled (recipe pg 196)

Filling
12 oz crunchy peanut butter (1¼ c)
8 oz Cool Whip or Riches Topping (whipped)
1 quart vanilla ice cream (softened)

Combine all until blended. Spoon into crusts and freeze until firm.
Let set out a little while before serving.

– Beulah (Rhodes) Burkholder

ICE CREAM PIZZA

Crust
½ cup corn syrup
½ cup peanut butter
3 cups Rice Krispies

Stir together until well coated. Press evenly onto round pizza
pan. Freeze until firm. Top crust with 1 quart vanilla ice cream,
strawberry topping, pecans, caramel sauce and chocolate chips or
chocolate topping. Freeze.

– Barbara (Rohrer) Eberly

MUD PIE BLIZZARD

1 gallon vanilla ice cream
⅓ cup instant coffee granules
50 Oreo cookies, crushed

Soften ice cream in fridge. Dissolve coffee in a little water. Combine
coffee mixture and ice cream. Stir in cookies. A delicious soft-
serve treat.

– Karen (Rohrer) Rohrer

Diet—something to take the starch out of you.

Honey Nut Pie

½ cup peanut butter
½ cup honey or light corn syrup
4 cups crushed honey nut cornflakes
Ice cream, vanilla or other flavor

Cream peanut butter and honey. Stir into corn flakes. Press into 2 greased 9" pie plates. Chill. Fill with ice cream. Cover and freeze.

Variation

Nutty Buddy Pie – Top ice cream with chocolate syrup and peanuts.

Chocolate Rice Krispie Pie

6 oz chocolate chips
¼ cup butter
1 Tbsp light corn syrup
4 cups Rice Krispies

Melt first 3 ingredients. Stir in cereal and press into a large buttered pie pan. Chill. Fill with 1 qt ice cream. Cover and freeze.

Grasshopper Pie

1 chocolate wafer crust (recipe page 196)
24 large marshmallows
½ cup milk
¼ cup creme de menthe syrup
1 cup heavy cream, whipped

Melt marshmallows and milk, while stirring, over low heat. Cool slightly. Fold in creme de menthe and whipped cream. Pour into crust and chill. Garnish with chocolate curls or mint leaves.

Diets are for people who are thick and tired of it.

MINCEMEAT PIE FILLING

Mince pies have been eaten at Christmas-time for hundreds of years. They were first made in England and contained mutton, instead of beef like we use today. They were called "mutton pies" until the early 1700's. The ingredients listed are my favorites. You may substitute your favorite ingredients and spices to make it tasty to you. I add a few cups of homemade grape wine to the filling.

4-5 lbs raw beef roast, cooked, cooled, and ground with coarse blade in meat grinder (Save broth for other uses.)
1 peck baking apples, peeled and sliced or chopped
10 cups water
4½ cups sugar
1 cup cornstarch
2 lbs raisins (dark or light)
6 oz frozen orange concentrate
6 oz frozen lemonade concentrate
6 oz frozen apple juice concentrate
2 large cans crushed pineapple
6 lbs drained sour cherries (frozen or canned)
2 lbs brown sugar
2½ Tbsp salt
2½ Tbsp cinnamon
2 tsp ginger
2 tsp cloves

Cook water, sugar, and cornstarch together, and stir over apples in a very large bowl. Then combine apple mixture, meat, raisins, thawed juices, pineapple, and cherries. Mix remaining ingredients and stir into mincemeat mixture. Freeze until needed. Makes 10 quarts.

You will notice I don't cook the entire mixture to reduce the liquids as we used to do. It always seemed to scorch easily, so I came up with a way to eliminate all the cooking and stirring. The cherries and apples will be bright colored and look tasty in your baked pies.

Oversleeping will never make our dreams come true.

MERINGUE PIE TOPPING

3 egg whites
¼ tsp cream of tartar
⅓ cup sugar
2 tsp cornstarch

Beat (room temperature) egg whites until frothy, add cream of tartar and continue to beat to a soft peak. Combine sugar and cornstarch and add gradually to egg whites while beating. Beat until meringue is stiff and glossy. Pile on top of pie, sealing around edges to help prevent shrinking. Bake at 325° for 15-20 minutes or until golden brown. (baking too fast will cause meringue to brown before egg whites are cooked)

Meringue may also be used to top cream pies. (See recipes on page 200) Pour hot pudding into prebaked crust. After it cools enough, spread meringue over top and bake as directed above.

LEMON MERINGUE PIE

Make pie crust and bake in 9" pan. Prepare Lemon Supreme Pie filling (recipe on page 207) and pour hot lemon pudding into pie crust. Let set until it begins to firm up and you can cover it with the above meringue. Bake as directed. Cool before serving.

ABOUT PASTRY FLOUR

Pie and pastry flour is milled from soft winter wheat. It has a very low gluten content, so it is the best flour to use for flaky crusts, and those kinds of cookies which we want to be crisp.

A man never discloses his own character so clearly as when he describes another person.

– J. P. Reicher

Who Is Rich?

There are over 1 billion people in North America, and over 6 billion people in the world.

If you have adequate clothing to protect you from the elements, you are in the top 15%.

If you have a regular annual income, you are in the top 14%.

If you have food enough for you and your family today and food stored for future use, you are in the top 6%.

If you have money in your pocket and in the bank, you're in the top 2% of the world's population.

If you have shelter that provides comfort from the elements and is shared only by parents, children or siblings, with privacy for all, you are in the top 1% of the world's population.

Give as you would to the Master
If you met His searching look;
Give as you would of your substance
If His hand the offering took.

Cakes
and
Frostings

Bake Day

Now it's bake day again, Oh, what shall I make?
  Be it custard or pies, or a coconut cake?
Our cookies are gone, they need a replacement,
  And alas, there're an item not found in the basement.
And while I am baking I think I shall try
  To replenish our bread, for we're short in supply.

…Now the bread is a'rising, the cookies are baked.
  The pies are cooling instead of a cake.
Thus the pantry is stocked from another bake day,
  We contentedly put all the dishes away.

— Hazel Horst

Her First Cake

She measured out the butter with a very solemn air;
The milk and sugar also, and she took the greatest care
  To count the eggs correctly, and to add a little bit
  Of baking powder, which you know, beginners oft omit;
Then she stirred it all together, and she baked it for an hour;
But she never quite forgave herself for leaving out the flour.

— Anonymous

Cakes and Frostings

ALMOND BRICKLE TORTE

1½ cups cake flour
1½ cups sugar
½ cup (8) egg yolks, beaten
¼ cup cold water
1 Tbsp lemon juice
1 tsp vanilla
1 cup (8) egg whites
1 tsp cream of tartar
1 tsp salt

Topping:
2 cups whipping cream or 16 oz. Cool Whip
½ cup sugar
1⅓ cups toffee bits (8 oz)
1½ cups sliced almonds

Sift flour and ¾ cup sugar in bowl. Make well in center, add egg yolks, water, lemon juice, and vanilla. Beat until smooth. In a separate bowl, beat egg whites, cream of tartar, and salt until very soft peaks form. Add ¾ cup sugar gradually and beat until stiff. Fold yolk mixture gently into meringue. Pour into ungreased tube pan and bake at 350° for 50-55 minutes or until top springs back when touched lightly. Cool, remove from pans, and split into 2 or 3 layers. Whip the cream and sweeten with ½ cup sugar. Fill with whipped cream or cool whip and sprinkle toffee between layers and on top of cake. Ice sides of cake with whipped cream and cover with lightly toasted sliced almonds.

This cake is pretty and delicious, and suitable for a special occasion.

Angel Food Cake

2 cups egg whites
2 tsp cream of tartar
½ tsp salt
½ tsp almond flavoring
1 tsp vanilla
2 cups sugar
1½ cups cake flour

Put egg whites, cream of tartar, almond and vanilla, and salt in large bowl, and beat until foamy. Add 1 cup sugar gradually. After last of sugar is in, beat until stiff. Sift together remaining sugar, flour (and cocoa for chocolate angel food). Fold into stiff egg whites. Put into tube pan. Bake at 350° for 60 minutes. Invert on a bottle to cool.
❖ To remove cake from pan, pull the top edges gently away from the pan sides with your fingertips. Then turn the pan upside down and tap it firmly against the countertop. Your cake will fall out onto your plate with nice smooth sides, and no knife marks.

To basic recipe, add the following for these variations:

Cherry Nut Angel Food Cake

½ cup chopped maraschino cherries
½ cup finely chopped pecans

Chocolate Angel Food Cake

3 Tbsp cocoa Leave out almond flavoring

Peppermint Angel Food Cake

2 to 4 drops of peppermint oil and fold in ½ - ¾ cup crushed peppermint candy. Leave out almond and vanilla flavoring

We always have time for the things we put first.

About Cake Flour

Cake flour is made from soft winter wheat, and is lower in protein and higher in starch than all-purpose flour. It helps give delicate cakes like angel food and sponge cakes, a fine texture and higher volume. All purpose flour works well for most cakes, especially sturdy or dense cakes such as applesauce, pound cake, chocolate, banana, carrot, red velvet, etc.

If you don't have cake flour replace 2 Tbsp cornstarch for 2 Tbsp flour in every cup of all purpose flour. To substitute cake flour for all purpose flour, use 1 cup plus 2 Tbsp cake flour for every cup of all purpose flour.

Blue Ribbon Banana Cake

¾ cup shortening
1½ cups sugar
2 eggs
1 cup mashed banana
2 cups flour
½ tsp salt
1 tsp soda
1 tsp baking powder
½ cup buttermilk
1 tsp vanilla

Cream shortening and sugar; add eggs and beat 2 minutes. Add banana. Add dry ingredients alternately with buttermilk and vanilla. Beat 2 more minutes and pour into greased, floured 9x13 pan. Bake at 375° for 25-30 minutes. This is a good way to use up ripe bananas. Icing suggestions are: Creamy Pecan Icing, Cream Cheese Icing, or Peanut Butter Frosting.

– *Ava (Eberly) Heatwole*

A dash of love, A pinch of cheer,
Adds spice to every day all year.

What's the Difference Between Baking Powder and Baking Soda?

Both create gas bubbles that make baked goods rise. Double-acting baking powder has two leavening agents. One is triggered by moisture, the other by heat. Baking powder loses potency with age, so if you're wondering whether yours is still active, place ½ tsp in ¼ cup hot water. If it fizzes nicely, it's fine.

Baking soda, on the other hand, produces gas when combined with an acid such as buttermilk, molasses, or yogurt. It starts to work as soon as it gets wet, so it should be mixed with the dry ingredients first for a dough or batter. Once the wet ingredients are added, the mixture should be baked immediately.

BAKING POWDER SUBSTITUTE

Combine 2 Tbsp cream of tartar, 1 Tbsp soda, 1 Tbsp cornstarch

BLUEBERRY COFFEE CAKE

¾ cup sugar
½ cup soft butter
1 egg
½ cup milk
2 cups flour
2 tsp baking powder
½ tsp salt
2 cups blueberries

Mix sugar, butter and egg. Stir in milk and dry ingredients. Last fold in blueberries. Pour into greased and floured 9x13 pan.

Topping

⅔ cup sugar
2 tsp cinnamon
⅔ cup flour
½ cup soft butter

Combine and sprinkle over batter. Bake at 350° for 45-50 minutes.

Fresh Apple Cake

¾ cup butter or oil
1 cup sugar
3 eggs
2 tsp vanilla
2 cups flour
2 tsp cinnamon
1 tsp soda
1 tsp salt
4 cups apples, peeled and diced
1 cup chopped nuts

Cream shortening and sugar. Add eggs and vanilla. Beat well. Add dry ingredients and mix well. Stir in apples and nuts. Bake in a greased and floured 9x13 or a jelly roll pan at 350°. Top with Caramel Icing.

– Linda (Wenger) Shank

Fresh Coconut Cake

Bake any yellow or white cake you like. Split the cooled layers and fill with cool whip, whipped cream or your favorite fluffy white icing. Cover layers, sides, and top of cake with a generous layer of fresh grated or frozen coconut. Store in fridge.

About Vanilla

Pure vanilla is made from the seed pod of an orchid. The pod, called a vanilla bean, is dried and cured, then finely chopped. Alcohol is circulated through the chopped bean to extract the flavor. Pure vanilla is my choice for baking. I use about half the amount requested in most recipes, for it is very flavorful and won't bake out like imitation vanilla.

*It takes very little effort to be nice to people
and kindness is usually returned tenfold.*

– Jeanne Shaheen

ORANGE SLICE CAKE

1 cup margarine
2 cups sugar
4 eggs
1 tsp soda
dash of salt
½ cup buttermilk
3½ cups flour
1 lb orange slices candy (cut into small pieces)
2 cups chopped nuts
1 cup chopped dates
1 cup flaked coconut

Cream margarine and sugar. Add eggs one at a time. Dissolve soda and salt in buttermilk; add alternately with 3 cups flour to creamed mixture. Dredge candy, nuts, and dates in ½ cup flour and add to mixture along with coconut. Bake in a greased and floured tube pan at 275° for about 1½ - 2 hours.

Topping
Mix 1 cup fresh orange juice and 2 cups powdered sugar thoroughly. Pour over cake as soon as it comes from oven. Let set in pan overnight. Remove and wrap in foil to mellow. Can be frozen.

– *Esther Rohrer*

UNBAKED FRUITCAKE

1 box (1 lb.) graham crackers
½ lb margarine
2 10 oz. bags marshmallows
2 16 oz. jars maraschino cherries
1 lb chopped dates
2 cups chopped nuts
2 cups golden or dark raisins

Crush or grind graham crackers. Drain cherries. Melt margarine and marshmallows over medium heat while stirring. Mix all ingredients and press into greased loaf pans. Store in refrigerator. Cut into thin slices to serve.

– *Esther Rohrer*

Sorrow looks back, worry looks around, faith looks up.

White Fruit Cake

1 lb candied pineapple
1 lb golden raisins
1¾ cups pineapple juice
1 lb soft butter
2 cups sugar
8 eggs
2 Tbsp lemon extract
4 cups flour
¾ tsp salt
2 tsp baking powder
1½ lbs candied cherries (red or green)
1 lb pecan pieces
½ lb English walnut pieces

Soak raisins in pineapple juice several hours or overnight. Cream together butter and sugar; gradually beat in eggs and lemon extract. Stir in raisins and pineapple. Add flour, salt, and baking powder. Stir in cherries and nuts. Pour into greased and floured loaf pans. Bake at 250°-275° until done. Don't overbake. Wrap in plastic wrap while still warm. Freezes well. Tastes better after a week or two.

Granny's Applesauce Cake

No eggs

2 cups sugar
1 cup butter
3 cups applesauce
2 cups raisins, plumped
½ cup nuts
4 cups flour
2 tsp soda
1 Tbsp cinnamon
1 tsp allspice
½ tsp nutmeg or cloves

Cream sugar and butter. Add rest of ingredients. Bake in greased and floured bundt or loaf pans at 275°-300° for 2 hours or until done. Test for doneness with a toothpick. This cake is delicious, and it makes a good fruitcake too. Just pack it with nuts and fruits.

– *Grandma Marie Rohrer*

Vanilla Butternut Pound Cake

3 cups sugar
½ tsp salt
1¼ cups butter
8 oz. cream cheese
2 tsp vanilla butternut flavoring
6 eggs separated*
3 cups flour

Cream sugar, salt, butter, and cream cheese until light and fluffy. Add flavoring. Beat in egg yolks, one at a time. Add flour and blend well. Last fold in stiffly beaten egg whites. Bake in a 10" tube or bundt pan at 300° for 1¾ hours or until done. May also be baked in layers or loaf pans. (*You may add ¼ tsp baking powder, and beat in the <u>whole eggs</u> if you prefer. The end result is about the same).

Fresh Coconut Pound Cake

Substitute coconut flavoring in Vanilla Butternut Pound Cake recipe, and fold in 2 cups fresh grated coconut.

My Aunt Frances' recipe calls for 1 cup milk instead of 8 oz cream cheese. Either way, it's a very special cake!

Carrot Cake

1 cup oil
2 cups sugar
4 eggs
3 cups grated carrots
2 cups flour
2 tsp baking powder
1 tsp salt
1 tsp each, cinnamon and cloves
½ tsp each, nutmeg, ginger, allspice
1 cup chopped nuts

Combine oil, sugar, and eggs. Beat well. Stir in carrots. Add rest of ingredients and beat thoroughly. Bake in layers or sheet pan at 350° until done. Frost with Cream Cheese Icing, and garnish with nuts.

EXCELLENT POUND CAKE

1 cup butter or margarine
2 cups sugar
6 eggs
1 cup sour cream
1 Tbsp vanilla
1½ Tbsp lemon or butter flavor
2½ cups flour
¼ tsp soda
¾ tsp salt

Cream butter and sugar well. Add eggs, flavoring, and sour cream. Add dry ingredients and beat well. Pour into greased tube pan or loaf pans. Bake at 300° until cake tester comes out clean. Don't overbake. Let set 10 minutes. Remove from pan. Cover when barely cool.
This is a versatile recipe and can be flavored any way you like. Jam or pureed fruit can be swirled into the batter after you pour it into the cake pan. Cinnamon-sugar and nuts can be layered into the batter. Use your imagination to make it special.

LEMON CAKE PUDDING

1 cup sugar
¼ cup flour
⅛ tsp salt
2 Tbsp melted butter
⅓ cup lemon juice
Grated rind of 1 lemon
3 eggs, separated
1½ cups milk

Combine first six ingredients. Beat egg yolks, add milk slowly, while stirring. Mix thoroughly into first mixture. Fold in stiffly beaten egg whites. Pour into greased 2 qt. casserole or bake dish. Set in a pan with an inch of hot water. Bake at 325° for 45 – 60 minutes until cake tests done.
It will have custard on the bottom and sponge cake on top.

Peanut Butter Fudge Cake

2 cups flour
2 cups sugar
1 tsp soda
1 cup butter
¼ cup cocoa
1 cup water
½ cup buttermilk
2 large eggs lightly beaten
1 tsp vanilla
1½ cups creamy peanut butter, reserved

Combine flour, sugar, soda. Set aside. Melt butter in heavy pan. Stir in cocoa, add water, buttermilk and eggs. Cook over medium heat stirring constantly until mixture boils. Add to flour mixture. Mix until smooth. Stir in vanilla. Bake in greased 9x13 or 10 x 15 pan at 350° for 20-25 minutes. Cool cake. Spread peanut butter over cake. Top with chocolate frosting for a decadent dessert.

Chocolate Frosting

¼ cup cocoa
½ cup margarine
⅓ cup buttermilk
1 lb sifted powdered sugar
1 tsp vanilla

Boil margarine, buttermilk, and cocoa, stirring constantly. Pour cocoa mixture over sugar. Mix until smooth. Add vanilla.

Chocolate Marshmallow Frosting

½ cup evaporated milk (or cream)
1 cup sugar
1 Tbsp butter
1 cup chocolate chips
1 cup mini marshmallows
½ cup pecans or walnuts

Bring sugar, butter, and milk to a boil. Cook 2 minutes. Add chocolate chips. Stir until melted. Add nuts and marshmallows. Blend and spread on cake while warm. This icing works best on a sheet cake.

CHOCOLATE LAYER CAKE

2¼ cups all purpose flour
2 cups sugar
1¼ tsp soda
1 tsp salt
½ tsp baking powder
2 eggs
1 tsp vanilla
1 cup water
¾ cup sour cream
¼ cup butter
4 oz bakers chocolate or German chocolate

Melt butter and chocolate together. Combine all dry ingredients in mixing bowl. Make a well in center of bowl. Add rest of ingredients. Stir well. Add chocolate mixture. Beat until light and fluffy. Bake in 2 round layers at 350° for 40-45 minutes.

– Maria (Eberly) Horst

These layers handle nicely and are sturdy enough to split and fill with any kind of filling you like; such as German Chocolate Topping, French Buttercream (see recipes), red raspberries and whipped cream, etc.

FAVORITE CHOCOLATE CAKE

2 cups flour
2 cups sugar
1 tsp salt
1 tsp baking powder
2 tsp soda
½ cup cocoa
1 cup salad oil
1 cup milk
2 eggs
1 cup hot coffee

Mix ingredients in order given, adding coffee last. Batter is thin. Bake at 350° for 40 minutes. Makes a 9x13 or two or three 8" layers. Frost with Chocolate Marshmallow Frosting.

– Neva Horst

Six Layer Toffee Torte

Bake Favorite Chocolate Cake or Chocolate Layer Cake (page 227) and make three 8" layers. When cakes are completely cool, split each layer horizontally in half to make six thin layers.

Filling:
3 cups whipping cream
1¼ cups brown sugar
1½ tsp instant coffee dissolved in a few drops of hot water
8 oz. toffee bits (you will have some left over)

Dissolve coffee in water, add to cream. Add brown sugar and whip cream until soft peaks form. Frost each layer with whipped cream filling and a sprinkle of toffee. Ice sides of cake and refrigerate until ready to serve.

Pumpkin Streusel Cake

3 cups flour
1 Tbsp cinnamon
2 tsp soda
1 tsp salt
1 tsp nutmeg
2 cups sugar
1 cup margarine
4 large eggs
2 cups pumpkin
1 cup sour cream
2 tsp vanilla

Streusel
1 cup brown sugar
4 tsp cinnamon
1 cup chopped pecans
¼ cup butter
Combine to make crumbs

Combine first five ingredients, set aside. Cream sugar and margarine until fluffy, add eggs and beat well. Stir in pumpkin, sour cream and vanilla. Beat well, last add flour mixture and mix well. Pour ⅓ of cake batter into greased and floured bundt pan, top with half of streusel, another ⅓ of batter, rest of streusel, and top with remaining cake batter. Bake at 325° for 1½ hours. Glaze with Caramel Icing if you like.

– *Ethel Shank*

God loves each of us, as if there were only one of us.

Hot Fudge Sundae Cake

1 cup flour
¾ cup sugar
2 Tbsp cocoa
2 tsp baking powder
¼ tsp salt
½ cup milk
2 Tbsp oil
2 tsp vanilla
1 cup brown sugar
¼ cup cocoa
1¾ cups <u>hottest</u> tap water

Mix all but the last 3 ingredients in a 9" square bake dish. Combine brown sugar and cocoa and sprinkle over dough. Pour water over all. Bake at 350° for 40 minutes. Serve warm with ice cream.

– *Annette Wenger*

Chocolate Bavarian Torte

1 Dark Chocolate cake mix or any chocolate cake
8 oz cream cheese
⅔ cup brown sugar
1 tsp vanilla
⅛ tsp salt
4 cups whipped cream (or Cool Whip)
2 Tbsp grated chocolate

Bake cake in round layers. Make filling by beating cream cheese, brown sugar, vanilla and salt until fluffy. Add whipped cream. Split layers and spread each layer with filling. Garnish top of cake with chocolate. Refrigerate or freeze until needed.

– *Esther Burkholder*

God gave us one tongue and two ears.
Perhaps we should listen more and talk less.

Chocolate Mayonnaise Cake

No eggs

1 cup sugar
2 cups flour
¼ cup cocoa
2 tsp soda
½ tsp salt
1 cup mayonnaise
1 cup water
1 tsp vanilla

Mix dry ingredients together in large bowl. Add wet ingredients and beat well. Pour into a greased and floured 9x13 pan. Bake at 350° for 30-35 minutes. Delicious with any fluffy white icing, especially Angel Food Icing. See recipe on pg 246.

– Esther Rohrer

Wacky Cake

No eggs

3 cups flour
2 cups sugar
½ cup cocoa
½ tsp salt
½ tsp baking powder
2 tsp baking soda
⅔ cup oil
2 cups cold water
2 tsp vanilla
2 Tbsp vinegar

Beat all ingredients together in mixing bowl until batter is smooth. Pour into a greased and floured 9 x 13 cake pan. Bake at 350° for about 30 minutes.

This is a good cake for a beginner to make. Quick and easy.

Fluffy Gingerbread with Lemon Sauce

2 cups sifted flour
1½ tsp baking soda
½ tsp salt
2 tsp ginger
1 tsp cinnamon
½ tsp cloves
½ cup butter
½ cup brown sugar
2 eggs, beaten
¾ cup sorghum molasses
1 cup boiling water

Sift dry ingredients together. Cream sugar and butter. Add eggs and ¼ flour mixture, then molasses. Add remaining flour. Beat well, and stir in boiling water until blended. Pour into greased 9" x 13" pan. Bake at 350° for 45 minutes. Serve warm cake with Lemon Sauce or whipped cream.

Lemon Sauce

2 Tbsp cornstarch
1¼ cups sugar
¼ cup lemon juice
1 Tbsp grated lemon rind
2 egg yolks
pinch salt
1½ cups boiling water
1 Tbsp butter (optional)

Combine starch, sugar, lemon juice and rind. Beat yolks and add to mixture. Gradually add boiling water, heat to boiling, and boil gently 2 minutes. Add butter. Serve warm over gingerbread.

Keep your words soft and sweet.
You never know when you'll have to eat them.

DELICATE WHITE CAKE

⅔ cup Crisco shortening
2 cups sugar
1 tsp vanilla
3 cups cake flour
¼ tsp salt
2 tsp baking powder
1 cup milk
4 egg whites
1 tsp baking powder

Cream Crisco shortening and sugar. Add vanilla. Combine dry ingredients and add alternately with milk. Beat egg whites until stiff. Stir in remaining teaspoon of baking powder. Fold into cake batter and blend well. Bake in two 9-inch or three 8-inch pans at 350° for about 30-40 minutes.

From the recipes of Grandmother Nettie Rhodes Wenger

HOT MILK CAKE

3 large eggs
2 cups sugar
2½ cups cake flour
1 cup milk
3 Tbsp butter
½ tsp salt
1 tsp vanilla
1 Tbsp baking powder
Beat eggs until light and foamy. Add sugar and flour, beating well to combine. Heat milk and butter to almost boiling. Pour gradually into egg mixture while stirring. Add salt and vanilla, then baking powder. Bake immediately at 350° in two 9-inch or three 8-inch pans or a 9x13. Bakes in 25-35 minutes, depending on pans. This cake is good with Caramel Icing or Broiled Topping, or with fresh strawberries and whipped cream.

People don't care how much you know,
until they know how much you care.

EASY STRAWBERRY SHORTCAKE

2 cups flour
½ cup sugar
1 Tbsp baking powder
pinch of salt
6 Tbsp cold butter
1 egg beaten
1 cup milk

Mix first 5 ingredients in bowl until crumbly. Add egg and milk. Stir just enough to moisten crumb mixture. Spread in a buttered 9" pie or cake pan. Bake at 350° for 18-20 minutes. Serve with crushed strawberries and milk or whipped cream.

YELLOW BUTTER CAKE

⅔ cup butter
2 cups sugar
4 eggs
3 cups flour
1 Tbsp baking powder
½ tsp salt
1 Tbsp vanilla
1 cup milk

Cream butter and sugar. Add eggs. Beat well. Add dry ingredients alternately with milk and vanilla. Makes a 9"x13" or two 8" layers. Bake at 350° for 30-40 minutes.

Giving is the secret of a healthy life....
not necessarily money,
but whatever a man has of encouragement
and sympathy and understanding.

– John D. Rockefeller, Jr.

LOVELIGHT CHIFFON CAKE

4 egg whites
½ cup sugar
2¾ cups cake flour
1½ cups sugar
4 tsp baking powder
1 tsp salt
½ cup oil
1⅓ cups milk
4 egg yolks, well beaten
2 tsp flavoring (vanilla, butter, coconut, or almond)

Beat egg whites until stiff and add ½ cup sugar gradually. Set aside. Sift dry ingredients into mixing bowl. Add oil and half of milk, beat 1 minute. Add remaining milk, beaten egg yolks, and flavoring. Beat 1 minute more. Fold in meringue. Bake in 2 greased, floured round layer pans or a 9x13 at 350° for 30-45 minutes. Makes three 8" layers or two 9" layers.

This cake is my choice for a fresh coconut cake. – Ethel Shank

ITALIAN CREAM CAKE

1 cup butter
2 cups sugar
5 eggs, separated
2 tsp vanilla
1 cup buttermilk
2 cups flour
1 tsp soda
½ tsp salt
1½ cups flaked coconut
1 cup chopped pecans

Cream butter and sugar. Beat in egg yolks. Stir in vanilla and buttermilk. Add flour, soda and salt. Fold in stiffly beaten egg whites, coconut, and pecans. Bake in 3 layers at 350° for 25-30 minutes. Frost with Cream Cheese Icing. Garnish with coconut and pecans on top of each layer.

Luscious Walnut Cake

1 cup butter
1 cup white sugar
1 cup brown sugar
1 tsp maple flavoring
1 tsp vanilla
5 egg yolks
2¼ cups cake flour
1½ tsp soda
½ tsp salt
1 cup buttermilk
1 cup crushed black walnuts
5 egg whites, stiffly beaten

Cream butter and sugars. Add egg yolks and flavorings. Beat well.
Add flour, soda, and salt alternately with buttermilk. Stir in walnuts.
Fold in egg whites. Pour into 3 greased and floured 9" cake pans.
Bake at 350° for 20-25 minutes. When cool, frost with Fluffy Maple
Frosting.

Oatmeal Cake

1½ cups boiling water
1 cup quick oats
½ cup brown sugar
1 cup sugar
½ cup butter
2 eggs
1½ cups flour
2 tsp cinnamon
1 tsp soda
½ tsp salt
1 tsp vanilla

Combine water and oats. Let set 20 minutes. Cream butter and
sugars. Add eggs. Stir in oatmeal mixture. Add vanilla and dry
ingredients. Bake in a greased and floured 9x13 pan at 350° for
30-35 minutes. Good with Broiled Topping.

This is my favorite cake; the good old-time recipes are still the best!

SHOO FLY CAKE

No eggs

4 cups flour
¾ cup butter
2 cups brown sugar
½ tsp salt
2 cups boiling water
½ cup sorghum molasses
½ cup dark corn syrup
1 Tbsp soda

Combine first 4 ingredients to form crumbs. Reserve 1 cup of them. To rest of crumbs in bowl add remaining ingredients. Mix well. Pour into greased and floured 9"x13" pan. Sprinkle crumbs on top. Bake at 350° about 40 minutes. May bake in 10"x15" pan for a coffee cake or make into cupcakes.

RED VELVET CAKE

½ cup shortening
1½ cups sugar
2 eggs
2¼ cups flour
1 scant tsp salt
¼ cup cocoa
2 tsp vanilla
1 cup buttermilk
2 Tbsp red food coloring
1 Tbsp vinegar
1 tsp soda

Cream shortening, sugar, and eggs. Combine flour, salt, and cocoa. Add alternately with buttermilk, vanilla, and red color. Last add soda and vinegar. Blend into batter. Bake in two 8-inch pans. Bake at 350° for 30-40 minutes. Frost with French Buttercream Icing.

The way out of trouble is never as easy as the way in.

SPONGE CAKE

5 eggs, separated
1 tsp cream of tartar
½ cup cold water
1½ cups sugar, divided
1½ cups cake flour
½ tsp baking powder
½ tsp salt
1 tsp lemon extract

Beat egg whites and cream of tartar until semi-stiff. Beat in ½ cup sugar. Set aside. Add water to egg yolks and beat well. Add 1 cup sugar and beat several minutes. Add flour, baking powder, salt, and lemon extract. Fold into egg whites and bake in a tube pan at 325° for an hour. This also works well for a jelly roll (line 10x15 pan with waxed paper), or it can be used for layer cakes or a 9x13. Make cupcakes if you have extra batter.

Cake Roll Suggestions
❖ Fill with lemon or pineapple filling (see recipes)
❖ Fill with cream filling and strawberries, etc.
Roll up and dust with powdered sugar before serving.

TURTLE CAKE

1 German Chocolate Cake mix
½ cup evaporated milk
14 oz bag of caramels
1 cup chopped pecans
1 cup chocolate chips (optional)

Melt caramels with milk in a double boiler. Prepare cake by directions on box; spread ½ of batter in a greased 9x13 pan, and bake at 350° for 15 minutes. Spread caramels, nuts, and chips on cake. Add the other ½ of batter and bake 30 minutes longer.

– Miriam (Rohrer) Martin

A temper is a valuable possession, don't lose it.

Pumpkin Roll Cake

¾ cup flour
1 tsp baking powder
½ tsp soda
2 tsp cinnamon
1 tsp ginger
½ tsp salt
3 large eggs
1 cup sugar
1 cup cooked pumpkin
1 cup chopped pecans (optional)

Line a greased 10"x15" jelly roll pan with waxed paper. Grease and flour paper. Turn oven to 375°.

Combine first 6 ingredients. Beat eggs and sugar in a large mixing bowl until thick. Beat in pumpkin. Stir in flour mixture and spread evenly in pan. Sprinkle with nuts. Bake 13-15 minutes until cake tests done. Invert cake onto a cloth or paper towels (dusted with powdered sugar) and peel off waxed paper. Roll up cake in towel, starting at narrow end. Cool completely.

Filling:
Drain one 20 oz can of crushed pineapple and squeeze out all the juice you can. Combine 2-3 cups cool whip and 8 oz soft cream cheese*. Stir in pineapple. Unroll cake and spread filling over all. Roll up and chill until served. Will keep several days in fridge. Dust with powdered sugar before serving. Serves 10-12.

*I use fat free cream cheese and you can not taste the difference. This makes a low fat, tasty dessert. (see picture on back cover)

*Put good food in your body
and good thoughts in your head.*

CHOCOLATE ROLL CAKE

¼ cup butter
1 cup chopped pecans
1⅓ cups coconut
1 can sweetened condensed milk
3 eggs
1 cup sugar
1 tsp vanilla
⅓ cup water
⅓ cup cocoa
⅔ cup flour
¼ tsp salt
¼ tsp soda
½ tsp baking powder

Line a 10 x 15 jelly roll pan with foil. Melt butter in pan. Sprinkle pecans and coconut over all, drizzle with condensed milk. In bowl, beat eggs until light and foamy. Gradually add sugar and beat well. Stir in water and vanilla. Combine dry ingredients and add. Beat well. Pour evenly into pan. Bake at 350° for 25 – 30 minutes or until it tests done. Sprinkle with powdered sugar and cover with a paper towel. Invert onto a cookie sheet, remove pan and foil. Starting on 10 inch side, roll up. When cool, slice and serve.

Patterns

It takes a blueprint to build a house
A pattern to sew a dress;
A recipe when you bake a cake,
If you would have success.
And those who build for eternity
Must follow a pattern too;
The blueprint's found in the Word of God,
It's tested and tried and true.

Pineapple Upside-Down Cake

2 Tbsp butter
½ cup brown sugar
5-8 slices pineapple
Maraschino cherries

Melt butter in a 9" or 10", round skillet or bake dish and add brown sugar. Place pineapple rings on brown sugar and a cherry in each. Pour cake batter on top and bake at 350° until cake tests done with a toothpick. Invert on a large plate. Serves 8.

Cake batter:
3 eggs, beaten
1 cup sugar
¼ cup milk
1 cup flour
1 tsp baking powder
½ tsp salt
1 tsp lemon or vanilla flavor
Combine all ingredients and pour over pineapple rings.

Pineapple Filling

½ cup sugar
½ tsp salt
3 Tbsp cornstarch
¾ cup pineapple juice
1 can (1 lb 4 oz) crushed pineapple
1 Tbsp butter
1 tsp lemon juice

Drain pineapple. Mix sugar, salt, and cornstarch in a saucepan. Slowly add juice, then crushed pineapple. Cook over low heat while stirring. Boil 1 minute. Add butter and lemon juice. Chill before filling cake.

Giving does not drain our resources,
but provides a space for us to refill.

LEMON FILLING

¾ cup sugar
3 Tbsp cornstarch
¼ tsp salt
¾ cup water
1 egg, slightly beaten
1 Tbsp butter
1-2 Tbsp grated lemon peel
⅓ cup lemon juice

Mix sugar, cornstarch and salt in a saucepan. Stir in water, bring to a boil while stirring. Boil one minute. Stir some of hot mixture into egg, then add egg to saucepan. Boil one minute while stirring. Remove from heat, add butter, lemon peel and juice. Chill, then fill cake.

CREAM FILLING FOR CAKE OR CREAM PUFFS

⅓ cup sugar
2 Tbsp flour
1 Tbsp cornstarch
½ tsp salt
1½ cups rich milk
1 egg, slightly beaten
½ tsp vanilla

Combine sugar, flour, cornstarch and salt. Gradually stir in milk. Cook ½ minute over medium heat, stirring constantly. Stir a bit of hot mixture into egg, then add egg to saucepan and stir while cooking, two minutes. Stir in vanilla or desired flavoring, and cool filling.

*The things we sweep under the rug
have a tendency of creeping out on the other side.*

CREAMY PECAN ICING AND FILLING

½ cup sugar
2 Tbsp flour
½ cup cream
2 Tbsp butter
½ cup chopped pecans
¼ tsp salt
1 tsp vanilla

Cook first four ingredients until thick. Add remaining ingredients.
Double the recipe for icing a layer cake.

GERMAN CHOCOLATE CAKE TOPPING

3 egg yolks, beaten
⅔ cup evaporated milk
½ cup butter
1 cup sugar
pinch of salt
1 tsp vanilla
1 cup chopped pecans
2 cups (or more) coconut

Cook milk, yolks, and butter in double boiler until thick. Add rest of
ingredients. Cool and spread on cake.

CHERRY BUTTER ICING

3 cups powdered sugar
¾ stick of butter
pinch of salt
1½ tsp almond or vanilla flavoring
3 ¾ Tbsp maraschino cherry juice

Combine all ingredients and beat until creamy.

There is no tranquilizer in the world that is more effective
than a few kind words.

Chocolate Glaze

¼ cup butter
¼ cup cocoa
3 Tbsp water
1 tsp vanilla
¼ tsp salt
2 cups powdered sugar

Melt butter, stir in cocoa and water. When it begins to thicken, remove from heat. Add vanilla, salt and sugar. Pour over cake while glaze is warm.

Chocolate Silk Frosting

3 cups powdered sugar
⅓ cup soft butter
¼ tsp salt
1 tsp vanilla
3 oz. unsweetened chocolate, melted
2-3 Tbsp milk

Blend sugar, butter, and salt. Add, vanilla, and melted chocolate. Add enough milk to make it spreadable, and beat until fluffy.

Chocolate Buttercream Frosting

6 Tbsp butter, softened
½ cup cocoa
⅛ tsp salt
2 ⅔ cups powdered sugar
⅓ cup milk
1 tsp vanilla

Cream butter, add cocoa, salt, and powdered sugar, alternating with milk and vanilla. Beat until good spreading consistency. Makes 2 cups.

Be kind; everyone you meet is fighting a hard battle.

LEMON ORANGE ICING

½ cup butter
3 Tbsp lemon juice
3 Tbsp orange juice
1-2 Tbsp grated lemon rind
1-2 Tbsp grated orange rind
¼ tsp salt
5½-6 cups powdered sugar

Combine and beat until creamy. Will frost a 2 or 3 layer cake. Use half recipe for sheet cake or bundt cake.

CREAMY WHITE ICING

2-4 Tbsp milk
1 cup Crisco shortening
1 tsp flavoring, your choice
½ tsp salt
1 lb (about 4 cups) powdered sugar

Combine and beat until creamy. Add more milk if needed.
Note: If using for decorating, sift sugar.

CREAM CHEESE ICING

8 oz cream cheese
¼ cup butter
3½ cups powdered sugar
1 Tbsp vanilla
½ tsp salt

Beat all together until light and creamy. May garnish with pecans. Variation: Substitute orange juice and grated orange rind for flavoring.

The smallest good deed is better than the grandest intention.

Fluffy Maple Frosting

1½ cups brown sugar
¼ tsp cream of tartar
¼ cup water
2 egg whites, unbeaten
½ tsp maple flavoring
⅛ tsp salt

Combine all ingredients in top of double boiler over boiling water. Beat while cooking until icing forms almost stiff peaks. Remove from heat. Beat until stiff.

Broiled Topping

1 cup brown sugar
½ cup melted butter
¼ cup cream
pinch of salt
1 tsp vanilla
1 cup nuts
1 cup coconut

Mix well. Spread on hot sheet cake and broil 2-4 minutes until golden brown. (Watch carefully at the last, it burns easily) Tastes wonderful on oatmeal or hot milk cake.

Caramel Icing

½ cup butter
1 cup brown sugar
pinch of salt
¼ cup milk
1¾ -2 cups powdered sugar

Melt butter. Add brown sugar and salt. Stir over low heat for 2 minutes. Add milk. Bring to a boil. Cool to lukewarm and add powdered sugar. Good on sheet cakes or cinnamon buns.

FRENCH BUTTERCREAM ICING

2 cups sugar
½ cup flour
½ tsp salt
1 cup milk
1 cup cold butter
1 cup Crisco shortening
2 tsp vanilla

Put sugar, flour, and salt in pan. Mix well. Slowly stir in milk. Cook over medium heat, stirring until thickened. Cool. Add ½ cup shortening at a time and beat until creamy. Add vanilla. Beat until fluffy like whipped cream. Chill a few minutes until ready to use. This icing is creamy and not too sweet. Perfect for Red Velvet cake.

PEANUT BUTTER FROSTING

½ cup butter, softened
1 cup creamy peanut butter
2 cups powdered sugar
¼ cup milk

Beat butter and peanut better together. Add sugar and beat until blended. Add milk and beat until frosting is fluffy and smooth. This will taste good on a banana or chocolate cake, or cupcakes.

ANGEL FOOD FROSTING

1 cup sugar
¼ tsp cream of tartar
1 Tbsp corn syrup
⅓ cup boiling water
½ tsp salt
1 tsp vanilla
2 egg whites

Stir together first six ingredients over simmering water in double boiler. Leave until clear. Remove from heat. Add egg whites and beat awhile. Put back over the water and beat 3 minutes longer, or until you have semi-stiff peaks. Can be put on cake while frosting is still warm.

– Marilyn Eberly

Cookies
and
Bars

Cookies

Eight Ways to Success and Mental Ease

Deal justly with your fellow man.
Work hard at making a happy home life.
Never get far from nature.
Keep busy.
Talk out your problems.
Do selfless deeds.
Pray for strength and guidance.
Believe in the future.

– James Bender

This Year

Mend a quarrel.
Seek out a forgotten friend.
Write a letter.
Share some treasure. Give a soft answer.
Encourage youth. Keep a promise.
Find the time. Forgive an enemy.
Listen. Apologize if you were wrong.
Think first of someone else.
Be kind and gentle.
Laugh a little. Laugh a little more.
Express your gratitude.
Gladden the heart of a child.
Take pleasure in the beauty and wonder of the earth.
Speak your love. Speak it again.
Speak it still once again.

– Anonymous

Cookies and Bars

Big Batch Cookies

2 cups oil
4 eggs
2 tsp vanilla
2 cups brown sugar
2 cups white sugar
4 cups flour
1 tsp salt
2 tsp soda
4 cups corn flakes
1½ cups oatmeal
1 cup pecans
2 cups (12 oz) chocolate chips

Slightly crush corn flakes. Blend oil, eggs, and vanilla. Add sugars. Beat well. Combine and add dry ingredients. Stir in the goodies. Drop onto greased cookie sheets and bake at 350°.

– *Karen (Rohrer) Rohrer*

Friends are the chocolate chips in the cookie of life.

Coconut Macaroons

2 egg whites
2 Tbsp cake flour
½ cup sugar
¼ tsp salt
½ tsp vanilla
2 cups coconut

Beat egg whites until stiff. Fold in flour, sugar, and salt. Add vanilla and coconut. Drop by teaspoons onto lightly greased parchment paper. Bake at 350° about 15 – 20 minutes. Makes 20.

Coconut Slabs

1 cup butter
4 cups sugar
1 pt dark corn syrup
1 tsp vanilla
12 oz fresh or frozen coconut
1½ tsp soda
½ tsp salt
6 cups (or more) flour

Mix and drop by spoonsful onto cookie sheet. Bake at 375° for 10-12 minutes, until just done. Cool and remove from tray. Store between layers of waxed paper.

Peanut Butter Cookies

1½ cups butter
3 cups brown sugar
3 eggs
1½ cups crunchy peanut butter
½ cup light corn syrup
1½ tsp vanilla
¾ tsp salt
1½ tsp baking powder
1 Tbsp soda
5½-6 cups flour; use ½ cake flour

Cream butter and sugar. Add eggs and beat well. Stir in peanut butter, syrup, and vanilla. Last add dry ingredients and mix well. Shape into 1" balls and flatten with a fork or potato masher. Bake at 350° until done. Makes 8 dozen.

LEMON CRACKERS

2½ cups sugar
1 cup butter
3 eggs
1 cup milk
1½ tsp baking ammonia
½ tsp salt
2 tsp lemon oil
8 cups all purpose flour

Cream together sugar and butter, add eggs, beat well. Heat milk to lukewarm, dissolve ammonia in it. Add lemon oil and salt. Combine all ingredients and stir in enough flour to make dough you can roll out ⅛-¼" thick. Cut into desired shapes.
Prick crackers with a fork and sprinkle with coarse sugar. Bake at 350° until done. I usually make a thicker cookie and brush it with a beaten egg white, then sprinkle with sugar. Colored sugar is nice for special occasions.

– Esther Rohrer

Note: Lemon oil comes in 1 dram bottles. You'll need two bottles. Bakers ammonia is a powder and can be bought at the pharmacy or bulk food store. This cookie was made in the early 1800's before there was baking powder.

FORGOTTEN PEPPERMINT COOKIES

2 egg whites
⅔ cup sugar
pinch of salt
1 tsp peppermint extract <u>or</u>
2 Tbsp crushed peppermint candy

Preheat oven to 350°. Beat egg whites until foamy. Gradually add sugar, beating until stiff. Add salt and peppermint. (Half cup chopped nuts and chocolate chips may be folded in if you want.) Drop cookies onto foil-lined cookie sheet. Put in oven and turn heat off right away. Leave overnight or until oven is cool.

– Zelda Rohrer

GRAHAM CRACKERS

Sylvester Graham, the man who promoted the use of graham flour, was a minister who lived in the early 1800's. He believed that to separate the bran from the rest of the wheat berry was wrong. Graham flour is whole-wheat flour milled with the coarse bran particles left in the flour.

1 cup butter
2 cups brown sugar
2 eggs
½ cup milk
1 tsp vanilla
1 tsp salt
1 tsp cinnamon
2⅓ cups white flour
4 cups coarse whole-wheat or graham flour
2 tsp soda
1 tsp baking powder

Cream sugar and butter. Add eggs, and beat well. Add milk and vanilla alternately with dry ingredients. Chill dough. Roll out ⅛ inch thick on a lightly floured surface. Cut in squares with pastry wheel or use cookie cutter. Brush with milk and sprinkle with cinnamon sugar before baking. Prick with a fork. Bake on a lightly greased sheet at 350° for (15-18 minutes). These are fiber-filled and very tasty. Try them for a healthy snack.

CHOCOLATE CHIP PIXIES

1 cup margarine
1½ cups brown sugar
2 eggs
1 tsp vanilla
2 tsp soda
3 cups flour
1½ cups chocolate chips

Cream margarine and sugar, add eggs and vanilla. Stir in dry ingredients, last add chips. Drop onto trays. Bake at 350° until done.

– Audrey and Amanda Wenger

Soft Chocolate Chip Cookies

1½ cups butter
¾ cup white sugar
1½ cups brown sugar
3 eggs
¼ cup light corn syrup
2 tsp vanilla
1½ tsp soda
1 tsp salt
4½-5 cups flour (use half cake flour)
1 lb chocolate chips

Cream shortening and sugars. Add eggs and beat well. Stir in syrup and vanilla. Add dry ingredients and mix well. Stir in chocolate chips. Drop onto cookie sheets. Bake at 350° for 8-10 minutes or until done. Don't overbake.

The secret to these cookies is in the corn syrup and cake flour.

Cowboy Cookies

2 cups sugar
2 cups brown sugar
2 cups butter
4 large eggs
2 tsp vanilla
2 cups all purpose flour
2⅓ cups cake flour
1 tsp salt
1 tsp baking powder
2 tsp soda
2 tsp cinnamon
4½ cups quick oatmeal
1 cup chopped pecans or walnuts
4 cups (1½ lbs) semisweet chocolate chips
2 cups raisins (soak in 2 cups of water and drain)

Cream together sugars and butter. Add eggs and vanilla and beat until fluffy. Stir in flours and next four ingredients. Last add oatmeal and the goodies. Drop onto greased cookie sheets. Bake at 350° for 10-13 minutes.

GRANDMA'S "MIKE-LIZZIE" BARS

2 lbs raisins
1 lb margarine
2 cups white sugar
2 cups brown sugar
6 eggs
2 cups sorghum molasses
2 tsp salt
1 Tbsp vanilla
3 Tbsp soda
½ cup boiling water
4½ lbs flour

Cook raisins in a small amount of water. Let set to cool. Drain.

Cream sugars and margarine. Add 5 of the eggs. Beat well. Stir in molasses, salt, and vanilla. Dissolve soda in boiling water. Mix into dough. Stir in flour to make a soft dough. Chill overnight.

Shape dough into rolls 1½" wide and ½" thick on greased baking sheets. Brush with a beaten egg before baking at 350° for 8-12 minutes. Bake until barely done. Let set on trays to cool. Cut into cookie sized pieces. Store in fridge with waxed paper between layers.

– Grandma Marie Rohrer

Grandma often had a plate of these waiting with a cup of coffee when we arrived to spend the day. This is a large recipe. You may want to make only half the first time. The second time you'll want to make a full recipe. ☺

*Keeping up with the Joneses isn't nearly as dangerous
as trying to pass them on a hill.*

Great Grandma Knicely's Soft Sugar Cookies

2 cups sugar
1 cup butter
2 eggs
1 cup sour cream
1 tsp vanilla
½ tsp salt
1 tsp cream of tartar
1 tsp nutmeg
2 tsp soda
7½ cups flour (use part cake flour)

Cream sugar and butter. Add eggs. Beat well. Stir in sour cream and vanilla. Add dry ingredients, saving out a little flour to use only if needed. Chill dough. Roll out, cut, and bake at 350° for 10-13 minutes. May be sprinkled with colored sugar before baking, or iced after baking. Use creamy bun icing on page 12.

Grandma made them thick and called them "sugar cakes."

Cherry Winks

5 cups cornflakes
1 cup sugar
¾ cup butter
2 eggs
1 tsp almond flavoring
2 Tbsp cream
2½ cups flour
1 tsp baking powder
½ tsp soda
½ tsp salt
1 cup chopped pecans
½ cup chopped maraschino cherries
15 cherries cut in quarters, reserved

Crush cornflakes into coarse crumbs, and set aside. Cream butter and sugar. Add eggs, cream and almond flavoring. Stir in dry ingredients. Add nuts and cherries last. Shape into balls. Roll in cornflake crumbs and top each cookie with ¼ cherry. Bake at 350° for 10-12 minutes. Makes 5 dozen.

DISHPAN COOKIES

2½ cups sugar
2 cups melted margarine
2 cups sorghum molasses
4 beaten eggs
¼ cup hot water
7½ - 8 cups flour
1 Tbsp salt
1 Tbsp ginger
2 Tbsp soda
8 cups oatmeal
3 cups raisins
2 cups chopped black walnuts or pecans

Soak raisins in water to plump. Then drain well.

Mix eggs, margarine, sugar, and molasses. Add dry ingredients. Last stir in raisins and nuts. Roll ¼" thick and cut with cookie cutter. Brush tops with water and sprinkle with coarse sugar. Bake at 350° for 8-10 minutes or until done.

– Esther Rohrer

This recipe came from a farm magazine many years ago. We cut them out with a wide mouth jar ring for a large, hearty snack. Children will like these with a glass of milk for an after school treat.

ROLLED OATMEAL SUGAR COOKIES

¾ cup butter
¾ cup sugar
1 egg
1 tsp vanilla
2 Tbsp milk
2½ cups flour
½ tsp salt
1 tsp baking powder
1 cup oatmeal

Cream butter and sugar. Add egg. Beat well. Add vanilla and milk. Stir in dry ingredients and oatmeal. Roll out thin and cut with cookie cutter. Sprinkle sugar on top. Bake at 350° until done. Simple and delicious. Good for a tea party.

Yummy Oatmeal Cookies

1 lb butter
2 cups brown sugar
2 cups white sugar
4 eggs
1 Tbsp vanilla
1½ tsp soda
1 tsp salt
4½ cups flour
4½ cups quick oats
1 cup chopped pecans

¾ cup sugar
3 Tbsp cinnamon

Cream sugars and butter. Add eggs and vanilla. Beat well. Stir in soda, salt, flour, oats and pecans. Roll into 1" balls. Coat with sugar-cinnamon mixture. Bake at 350° for about 12 minutes.

Quaker's Best Oatmeal Cookies

1¼ cups butter
¾ cup brown sugar
½ cup sugar
1 egg
1 tsp vanilla
1½ cups flour
1 tsp soda
1 tsp salt
1 tsp cinnamon (optional)
¼ tsp nutmeg (optional)
3 cups quick or old-fashioned oats
1 cup plumped raisins (optional)

Beat butter and sugars until fluffy. Beat in egg and vanilla. Add combined flour, soda, salt, and spices. Mix well. Stir in oats and raisins. Drop by rounded spoonsful onto ungreased cookie sheet and bake at 350° for 8 to 9 minutes for a chewy cookie, 10-11 minutes for a crisp one. Cool 1 minute on cookie sheet, and remove to wire rack or baking cloth to cool. Makes 4½ dozen.

MOLASSES CRINKLES

¾ cup shortening
1 cup brown sugar
1 large egg
¼ cup sorghum molasses
2¼ cups flour
2 tsp baking soda
½ tsp salt
1 tsp cinnamon
1 tsp ginger
½ tsp cloves

½ cup sugar

Cream shortening and brown sugar. Add egg and molasses, mixing well. Combine flour and next 5 ingredients; add to shortening mixture, mixing well. Cover. Chill 2 hours. Shape dough into 1" balls, and roll in sugar. Place on lightly greased cookie sheets. Bake at 350° for 12-15 minutes.

– Alice Rhodes

CRACKLE-TOP GINGER COOKIES

1 cup shortening, (butter or margarine)
2 cups brown sugar
1 egg, beaten
1 cup sorghum molasses
4 cups sifted flour
½ tsp salt
2 tsp soda
1 tsp ginger
1 tsp vanilla
1 tsp lemon extract

Cream shortening, gradually add brown sugar. Blend in egg and molasses, beat until fluffy. Sift dry ingredients, blend into mixture. Dough should be soft but not sticky. Add vanilla and lemon extract. Chill. Shape into balls, dip in granulated sugar. Bake at 350° for 12-15 minutes.

– Fran Good

SPRITZ COOKIES

2 cups soft butter
1 cup sugar
2 eggs
2 tsp flavoring (vanilla _or_ almond)
4¾ cups flour
1 tsp salt
few drops of coloring if desired

Cream butter and sugar. Add eggs, and beat well. Add rest of ingredients. Put dough in cookie press. Press onto _cold_ trays so cookies will stick. Bake fast, about 400° for 6-9 minutes. Store in airtight container. Yields approximately 10 dozen.

GINGERBREAD BOY COOKIES

1 cup sugar
1 cup margarine
1 cup sorghum molasses
1 Tbsp vinegar
1 egg beaten
4¾ cups flour
2 tsp soda
1 tsp salt
1½ tsp ginger
1 tsp cinnamon

Cream sugar and margarine. Add molasses, vinegar and egg. Stir in rest of ingredients. Chill dough. Roll dough about ¼ - ⅛" thick. Cut and bake at 350° until done. We use cinnamon heart candy to create eyes, nose, buttons, etc. before baking.

Royal Icing (for decorating gingerbread houses and cookies)
3 egg whites
1 lb plus 1 cup powdered sugar
½ tsp cream of tartar

Beat until stiff. Cover until ready to use. (Dries out fast.) Can be used to hold your house together and make windows, snow on the roof, etc. Add a few drops of water if it gets too dry while you are working.

– *Lois and Alice Rhodes*

HOBO COOKIES

2 cups margarine
3½ cups sugar
1 cup sorghum molasses
5 eggs
6 cups flour
4 tsp soda
1 tsp salt
1 tsp ginger
4 tsp cinnamon
2 tsp cloves
5 cups oatmeal

Cream margarine and sugar. Add molasses and eggs. Mix well. Combine dry ingredients and stir into creamed mixture. Last, stir in oatmeal. Drop by teaspoon or cookie dipper onto greased cookie sheet. Bake at 350° for 10-12 minutes.

Variation: Using half cake flour makes a thicker cookie. This makes a great oatmeal sandwich cookie when filled with this filling:

Fluffy White Cookie Filling
2 egg whites beaten
2 cups powdered sugar
1 tsp vanilla
1 cup Crisco shortening
pinch of salt

Mix all together and beat until fluffy.

Did you ever wonder why some cookie recipes request corn syrup? Corn syrup is an invert sugar and will absorb moisture from the air into your baked goods. Honey and molasses have the same properties.

Whoopie Pies

4 cups flour (I use half cake flour)
1 cup cocoa
2 tsp soda
½ tsp salt
1 cup shortening
2 cups sugar
2 large eggs
2 tsp vanilla
1 cup cold water
1 cup buttermilk

Mix all dry ingredients together with wire whisk. In mixing bowl, cream shortening and sugar. Add eggs and vanilla. Mix flour alternately with water and buttermilk. Drop dough with cookie scoop onto cookie sheet. Bake at 350° until no dent remains in top when touched. (15 minutes or more) Cool. Sandwich cookies together with Fluffy White Cookie Filling. (Recipe with Hobo Cookies.)

Monster Cookies

2 cups brown sugar
2 cups white sugar
1 tsp salt
½ lb margarine
1½ lbs peanut butter
6 eggs
2 Tbsp light corn syrup
1 Tbsp vanilla
4 tsp soda
1 cup flour
7 cups quick oatmeal
1 lb M&M candy
1 cup chocolate chips

Mix ingredients in order given in large bowl. Drop by spoonfuls onto greased cookie sheet. Bake at 350° about 10-12 minutes.
– *Linda (Wenger) Shank*

To a child, a balanced diet is a cookie in each hand.

Pecan Puffs, Walnut Puffs, Peppermint Puffs

1 cup butter
½ cup powdered sugar
1 tsp vanilla
¼ tsp salt
2¼ cups flour
¾ cup chopped pecans

Mix all together. Shape into 1" balls. Bake at 350° until golden (10-12 minutes). Roll in powdered sugar. Cool and roll in sugar again.

Walnut Puffs

Use almond flavoring and black walnuts.

Peppermint Puffs

Use 1 tsp peppermint flavoring and 1 cup crushed peppermint candy. Omit nuts.

Snickerdoodles

½ lb butter
1½ cups sugar
2 eggs
2¾ cups flour
2 tsp cream of tartar
pinch of salt
1 tsp soda
1 tsp vanilla

Cream butter and sugar. Add eggs and beat well. Add rest of ingredients. Roll balls of dough in a mixture of ⅓ cup sugar and 5 teaspoons of cinnamon. Bake at 350° until done.

Never ruin an apology with an excuse.

RAISIN FILLED COOKIES

Filling

2¼ cups raisins
1½ cups brown sugar
1¾ cups water
¼ cup cornstarch
¼ tsp salt
1½ tsp lemon extract

Mix all filling ingredients in saucepan. Cook while stirring until it thickens. Set aside to cool.

Cookies

2 cups brown sugar
1 cup sugar
1½ cups margarine
6 eggs
1½ tsp vanilla
7 cups flour
1 tsp salt
2 tsp soda

Cream sugars and margarine. Add eggs and vanilla and mix well. Stir in dry ingredients and blend well. Chill dough. Roll out ⅛"- ¼" thick. Cut with round cutter. Place on greased cookie sheets. Put 1 rounded teaspoon of filling on each. Top with another circle of dough. Press edges. Bake at 350° for 10-15 minutes.
Note: Use as little flour as possible to roll out cookie tops so they'll bake into the bottom half. Use an empty plastic thread spool with the paper removed from the ends to make a flower design on your cookie tops. Makes 4 dozen large cookies.

Enrich someone's life today with a warm word of sincere praise.
Both of you will be better for it.

What is Biscotti?

Italian cookies which are baked twice. A good cookie for dunking, and they keep well for 4-6 weeks in your cookie jar…at least if you can keep your hands out of it. I make these in December for holiday gifts.

CRANBERRY ORANGE BISCOTTI

1¼ cups sugar
½ cup butter
2 large eggs
2½ cups flour
1 tsp baking powder
½ tsp salt
1 cup dried cranberries
2 Tbsp grated orange rind
½ tsp orange oil

Combine butter and sugar. Add eggs and beat well. Stir in dry ingredients, cranberries and flavorings. Mix until well blended. Chill dough. Divide dough in half. Using floured hands shape each piece into a 2½" wide, 10" long, 1" high log. Transfer to a parchment lined cookie sheet and bake at 350° about 45 minutes, or until they test done with a toothpick. Cool, then slice ½"-¾" thick and arrange biscotti with space between pieces on cookie sheets. Rebake at 250° 10-15 minutes to crisp. Store in a tight container. Makes 30.

CINNAMON SUGAR BISCOTTI

2 cups flour
2 tsp cinnamon
1 tsp baking powder
½ tsp salt
1 cup sugar
6 Tbsp butter
2 large eggs
1 tsp vanilla
½ cup finely chopped pecans

Cinnamon Sugar Mixture:
1 cup sugar
4 tsp cinnamon

Combine first four ingredients and set aside. Cream together sugar and butter until fluffy. Add eggs and beat well. Stir in vanilla and dry ingredients, Stir in nuts. Chill dough several hours. Divide dough into two pieces. Shape each into a log about 2½" x 10" x 1" high. Place each on a parchment lined baking sheet and bake at 350° until dough is firm to touch. Cool and slice about ¾" thick. Sprinkle each slice on cut side with cinnamon sugar mixture. Rebake at 250° until crisp. Store in an airtight container. Makes about 30.

DOUBLE CHOCOLATE WALNUT BISCOTTI

¾ stick butter (6 Tbsp)
1¼ cups sugar
2 large eggs
2 cups flour
½ cup cocoa
1 tsp soda
½ tsp salt
1 cup chopped English walnuts
¾ cup semisweet chocolate chips

Cream butter and sugar. Add eggs and beat well. Stir in dry ingredients. Last add nuts and chips. Combine well. Chill dough. Divide dough in half. Using floured hands, shape each piece into a 2½"x10" log. Bake on parchment lined cookie sheet at 350° about 45 minutes or until they test done with a toothpick. Cool and slice about ¾" thick. Rebake biscotti at 250° until crisp (about 10-15 minutes). Keep in an airtight container. These are real pretty when drizzled with melted white chocolate. Makes about 30.

When you give what you make with your hands,
you share your heart.

LAYERED CHOCOLATE BARS

First Layer

- ½ cup butter
- 1½ cups sugar
- 2 eggs
- 1 cup water
- ½ cup vegetable oil
- 1 tsp vanilla
- 2 cups flour
- 3 Tbsp cocoa
- 1 tsp soda

Cream butter and sugar, beat in eggs. Add water and oil, stir in vanilla and dry ingredients. Beat well. Bake in 10 x 15 prepared pan, at 350° for 20-25 minutes. Don't over bake. Cool.

Second Layer

- 1 cup Crisco shortening
- ¾ cup sugar
- ½ cup milk
- 1 Tbsp water
- 1 tsp vanilla
- ½ tsp salt
- 1 cup powdered sugar

Combine first six ingredients and beat together 5 minutes. Add powdered sugar, beat well. Spread on cooled cake

Third Layer

- ¾ cup sugar
- 6 Tbsp butter
- 6 Tbsp milk
- 1¼ cups chocolate chips

Combine sugar, butter and milk in saucepan over medium heat and stir until it's bubbly. Remove from heat, stir in chocolate chips. Beat until right consistency, frost cake. Cut into bars.

– Karen (Nolt) Martin

Life is fragile, handle with prayer.

Chewy Granola Bars

⅓ cup brown sugar
¼ tsp salt
⅔ cup crunchy peanut butter
½ cup light corn syrup
1 Tbsp vanilla
¼ cup margarine
3 cups quick oats
1 cup Rice Krispies cereal
½ cup coconut
½ cup chocolate chips or M&M's
½ cup marshmallow bits (optional)

Blend first six ingredients in large bowl. Add rest of ingredients and mix well. Press into greased 9x13 pan. Bake at 300° for 10-12 minutes. Cool. Cut into bars.

– Ethel Shank

Oatmeal Chocolate Chip Bars

1½ cups brown sugar
¾ cup sugar
1 cup oil
3 eggs
¾ cup milk
2 tsp vanilla
2¼ cups flour
1 tsp soda
1 tsp salt
1½ tsp cinnamon
4 cups oatmeal
12 oz chocolate chips

Combine sugars, oil, and eggs. Beat well. Stir in milk and vanilla. Add dry ingredients and oatmeal. Last stir in chocolate chips. Bake in greased and floured 10 x 15 pan at 350° for about 30 minutes. Cut into bars. Keep in a tight container.

Hardship makes character.

YUMMY GRANOLA BARS

1½ lbs marshmallows
¼ cup margarine or butter
¼ cup oil
½ cup honey
½ cup peanut butter
9½ cups Rice Krispies
2 cups graham cracker crumbs
4 cups oatmeal
1 cup chopped peanuts or pecans
1 cup coconut
1-2 cups chocolate chips or M&M's

Melt butter, oil, and marshmallows over low heat, stirring until melted. Turn off heat. Add honey and peanut butter. In large bowl mix remaining ingredients. Pour melted mixture over dry ingredients, stirring all the while. Keep from side of pan as it gets very hard and difficult to mix. Spread quickly in 2 large greased sheet pans (10 x 15). Press down with palm of hand or roll with rolling pin to flatten. Makes a large batch.
Note: You may want to add the chocolate chips last, after mixing in the syrup. They melt a bit when the hot syrup coats them.

– Esther Rohrer and Zelda Rohrer

PUMPKIN BARS

4 eggs beaten
1 cup salad oil
2 cups sugar
2 cups pumpkin
1 tsp salt
1 tsp soda
1 tsp baking powder
2 tsp cinnamon
2 cups flour

Combine all ingredients. Pour into greased and floured 10 x 15 sheet pan. Bake at 350° for 20-25 minutes. Frost with Cream Cheese Icing. Decorate bars with a pecan half or corn candy.

QUICK OATMEAL BARS

¾ cup butter
1 cup brown sugar
1¼ cups flour
1 tsp salt
½ tsp soda
2 cups oatmeal
½ cup light corn syrup
1 tsp vanilla

Topping
1¼ cup chocolate chips
½ cup peanut butter

Melt butter. Add sugar and stir until dissolved. Stir in dry ingredients. Add corn syrup and vanilla. Mixture will be dry and crumbly. Press into greased 9x13 pan. Bake at 350° for 20-25 minutes. Don't overbake. Melt chocolate chips and stir in peanut butter. Spread over warm bars. Cut when cool.

– Cornelia (Shank) Good

SURPRISE BROWNIES

1 cup butter, melted
3 cups sugar
1 Tbsp vanilla
5 eggs
2 cups flour
⅔ cup cocoa
1 tsp baking powder
1 tsp salt
24 thin peppermint patties
1 cup black walnut pieces

Cream butter, sugar, and vanilla. Add eggs and beat well. Stir in dry ingredients. Reserve 2 cups batter. Spread remaining batter in a greased 9x13 pan. Arrange peppermint patties in a single layer over pan. Sprinkle nuts over patties. Cover with 2 cups batter. Bake at 325° for 45-50 minutes.

Variation: You may add 1 tsp peppermint extract to dough instead of layering with peppermint patties.

Blonde Brownies

2 sticks (1 cup) butter
2 cups brown sugar
3 large eggs
2 tsp vanilla
2 cups flour
2 tsp baking powder
1 tsp salt
2 cups goodies (semi-sweet chocolate chips, nuts, etc.)

Melt butter and brown sugar stirring over medium heat until bubbly. Whisk eggs and vanilla together in a large mixing bowl. Slowly add hot butter mixture while stirring to blend. Add flour, baking powder and salt. Add goodies last. Bake in a greased and floured 9 x 13 pan at 325° until dough is set (30-40 minutes). May bake in 10 x 15 pan for 20-25 minutes. Cut into squares.

– *Clarence Rohrer*

Peanut Butter Brownies

1¼ cups sugar
¾ cup brown sugar
½ cup crunchy peanut butter
¼ cup butter
3 eggs
½ Tbsp vanilla
2 cups flour
2½ tsp baking powder
¾ tsp salt
¼ cup chopped peanuts (optional)

Cream first four ingredients. Add eggs, beat well. Stir in vanilla and dry ingredients. Spread in a lightly greased 9x13 or 10x15 pan. Sprinkle peanuts on top. Bake at 350° for about 25 minutes.

– *Evaleen Rohrer*

A good neighbor, like an apron,
is comforting, protecting and appreciated a lot.

FROSTED ZUCCHINI BROWNIES

No eggs

2 cups flour
⅓ cup cocoa
1½ tsp soda
1 tsp salt
2 cups shredded zucchini
1½ cups sugar
¾ cup oil
½ cup chopped walnuts (optional)
2 tsp vanilla

Mix first four ingredients. Mix remaining ingredients together and add to dry ingredients. Put in a greased and floured 9x13 pan and bake at 350° for 35-40 minutes.

Frosting
¼ cup butter
1 cup sugar
¼ cup milk
1 tsp vanilla
½ cup chocolate chips
½ cup mini marshmallows
½ cup walnuts (optional)

Melt butter. Stir in sugar and milk and bring to a boil over medium heat. Boil and stir 1 minute. Remove from heat and add rest of ingredients. Spread over brownies. Eat.☺

– *Hazel (Rohrer) Horst*

A good friend is like a teddy bear;
They are both good listeners,
No one cares how chubby they are,
And they both grow more valuable as time passes.

DOUBLE CHOCOLATE BARS

½ cup butter
¾ cup sugar
2 eggs
1 tsp vanilla
¾ cup flour
½ chopped pecans
2 Tbsp cocoa
¼ tsp baking powder
¼ tsp salt
3 cups miniature marshmallows
1 cup chocolate chips
1 cup peanut butter
1½ cups Rice Krispies

Cream butter and sugar. Beat in eggs and vanilla. Stir together flour, nuts, cocoa, baking powder and salt. Stir into egg mixture. Spread into a greased 9 x 13 pan. Bake at 350° for 15-20 minutes or until done. Sprinkle marshmallows over top. Bake 3 minutes more. Spread marshmallows evenly with a knife. Cool. In a small sauce pan, combine chocolate chips and peanut butter. Cook and stir over low heat until chocolate is melted. Stir in cereal, spread mixture on top of cooled bars. Cool, cut into bars.

– *Linda (Wenger) Shank*

CHOCOLATE CHIP CREAM CHEESE BARS

18½ oz chocolate cake mix
1 egg
⅓ cup vegetable oil
8 oz soft cream cheese
⅓ cup sugar
1 egg
1 cup chocolate chips

Mix first three ingredients together until crumbly. Pat all but 1 cup of crumbs into a 9x13 pan. Bake 15 minutes at 350°.
Beat together remaining ingredients until light and smooth. Stir in 1 cup chocolate chips. Spread over baked layer. Sprinkle crumbs on top. Bake 15 more minutes. Cool and cut.

– *Neva Horst*

BLACK-BOTTOM BANANA BARS

½ cup softened butter
1 cup sugar
1 egg
1 tsp vanilla
1 ½ cups mashed bananas
1 ½ cups all-purpose flour
1 tsp baking powder
1 tsp baking soda
½ tsp salt
¼ cup cocoa, reserved

Cream butter and sugar. Add egg and vanilla; beat until thoroughly combined. Blend in the bananas. Combine dry ingredients; add to creamed mixture and mix well. Divide batter in half. Add cocoa to half. Spread into a greased 9x13 pan. Spoon remaining batter on top and swirl with a knife. Bake at 350° for 25 minutes or until done.

– Frances Martin

TOFFEE TOP BARS

1½ cups brown sugar
2 cups flour
½ cup butter
1 tsp baking powder
½ tsp salt
1 tsp vanilla
1 cup milk
1 large egg
1 cup semi sweet chocolate chips
½ cup chopped walnuts
¼ cup unsweetened coconut

Combine sugar and flour. Cut in butter to make coarse crumbs. Reserve 1 cup crumbs for topping. To rest of crumbs, add the next 5 ingredients and stir until smooth. Spread in a greased 9x13 pan. Sprinkle with reserved crumbs. Combine chips, nuts, and coconut, and sprinkle over all. Bake at 350° for 30-35 minutes.

– Mary Alice Horst

MINCEMEAT COFFEE CAKE BARS

Dough

¾ cup milk
½ cup sugar
½ tsp salt
¼ cup butter
¼ cup very warm water
1 Tbsp yeast
1 egg (well beaten)
4 cups sifted flour

1 quart mincemeat for filling

Mix dough as usual for yeast dough. Let rise until double. Divide and roll into 2 large rectangles to cover a large baking sheet. Spread mincemeat over dough to ½ " from edges. Cover with other half of dough and pinch edges to seal. Cover and let rise until doubled. Bake at 350° for 20-30 minutes. Ice with the following while still warm:

Glaze

1 cup powdered sugar
1½ Tbsp cream
½ tsp orange or lemon extract
pinch of salt

– Rosanna (Rhodes) Martin

*There is a serene and settled majesty to woodland scenery
that enters into the soul and delights and elevates it,
and fills it with noble inclinations.*
– Washington Irving

Delicate Lemon Squares

Crust

1 cup all purpose flour
¼ cup powdered sugar
½ cup butter

Filling

2 eggs
¾ cup sugar
3 Tbsp fresh lemon juice
2 Tbsp all purpose flour
½ tsp baking powder
powdered sugar

Stir together flour and powdered sugar. Cut in butter. Pat into an ungreased 8x8x2 baking pan. Bake at 350° for 10-12 minutes.

Beat eggs in mixing bowl; add sugar and juice. Beat until thick and smooth. Stir together flour and baking powder; add to egg mixture, blending well.   Pour egg mixture gently over baked crust layer. Bake at 350° for 20-25 minutes. Cool slightly. Sift powdered sugar over top. Yields about 3 dozen.

– Ava (Eberly) Heatwole

Energy Bars

2 cups quick oats
3 Tbsp butter
¼ cup honey
½ cup chunky peanut butter
3 cups mini marshmallows
1 cup chopped peanuts

Toast oats in 350° oven for 15 minutes. Melt butter in large saucepan over low heat. Add honey, peanut butter and marshmallows; stirring until melted. Stir in oats and peanuts. Press into a greased 9" square pan. When cool, cut into bars.

– Millard Rohrer

A good snack for hunters in the woods. ☺

SHORTBREAD LEMON BARS

Crust:

1½ cups flour
½ cup powdered sugar
1 tsp lemon peel
1 tsp orange peel
¾ cup butter

Filling:

4 eggs, beaten
2 cups sugar
⅓ cup lemon juice
¼ cup flour
1 tsp baking powder
2 tsp lemon peel
2 tsp orange peel

Topping:

2 cups sour cream
⅓ cup sugar
½ tsp vanilla

For crust, combine flour, powdered sugar, lemon and orange peel. Cut in butter until crumbly. Pat into greased 9" x 13" pan. Bake at 350° for 14 minutes. Combine filling ingredients, mixing well. Pour over hot crust. Return to oven for 16-20 minutes or until set. Mix topping ingredients and spread over filling. Bake for 8 minutes. Cool and refrigerate overnight.

– *Suetta (Rohrer) Horst*

When speaking, use a grain of sugar;
when listening, use a grain of salt.

Candy
and
Snacks

The Things That Count

Not what we have, but what we use
Not what we see, but what we choose.
These are the things that mar or bless,
The sum of human happiness.

The things nearby... not things afar
Not what we seem, but what we are;
These are the things that make or break...
That gives the heart its joy or ache.

Not what seems fair, but what is true
Not what we dream, but what we do.
These are the things that shine like gems
Like stars in fortune's diadems.

Not as we take, but as we give–
Not as we pray, but as we live...
These are the things that make for peace
Both now and after time shall cease...
~ These are the things that count. ~

– Author Unknown

Candy and Snacks

ALMOND BUTTER CRUNCH

1½ cups sliced almonds
¾ cup butter
1½ cups sugar
1 Tbsp light corn syrup
3 Tbsp water

Melt butter in saucepan. Add sugar, syrup, and water. Stir until dissolved. Boil to hard crack (290°) without stirring. Remove from heat. Add nuts and stir to coat. Pour onto greased cookie sheet and spread thin. Cool and break into pieces. Makes 1½ lbs of candy.

– *Esther Rohrer*

The Crown of the house is Godliness...
The Beauty of the house is order...
The Blessing of the house is contentment...
The Glory of the house is hospitality.

Brittle Butter Crunch

½ cup butter
½ cup white sugar
3 Tbsp brown sugar
1 Tbsp light corn syrup
1 Tbsp water
¼ tsp soda
1 tsp vanilla
8 oz chocolate chips, melted

Melt butter. Add sugars, syrup, and water. Bring to a boil, stirring constantly. Cook to 290°. Remove from heat, and stir in soda and vanilla. Pour into a buttered jelly roll pan. Cool. Spread melted chocolate over all. Break into pieces.

– Esther Rohrer

Terrific Toffee

1 cup chocolate chips
1 cup pecans, coarsely chopped
1 cup butter
1 cup sugar
3 Tbsp water

Line a 9x13 pan with foil or parchment. In a heavy 2 qt sauce-pan, combine butter, sugar, and water. Cook over medium heat to boiling, stirring to dissolve sugar. Place candy thermometer in pan and continue stirring often until it reaches 290°. Pour into prepared pan and quickly spread. Sprinkle nuts and chips over toffee. You may prefer to just put ¾ cup of melted chocolate on top of toffee and sprinkle with pecans. It's also good with no toppings. Cool about an hour until it breaks up easily. (If necessary, chill to harden chocolate.)

Praise to a child is like water to a thirsty plant.

PEANUT BRITTLE

3½ cups sugar
¾ cup water
1 cup light corn syrup
¾ tsp salt
1 lb raw peanuts
4 Tbsp butter
1 tsp vanilla
1 Tbsp soda

Combine sugar, water, syrup and salt. Boil rapidly to 230°. Add peanuts, stir constantly to 290° (hard crack). Remove from heat, add butter and vanilla. Add soda and stir briskly to blend well. Pour onto buttered or parchment lined sheet pans. Spread as thin as possible. Break into pieces when it hardens. Makes 2½ lbs.

CANDY PLAY DOUGH

1 cup peanut butter
⅓ cup honey
1 cup dry milk

Mix together. Blend well. Roll out like cookie dough and cut with cutters or mold into interesting shapes. Use powdered sugar for easier handling. Amuses children (and others) while you cook... and tastes delicious!

– Lois Y. Wenger

Correction does much,
but encouragement does more.
Encouragement after censure is like the sunshine after a shower.
– Goethe

CARAMEL CANDY

1½ cups white sugar
½ cup brown sugar
1 cup cream
1 tsp butter
1 tsp vanilla
½ cup chopped nuts if desired

Boil sugar and cream to 234° or until candy forms soft ball in cold water. Remove from heat. Add butter and vanilla. Cool to lukewarm and beat until candy loses gloss. Pour into 8"x8" buttered pan. Press nuts on top.

– Rebecca (Shank) Shank

CREAM CARAMELS

2 cups white sugar
2 cups light corn syrup
⅛ tsp salt
2 cups cream
½ cup butter
1 tsp vanilla

Boil sugar, corn syrup, and salt to 245°. Add butter and cream gradually, keeping mixture boiling continuously. Cook rapidly to the firm ball stage (245°), stirring all the time. Add vanilla. Pour into buttered 9x13 pan. Cut into squares, and wrap in waxed paper. For chocolate caramels, stir in 3 squares bakers chocolate.

CARAMEL PECAN TURTLES

Wrap softened caramels around pecan halves. Dip in melted chocolate. Good made with peanuts, too.

A man's true wealth is the good he does for others.
– Bendixline

DELECTABLE DIVINITY

3 cups sugar
¼ tsp salt
¾ cup light corn syrup
½ cup water
2 egg whites, stiffly beaten
1 tsp vanilla
1 cup broken walnuts or pecans

Mix sugar, salt, corn syrup, and water in saucepan. Stir to dissolve sugar over low heat. Then cook without stirring to hard ball
(260°). Remove from heat and pour in a thin stream into beaten
egg whites, beating constantly. Add vanilla and beat until stiff.
Fold in nuts. Spread in a buttered 11x7 pan. Cut into squares
when firm. If using a hand beater, this is a 2-person job, but well
worth the effort!

HOLIDAY FONDANT

3 cups sugar
¾ cup light corn syrup
½ cup water
2 egg whites, beaten
dash of salt

Boil sugar, corn syrup, and water together to 240°. Then pour in
a thin stream over egg whites, beating continuously. Beat awhile
until stiff. When mixture cools, you can chill it for several hours
to make it easier to handle. Mold the fondant around cherries,
nuts, etc. to form balls. Flavor with peppermint for a special treat.
(Dust your fingers with cornstarch if they get sticky.) Dip in melted
chocolate. Drop onto waxed paper.
Note: If beating by hand, you'll need a helper to make this.

I have fond memories of helping Mom make these when we were
young. They were a holiday favorite in our family.

ALMOND JOYS

½ lb butter
1 lb powdered sugar
1 lb flaked coconut
½ can sweetened condensed milk
1 tsp vanilla
1 tsp almond flavoring
¼ tsp salt

Whole almonds for topping candy
1 lb dark chocolate, melted in 140° oven

Mix all together and shape as you like. Top with an almond and dip into melted chocolate. Cool on waxed paper.

CHOCOLATE MALLOW FUDGE

¾ cup evaporated milk
1⅔ cups sugar
½ tsp salt
2 cups mini marshmallows
1 cup chocolate chips
1 tsp vanilla
2 Tbsp butter
½ cup chopped walnuts or pecans

Mix sugar and milk in heavy saucepan over medium heat. Stir until it boils, then cook about 5 minutes, or until 234° (soft ball stage) stirring constantly. Remove from heat and add rest of ingredients. Stir to melt marshmallows. Add nuts last. Pour into buttered 9"x9" pan. Cool and cut.

Families are like fudge, mostly sweet with a few nuts.

HOMEMADE SNICKER BARS

1 cup (6 oz) milk chocolate chips
¼ cup butterscotch chips
¼ cup creamy peanut butter

Filling
¼ cup butter or margarine
1 cup sugar
¼ cup evaporated milk
1½ cups marshmallow crème
¼ cup creamy peanut butter
1 tsp vanilla
1½ cups salted peanuts

Caramel Layer
1 pkg (14 oz) caramels
¼ cup whipping cream

Icing
1 cup (6 oz) milk chocolate chips
¼ cup butterscotch chips
¼ cup creamy peanut butter

Combine first three ingredients in small saucepan; stir over low heat until melted and smooth. Spread onto bottom of lightly greased 9x13x2 pan. Refrigerate until set.

Melt butter in heavy saucepan over medium-high heat. Add sugar and milk. Bring to a boil; boil and stir 5 minutes. Remove from heat; stir in marshmallow crème, peanut butter, and vanilla. Add peanuts. Spread over first layer. Refrigerate until set.

Combine the caramels and cream in saucepan; stir over low heat until melted and smooth. Spread over filling. Refrigerate until set.

In another saucepan, combine chips and peanut butter; stir over low heat until melted and smooth. Pour over caramel layer. Refrigerate for at least one hour. Cut in 1 inch squares. Store in the refrigerator. Yields about 8 dozen. Then wash all the saucepans so you have something to cook supper in. ☺

– *Sharon (Knicely) Horst*

The Mars family created their famous candy bar over 50 years ago. They named it for their family pet, a horse named Snickers.

CHOCOLATE MARSHMALLOW CLUSTERS

½ cup sugar
½ cup evaporated milk
1 Tbsp light corn syrup
16 oz chocolate (chips or other)
1 cup chopped walnuts
1 cup miniature marshmallows

In a heavy 2 quart saucepan, combine sugar, milk and syrup. Bring to full boil, stirring constantly. Boil 2 minutes. Remove from heat, add chocolate and stir until melted. Let mixture cool for 10 minutes. Stir in nuts and marshmallows. Drop by small clusters on waxed paper. Cool until firm.

CHOCOLATE TRUFFLES

1½ lbs milk or dark chocolate pieces
1 cup heavy cream
1½ tsp vanilla or orange flavoring
pinch of salt
¾ lb milk or dark chocolate for dipping

Melt chocolate in 140° oven. Add cream to chocolate, stirring to blend well. Add vanilla and salt. Let cool. Shape into bite-sized pieces. You may use powdered sugar or cocoa to help keep it from sticking to your fingers. Nuts may be added. Dip in melted chocolate. These are extremely hard to resist!

STAINED GLASS WINDOWS

10½ oz. pkg colored mini marshmallows
12 oz. pkg semi-sweet chocolate chips
1 stick butter (½ cup)
1-2 cups powdered sugar

Melt butter and chocolate chips in top of double boiler. Remove from heat. Pour over marshmallows in a bowl and stir to coat. Form into two 16" rolls on waxed paper. Roll each into a cylinder and chill. When firm, roll in powdered sugar and slice into ½" slices.

Peanut Butter Cups

7 cups powdered sugar
½ lb margarine
2 cups crunchy peanut butter
1 Tbsp vanilla
1 tsp salt

Blend ingredients thoroughly. Shape into desired shapes. Dip in 1 lb melted chocolate. Chocolate may be melted in a 140° oven.

Yummy Peanut Butter Bars

2 cups peanut butter
¾ cup butter
1 lb powdered sugar
2 tsp vanilla

Melt butter in saucepan. Stir in peanut butter. Remove from heat. Stir in vanilla and sugar. Press into a buttered 9x13 pan. Mixture is very stiff. Make topping and spread over peanut butter mixture. Cool and cut. Makes 4-6 dozen.

Topping

1 cup milk chocolate chips
1 cup semi-sweet chocolate chips
¼ cup butter
1 tsp vanilla

Melt butter in a saucepan over low heat. Stir in chips until smooth and melted. Add vanilla.

A good mother is like a quilt—
she keeps her children warm
but she doesn't smother them.

KETTLE CORN

2 Tbsp oil
2 Tbsp sugar
¼ tsp salt
½ cup popcorn kernels

Put all ingredients in popcorn kettle. Pop over med-high heat, stirring constantly until popping stops. Pour at once into a serving bowl. (scorches easily)

CRAZY CRUNCH

1⅓ cups sugar
1 cup butter, no substitutes
½ cup light corn syrup
2 tsp vanilla
6 quarts popped corn
1 cup peanuts
1 cup pecans

Boil sugar, butter, and corn syrup together to hard crack stage (290°). Add vanilla after removing from heat. Pour over mixed corn, peanuts, and pecans.

– Esther Rohrer

POPCORN CAKE

4 quarts popped corn
1 lb small spiced gum drops
1 cup salted peanuts
½ cup butter or margarine
½ cup salad oil
1 lb marshmallows

Melt butter, oil, and marshmallows in saucepan. Stir frequently. Pour over popcorn, candy, and nut mixture. Stir well. Press mixture into greased tube pan. Cover with foil to keep moist. Refrigerate several hours. Dip pan in hot water 5-10 seconds to unmold. Turn out and decorate with gumdrop flowers. Cut gumdrops into slices and create flowers over top of cake.

– Esther Rohrer

CREAMY MINTS

8 oz cream cheese
2 lbs powdered sugar
small amount of peppermint or wintergreen oil

Combine all ingredients. Mix well. Shape into long thin rolls. Cut in pieces or put into candy molds. These are also good coated in chocolate. Spread out on sheet to dry a little before bagging.

– Zelda Rohrer

FESTIVE BUTTER MINTS

⅓ cup (¾ stick) butter
¼ cup whipping cream
¼ tsp salt
1 lb (4 cups) powdered sugar
½ tsp mint extract
1 to 2 Tbsp corn syrup
food coloring of choice

Heat butter, cream, and salt in medium saucepan over medium heat just until simmering. Add sugar and extract, mixing until well blended. Add a few drops of food coloring to portions of mixture, as desired. Knead on surface dusted with additional powdered sugar until smooth. Roll into balls or ropes, snowmen, candy canes, etc. Add 1-2 Tbsp corn syrup if mixture is difficult to roll into shapes. Make logs and slice for peppermint patties.
Store in sealed containers for soft mints or loosely covered for dry mints.

– Lorna (Good) Wenger

Volunteers are unpaid, not because they are worthless,
but because they are priceless.

SNACK MIX SQUARES

2½ cups halved pretzel sticks
3 cups Corn Chex cereal
1½ cups M & M's
½ cup butter
⅓ cup peanut butter
5 cups mini marshmallows

Combine pretzels, cereal, and M & M's in a large bowl. Melt butter and peanut butter over medium heat. Add marshmallows and stir until melted. Pour over cereal mix and toss to coat. Press into a greased 9x13 pan. Cut into squares when cool.
— *Melissa (Rohrer) Wenger and Wanda (Rohrer) Good*
— *Austin and Marie Eberly*

You'll have to use discipline when these are in your house – they're irresistible!

RICE KRISPIE SQUARES

¼ cup butter
½ lb marshmallows
½ tsp vanilla
6 cups Rice Krispies cereal

Melt butter and marshmallows in a large pan. Stir in vanilla and remove from heat. Add cereal and mix well. Press into a greased 9x13 pan. Cut into squares. For special occasions, press into 10 x 15 pan. Smooth with a rolling pin and cut into shapes with cookie cutters.

Super Squares
Melt chocolate or butterscotch chips and spread on top of bars.

How seldom we weigh our neighbor
in the same balance with ourselves.
— *Thomas á Kempis*

QUAKER OAT CEREAL SNACK

8 cups Quaker Oat Squares
2 cups pecans
½ cup corn syrup
½ cup brown sugar
¼ cup margarine
1 tsp vanilla
½ tsp soda

Bring sugar, syrup, and margarine to a boil. Add vanilla and soda.
Coat cereal and nuts and bake at 250° for 1 hour. Stir often.
– Barbara (Rohrer) Eberly

CHEERIO SQUARES

1½ cups white sugar
2 cups light corn syrup
1¼ cups butter or margarine
1⅔ cups peanut butter
16 cups Cheerios or other cereal

Combine sugar, syrup, and butter in saucepan and bring to a boil.
Remove from heat; add peanut butter and stir until smooth. Pour
boiled mixture over Cheerios. Mix well. Press into greased pans.
Cool and cut into squares. Refrigerate for chewier bars.

Individuals can change things...
If everyone will just do their little part,
we can make a tremendous difference in the lives of other people.
– Sarah Purcell

Party Mix

1 large box Crispix cereal
1 large box Corn Chex
1 large box Rice Chex
1 large box Cheerios
2 lbs pretzel sticks or mini pretzels
2 lbs mixed nuts
1 lb butter
¼ cup Worcestershire Sauce
1 Tbsp celery salt
1 Tbsp onion salt

Mix cereals, pretzels, and nuts in your biggest bowl. Dump into a large plastic bag. Melt butter and add Worcestershire Sauce. Pour over cereals in bag. Close the top and toss well in the bag. Combine seasoning salts and sprinkle over cereal mixture. Toss well to coat evenly. Bake on large baking pans at 250° for 1½ hours, stirring every 15 minutes. Store in tight container.

Spiced Pecans

1 cup sugar
1 tsp cinnamon
¼ tsp salt
6 Tbsp milk
1 tsp vanilla
2 cups pecan halves or large pieces

Mix milk, sugar, cinnamon, and salt. Boil to soft ball stage (236°). Add vanilla. Stir in pecans. Pour out on wax paper lined tray. Break apart when cool. These taste like pralines. Sweet and yummy!

Itching for what you want doesn't do much good;
You've got to scratch for it.

Salt Water Taffy

1 cup corn syrup
2 cups sugar
¾ cup water
1 Tbsp cornstarch
1 Tbsp butter
1 tsp salt

Combine all, and cook in heavy saucepan until syrup forms a hard ball when dropped in cold water. (248°-254°) Remove from heat and add 1 tsp flavoring if desired. Pour into greased pie pans. Let cool until you can handle it. Pull until light and non-glossy. Cut into pieces, and wrap in pieces of waxed paper.

School Days Taffy

1 cup cream
½ cup butter
¾ cup light corn syrup
3 ½ cups sugar

Boil to hard ball stage (248°-254°) Pour into greased pie pans. Let cool until you can handle it. Pull until light and non-glossy. Cut into pieces, and wrap in pieces of waxed paper.

A horse can't pull while kicking,
This fact I merely mention.
And he can't kick while pulling,
Which is my chief contention.
Let's imitate the good old horse
And lead a life that's fitting.
Just pull an honest load and then
There'll be no time for kicking.

SPICY CRUNCH SNACK

½ cup butter
½ cup brown sugar
½ cup honey
2 tsp cinnamon
½ tsp salt
3 cups Cheerios
2 cups Rice Chex
2 cups Corn Chex
2 cups Crispix
1 cup pecan pieces
1 cup raisins (optional)

Mix first 5 ingredients together and boil 3 minutes. Drizzle over remaining ingredients and stir to coat cereal. Bake at 275° for 20 minutes, stirring occasionally.

One of my students gave me this recipe years ago when I taught school. It's a simple, tasty and healthy snack mix.

CRANBERRY ALMOND SNACK

1 box (17.6 oz) Chex cereal (Rice, Corn, or Crispix)
2 ¾ cups sliced almonds
¾ cup chopped craisins (dried cranberries)

1 cup sugar
1 cup light corn syrup
¾ cup butter
½ tsp vanilla
½ tsp almond flavoring

Pour cereal into a large bowl and set aside. Prepare syrup. Bring sugar, syrup and butter to a boil over medium heat, stirring occasionally. Cook to 250° or hard ball stage. Remove from heat and add flavoring. Pour over cereal and mix well. Stir in nuts and craisins. After it cools, break up into chunks and store in containers with tight lids. This snack mix won't last long!

Relishes, Sauces, Dips, and Miscellaneous

Success

Success is in the way you
    Walk in the paths of life each day.
It's in the little things you do,
    And in the things you say.
Success is not in getting rich,
    Or rising high to fame.
It's not alone in winning goals,
    Which all men hope to claim.
Success is being big of heart,
    And clean and broad in mind;
It's being faithful to your friends,
    And to the stranger, kind.
It's in the children whom you love,
    And all they learn from you;
Success depends on character,
    And everything you do.

Be Careful

Be careful of your thoughts
    For your thoughts become your words.
Be careful of your words
    For your words become your actions.
Be careful of your actions
    For your actions become your habits.
Be careful of your habits
    For your habits become your character.
Be careful of your character
    For your character becomes your destiny.

–Author Unknown

Relishes, Sauces, Dips and Miscellaneous

PIMENTOS

12 large red peppers
1 cup vinegar
1 cup sugar
2 tsp salt

Remove seeds from peppers, and grind the peppers fine. Put all ingredients in kettle. Simmer 1 hour. Can in half-pint jars. Boil 10 minutes in hot water bath.

RED HOT-PEPPER SAUCE

2 qts chopped tomatoes
1½ cups hot peppers, halved
1 cup vinegar
1 cup sugar
1 Tbsp salt
2 Tbsp pickling spice (tied in a bag)
1 cup vinegar

Combine tomatoes, peppers and 1 cup vinegar. Cook until peppers are tender. Sieve and add sugar, salt, spice bag, and 1 cup vinegar. Simmer until thickened. Put in small jars, hot water bath for 10 minutes. Tastes good on eggs, meat dishes, fried potatoes, etc.

Zesty Hot Dog Relish

3 cups shredded zucchini or cucumbers
1 cup grated cabbage
1 cup chopped onions
1 cup chopped red peppers
4 tsp salt
⅔ cup vinegar
1½ cups sugar
2 Tbsp cornstarch
½ tsp celery salt
⅛ tsp black pepper
¼ tsp dry mustard

Mix vegetables and salt and let set overnight. Next morning, rinse and drain thoroughly. Make a thickened syrup of the remaining ingredients. Stir into vegetable mixture and bring to a boil. Pack into jars, and hot water bath for 15 minutes. Makes about 4 pints.

Burke's Garden Hot Pepper Relish

10 cups sweet pepper pieces
2 cups hot pepper pieces (or more)
4 cups onions
5 cups sugar
2 cups vinegar
2½ Tbsp salt
1 Tbsp celery seed

Grind peppers and onions. Pour boiling water over them. Drain after 5 minutes. Add remaining ingredients. Stir well to dissolve sugar and salt. Put into pints and seal. Cook 10 minutes in hot water bath. Delicious when served with meatloaf, hamburgers, hot dogs, barbecued meats, and with meaty soups.

Do your best, and rejoice with him who can do better.

CRISP LIME PICKLES

Wash and slice freshly picked cucumbers until you have 7 lbs. Soak in 1 gallon cold water and 1 cup pickling lime. Let set 24 hrs in fridge or a cool place. Drain. Rinse in cold water 3 times. Cover with ice water. Let set an hour. Drain. Heat to a boil the following: 5 cups vinegar (half white and half cider vinegar), 8 cups sugar, 1 Tbsp salt, and ⅓ cup mixed pickling spice. (Tie spices in a nylon net bag.) Pour over cukes and let set overnight at room temperature. Simmer all together 30 minutes and pack in pint jars. Seal. Hot water bath for 10 minutes. These are good served with any meat or chopped up in chicken salad.

MIXED VEGETABLE PICKLES

3 gal assorted vegetables
6 cups sugar
2 Tbsp salt
3 cups water
3 cups white vinegar

Wash and chop or slice your favorite vegetables, such as these: carrots, pearl onions, green, yellow, and red peppers, cabbage, celery, cucumbers, cauliflower, green beans, or limas. Boil each separately until tender-crisp; drain.

Heat the remaining ingredients to boiling for a brine. Pack vegetables in pint jars, and pour brine to ½" from top. Seal and boil in a hot water bath for 10 minutes.

– Grandma Marie Rohrer

Grandma's mixed pickles were especially tasty. One day I sat down with her to learn her secrets. "Use plenty of sweet and plenty of sour," she advised. This is the recipe we came up with.

A promise should be given with caution and kept with care.

RED BEET PICKLES

4 qts small beets
2½ cups vinegar
2½ cups sugar
1 cup water
2 cups beet juice
2 tsp salt
2 sticks cinnamon
8 whole cloves

Boil beets until just done. Slip off skins and reserve 2 cups beet juice to add to your brine for color. Bring rest of ingredients to a boil and simmer 10 minutes. Pack beets in 8 pint jars, fill with brine. Seal and hot water bath 10 minutes.

RED BEET PICKLED EGGS

2 dozen peeled hard-boiled eggs
2 cups (or more) red beet juice
1½ cups vinegar
2 cups sugar
1 Tbsp salt
red food coloring if desired

Dissolve sugar and salt in vinegar. Add beet juice and bring to a boil. Pour over eggs and stir occasionally for even coloring of eggs. You may need to add more water so juice covers eggs. Refrigerate when mixture cools. These keep several weeks in fridge. Cooked beets may be pickled in the same jar with the eggs.

Too little to save, Too much to dump;
That's what makes the housewife plump.

KETCHUP

2 gallons <u>thick</u> tomato juice
4 large onions, chopped
2 cups sugar
4½ cups brown sugar
¼ cup salt
2 tsp cinnamon
½ tsp cloves
2 Tbsp prepared mustard
3 cups cider vinegar
2 cups tapioca starch or clearjel

Cook and sieve <u>ripe</u> tomatoes and onions. Let juice set awhile.
Dip off clear liquid to make the remaining juice <u>thick</u>. Poor into a
12 quart kettle. Add other ingredients (except vinegar and starch)
and bring to a boil. Make a batter of the vinegar and starch. Thicken
juice with it. Boil while stirring about 5 minutes. Put into 16-18 pint
jars. Seal. Place in hot water bath and boil for 15 minutes.

CHUNKY SALSA

16 lbs peeled fresh tomatoes (about 2 gallons)
1 lb chopped hot peppers
4 med chopped onions
1½ cups brown sugar
1 cup instant clearjel
¼ cup vinegar
¼ cup salt
1 tsp black pepper
½ Tbsp basil flakes
2 Tbsp chopped, fresh parsley

Crush tomatoes with your hands or potato masher. Sauté peppers
and onions in a little oil. Combine brown sugar and instant clearjel.
Blend all ingredients and pack in pint jars. Process in a boiling
water bath for 20 minutes. Makes 16 pints. Herbs may be adjusted
to suit your taste.

A peck of common sense is worth a bushel of learning.

Pizza Shop Style Pizza Sauce

5 quarts tomato juice
4 onions, chopped
2 green peppers
¾ cup sugar
½ Tbsp Italian Seasoning
1 Tbsp crushed red pepper
1 Tbsp oregano flakes
1 Tbsp basil flakes
1½ tsp Pizza seasoning
½ tsp garlic powder
¼ cup salt
1 cup oil
3 bay leaves, crushed
½ gallon tomato paste

Cook tomato juice, onions, and peppers together for 1 hour. Sieve. Return to kettle and add remaining ingredients. Cook slowly for an hour. Can and seal. Process in hot water bath for 10 minutes. Makes 12 pints.

– Karen Shank

Pizza Sauce

2 or 3 large onions, chopped
½ cup oil
8 cups tomato pulp
1 Tbsp basil
1 Tbsp oregano
1 Tbsp garlic salt
¼ cup sugar
1 Tbsp salt

Sauté onions in oil. Mix in remaining ingredients and simmer 35 minutes. Bottle and seal. Process in hot water bath for 10 minutes.

Every time we say no to temptation, we become stronger.

HORSERADISH SAUCE

¼ cup horseradish
1 cup mayonnaise

Mix together and enjoy on roast beef or as a sandwich spread.

TANGY MUSTARD SAUCE

3 Tbsp butter
½ cup brown sugar
½ tsp salt
¼ cup cider vinegar
1 cup half and half
2 Tbsp flour
¼ cup dry mustard

Melt butter, brown sugar and salt in saucepan. Make a batter of everything else and shake well to dissolve lumps. Stir into saucepan gradually and cook over medium heat until thick. (You may use prepared mustard and 1 Tbsp less vinegar.)

CHEESE SAUCE

1 cup butter
3 cups milk
1 tsp salt
½ cup flour
2 lbs Velveeta cheese, cubed

In a saucepan over medium heat, melt butter, add half of milk and salt. Put rest of milk in batter shaker. Add flour and shake to blend. Add to hot mixture and stir until thick and bubbly. Add cubed cheese, and stir constantly until melted. Good over hot vegetables or as a dipping sauce for soft pretzels.

Temptation becomes a sin only when we yield to it.

Hot Fudge Sauce

1¾ cups sugar
½ cup flour
⅔ cup cocoa
¾ tsp salt
2 cups water
2 Tbsp butter
1 tsp vanilla
½ cup semisweet chocolate chips

Mix first 4 ingredients in saucepan. Gradually add water and stir while heating to a boil. Add butter, vanilla, and chocolate chips. Store in fridge, and heat to serve over ice cream.

– Ethel Shank

Chocolate Syrup

3 cups sugar
1 cup cocoa
pinch of salt
2 cups water

Combine sugar, cocoa, and salt. Stir in water. Boil 5 minutes. Store in fridge. Makes good chocolate milk.

Caramel Sauce

1 cup brown sugar
½ cup cream
½ cup light corn syrup
1 Tbsp butter
½ tsp salt
1 tsp vanilla

Boil over low heat for 5 minutes. Makes 1 cup. Serve over ice cream. You may add chopped walnuts or pecans for a real treat.

If anyone speaks evil of you, live so that none will believe it.

Pancake Syrup

1 cup brown sugar
1 cup white sugar
1 cup water
1 cup light corn syrup
pinch of salt
1 tsp maple flavoring

Combine and boil 5 minutes. Add maple flavoring after removing from heat.

Honey Butter

Beat 1 cup cold butter and 1 cup clover honey until light and creamy.   Keep in refrigerator. Delicious on homemade bread and rolls, toast, crepes, pancakes, or waffles.

Cinnamon Butter

2 sticks butter, softened
1½ cups powdered sugar
3 Tbsp cinnamon

Sift sugar and cinnamon, combine with butter. Refrigerate. Very good on toast, muffins, pancakes, sweet potatoes, etc.

Fresh Fruit Dip

1 cup sour cream
¼ cup brown sugar

Stir together. Delicious with strawberries, apples, kiwi, bananas, oranges, grapes, pineapple, peaches, pears, etc.

A rumor is as hard to unspread as butter.

STRAWBERRY CREAM SPREAD OR DIP

softened cream cheese
fresh strawberry jam

Combine and stir until smooth and creamy. Spread on rolls, quick breads, toast, etc. Add marshmallow crème for a tasty dip for fruit.

PARTY SHRIMP DIP

4 oz cooked salad shrimp
1 tsp Old Bay Seasoning
8 oz cream cheese
3 Tbsp cocktail sauce

Rinse shrimp and drain well. Bring to a boil in 1 cup water and Old Bay. Drain again and cool shrimp. Combine shrimp and softened cream cheese. Spread in a shallow flat dish. Top with cocktail sauce. Serve on crackers.

– Ava (Eberly) Heatwole

SHRIMP DIP

1 lb cooked salad shrimp
1¼ cups diced celery
¼ cup minced fresh onion
8 oz softened cream cheese
1¼ cups Miracle Whip
1 tsp salt
1 tsp sugar

Rinse cooked shrimp under cold water and drain well. Add rest of ingredients. Serve on crackers. May be made a day ahead of serving.

He who can take advice is sometimes superior to him who gives it.

VEGETABLE DIP

1 cup sour cream
1 cup mayonnaise
½ tsp onion salt
1 tsp dill weed
1 tsp parsley flakes
½ tsp Beau Monde Seasoning or celery salt
Mix all ingredients well.

– Lois Rhodes

VEGGIE DIP

16 oz cream cheese, softened
1 tsp horseradish
1 cup ketchup
1-2 tsp Worcestershire Sauce
parsley, garlic, and onion powder to taste

Combine all of the ingredients and stir until creamy.

– Wanda (Rohrer) Good

HOT CHIPPED BEEF DIP

16 oz cream cheese
1 cup sour cream
¼ cup fresh minced onion
¼ cup milk
¼ tsp garlic powder
5 oz finely chopped dried beef

Combine all and blend well. Put in a shallow bake dish and bake at 350° for 20 minutes. Serve warm with your favorite chips or crackers.

Be cheerful. Of all the things you wear,
your expression is the most important.

SWEETENED CONDENSED MILK

1 cup instant nonfat dry milk
⅔ cup sugar
½ cup boiling water
3 Tbsp melted margarine or butter

Combine and beat until smooth. Makes 1¼ cups or the equivalent of 1 can.

Gail Borden created sweetened condensed milk, and Civil War soldiers were among the first to use it. After the war, homemakers discovered the convenience of a milk product which didn't spoil quickly.

YOGURT

3 quarts milk
1 cup unflavored yogurt
¼ cup water
1 Tbsp gelatin

Heat milk to about 165°. Meanwhile soften gelatin in water. Stir into hot milk. Let cool to about 120°. Stir in yogurt, blend thoroughly. Set in warm oven, or wrap in towels and let set on counter until it thickens 6-8 hours). Refrigerate. You may sweeten or flavor yogurt to your liking. (For creamier yogurt, add a cup of powdered milk before heating and cooling the 3 quarts milk.)

SODA CHEESE

Stir ½ cup buttermilk or unflavored yogurt into 1 gallon fresh warm milk. Cover and let set until it thickens (12-24 hours).

Cut through milk with a knife to form cubes, and stir while heating to 140°-150°. Drain well in a cheesecloth bag. Save ½ cup whey for starter for the next time you make soda cheese. Mix 1 tsp soda into crumbs with your hands. Cover and let set until curds are soft (3-5 hours).

Melt slowly over low heat, stirring until curds are all melted. Add rich milk or cream (1 to 1½ cups) and 1 beaten egg. Heat to almost boiling while stirring. Then remove from heat. Add salt to taste (1 tsp). Pour into containers, cover, and cool. Finished soda cheese freezes well for up to a year.

HOMEMADE BUTTER

Churning butter Is an almost forgotten job these days. Once in a while we get an urge to fill Grandma's churn with cream and crank out some tasty homemade butter.

Use fresh "top-cream" from unpastuerized milk. Let set in a cool place, 50°-52° for a day or two for enzyme action to begin. Before beginning to churn, set cream out to begin warming. Cream at 62 ° is ideal to begin churning.

When butter forms, gather it into a large bowl. Add ice water and work it with your hands to remove as much whey as you can. Add salt to your liking and refrigerate. Use the buttermilk for baking, etc.

FRESH STRAWBERRY JAM

1 box Sure-Jell (for low sugar recipes in pink box)
3 pts strawberries (or enough to make 4 cups crushed berries)
1 cup water
3 cups sugar

Remove caps from strawberries, wash and drain well. Crush with a potato masher. Add sugar to Sure-Jell and stir in water. Bring to a boil over medium heat, stirring constantly. Boil and stir 1 minute. Pour into berries, stirring quickly to mix well. Pour into cup or pint containers. Cover. Let stand at room temperature until it jells. Keeps in refrigerator up to 3 weeks. Freeze for later use. Keeps well up to 2 years.

HORSERADISH-DRIED BEEF CHEESE BALL

1 lb cream cheese
1 Tbsp horseradish
1 cup chopped dried beef

Combine and blend until smooth. You may season it with a sprinkle of hickory smoke salt or your favorite seasoned salt. Using a piece of saran wrap is a big help when shaping a cheese ball.

Pineapple Cheese Ball

8 oz cream cheese, softened
½ cup drained crushed pineapple
¼ cup chopped green peppers
1 Tbsp chopped onion
1 tsp salt

Combine all ingredients and shape into a ball. Cover with plastic wrap and refrigerate. Roll in 1 cup chopped pecans before serving.

Cheese Ball

2 (8 oz) pkg cream cheese
1 jar Old English cheese spread
2 Tbsp pimentos
1 Tbsp onion
1 tsp sugar
1 tsp parsley

Combine all ingredients. Roll ball in parsley or chopped nuts.

– Sharon (Wenger) Good, Karen (Nolt) Martin

Holiday Cheese Ball

2½ lbs cream cheese
1 lb Sharp Cheddar, grated
1 lb Sharp Cheddar Cheese Spread (Wispride or other)
3 Tbsp finely grated raw onion
1½ cups home-canned Pimentos (see recipe pg 291)
1 tsp salt
1 Tbsp sugar

Warm cheese to room temperature. Mix all. Chill. Shape into balls or logs. May roll in chopped pecans before serving .Using a piece of saran wrap is a big help when shaping a cheese ball.

This makes 5 lbs of yummy stuff, so there's plenty for gifts for your friends and neighbors.

LAUNDRY STAIN REMOVER

1 cup water
1 cup liquid dish soap
1 cup ammonia

Combine in a spray bottle, and shake well. Use on collars, cuffs, underarms, and stains.

HOMEMADE LAUNDRY SOAP

6 qts rain water or soft water
5 qts liquid grease (melted but not hot)
3 cups 20 Mule Borateem
3 cups Tide powder
1 pt ammonia (unscented)
24 oz lye (or 2 13-oz cans Red Seal Lye)

Use stainless steel or plastic bucket and a wooden stirrer. Mix grease, Borateem, Tide, and ammonia. Stir in the soft water. Put on rubber gloves. Add lye slowly while stirring. Stir until it starts to thicken, then every 5 minutes until like thick honey. Pour into molds. (Molds can be made by lining cardboard boxes with plastic.) Pour soap about 3" deep. Cut after several hours. Separate bars, and let it dry several weeks to harden. Soap may be grated for use in automatic washers. Good for cleaning tough stains.

– *Neva Horst*

Grandmother Wenger added oil of sassafras or cloves to her soap. I always enjoyed using her scented homemade soap.

SPRING TONIC "JOGGIN' IN A JUG"

1 qt apple juice
1 qt purple grape juice
1 cup apple cider vinegar

Combine. Store in fridge. Drink ½ cup each day.
This is supposed to have a blood-thinning effect, similar to that of taking an aspirin a day. Folks with arthritis use this as a home remedy also.

Play Dough

1½ cups salt
3 cups flour
2 Tbsp cream of tartar
⅓ cup vegetable oil
3 cups water
1 tsp food coloring

Mix together salt, flour and cream of tartar. Add oil, water and color. Cook over medium heat while stirring, until it forms a soft ball. Knead on a floured surface for a minute. Store in an airtight container.

– Evaleen Rohrer

Bird Pudding – for Feeding Birds

3 cups melted suet (or other fat)
¼ cup peanut butter
3 cups dry bread crumbs
1 cup whole-wheat flour
1 cup cornmeal
½ cup sugar
1 cup oatmeal
1 cup sunflower seeds

Mix all ingredients into melted fat. Pour into a bread pan or muffin tins and chill. Tie it to a tree branch in an onion bag, or put a piece in your feeder tray. The birds will love it.

Hummingbird Nectar

3 cups boiling water
1 cup sugar
2 drops red food coloring

Combine and stir to dissolve sugar. Cool and put in feeder. Change weekly if any remains in feeder. It will ferment after that time.

Nature gives to every season some beauties of its own.– Charles Dickens

Beverages

Ah, Those Pills

A row of bottles on the shelf
Caused me to analyze myself.
One tiny, yellow pill I pop
Goes to my heart so it won't stop.
A little white one that I take
Goes to my hands so they won't shake.
The blue ones that I use a lot
Tell me I'm happy when I'm not.
The purple one goes to my brain
And tells me that I have no pain.
The capsules tell me not to sneeze,
Or cough, or choke, or even wheeze.
The green one, smallest of them all
Goes to my blood so I won't fall.
The orange ones are so big and bright
And stop my leg cramps in the night.
Such an array of brilliant pills
Help me to cure all kinds of ills,
But what I'd really like to know –
Is what tells each one where to go!

– Author Unknown

Beverages

FAVORITE ICED TEA

Pour one quart boiling water over ⅓ cup Lipton Loose-leaf tea or a gallon size Lipton tea bag. Steep 6-8 minutes. While you wait, slice ½ lemon (and ½ orange – optional) into a bowl. Add 1¼ cups sugar and squish it all together with your gloved hand to remove juices from citrus. Pour tea through a strainer into sugar mixture and stir to dissolve sugar. Pour into a gallon pitcher. Fill with water and ice. Keep in fridge.

ICED TEA FOR A CROWD

Pour 2½-3 quarts boiling water over 1½ cups Lipton Loose-leaf tea in a glass or stainless metal container. You may use four or five 1 gallon size Lipton tea bags if you prefer. Let tea steep 7 – 8 minutes, stir once or twice. If using gallon tea bags, rebrew them using half the amount of water. Add this to your tea for extra strength.
Dissolve 5 cups sugar in cold water. Strain tea to remove leaves, stir into sugar water. Add water to make 4 gallons of tea. Serve over ice. Serves 28-30.

The secret to making bright, clear tea that doesn't turn cloudy is using soft water.

GARDEN MINT TEA CONCENTRATE

4 qts water
4-6 cups tea leaves
4 cups sugar

Bring cold water to a rolling boil. Turn off heat, add tea leaves. Cover and steep 15 minutes. Remove leaves, stir in sugar. To serve add 3 qts water to 1 qt concentrate. Concentrate may be frozen for future use.

FRESH SQUEEZED LEMONADE

Wash and slice 4-5 large lemons into a bowl. Add 1½ cups sugar, and squeeze lemons and sugar together with your gloved hand. This releases the juice and lemon oil. Add about a quart of water, and stir to dissolve all the sugar. Strain into a gallon container. Fill with water. For a quicker, less messy version, juice 5 lemons with your lemon reamer.

EGG NOG

4 eggs, beaten
½ cup sugar
¼ tsp salt
3 cups milk
2 tsp vanilla
½ tsp rum flavor
3 cups cold milk
1 cup whipping cream (optional) for garnish

Combine eggs, sugar, salt and milk in top of a double boiler. Cook over boiling water until mixture is creamy (160º). Remove from heat and cool quickly. Stir in flavoring and refrigerate. At serving time beat chilled custard until smooth and frothy. Stir in cold milk. Whip cream, sweeten with a little sugar and drop spoonfuls to float on the nog. Garnish with nutmeg. Makes 7 servings.

Orange "Pick Me Up" Drink

2 cups milk
¼ cup sugar
⅔ cup frozen orange juice concentrate
10-12 crushed ice cubes

Combine and beat until smooth and frothy.

Frosty Banana Slush

6 cups boiling water
4 cups sugar
5 cups mashed bananas
6 oz can frozen lemonade
6 oz can frozen orange juice
46 oz pineapple juice
2 two liter jugs ginger ale

Combine water and sugar. Cool. Mix with fruit and juices. Pour into 2 containers and freeze. Stir occasionally until frozen. Remove from freezer several hours before serving. Break mixture up into slushy chunks. To each container add 1 jug of chilled ginger ale. Stir and serve as a refreshing drink.

– *Carolyn (Black) Shirkey*

Variation:
Substitute 48 ounces more pineapple juice for water and sugar. Use orange soda instead of ginger ale.

*Remember the banana—
when it left the bunch, it got skinned.*

CANNED GRAPE JUICE

Wash and de-stem Concord grapes. Put 1½ cups grapes and ½ cup sugar in a quart jar. Fill with warm water. Seal and hot water bath for 25 minutes. After two weeks it's ready to pour over ice and drink.

TANGY FRUIT PUNCH

46 oz Hawaiian (or similar) punch
46 oz pineapple juice
12 oz frozen orange juice concentrate
12 oz frozen lemonade concentrate
2-3 liters ginger ale

Combine juices and chill. When ready to serve, add ginger ale and ice.

PARTY PUNCH

12 oz frozen orange juice
12 oz frozen lemonade
1 qt unsweetened pineapple juice
1 qt cranberry juice
1 gallon water
sugar (optional)
2 liters ginger ale

Combine all ingredients except ginger ale. Chill. Add ginger ale just before serving.

– Beulah (Rhodes) Burkholder

To be a Christian is to obey Christ, no matter how you feel.
– H. W. Beecher

Pink Punch

2 pkg red Kool-Aid
1 gallon water
2 cups sugar
46 oz pineapple juice
2 liters ginger ale

Combine all except ginger ale, and chill. Add ginger ale just before serving. Also good to substitute Hawaiian punch for pineapple juice.

– Austin and Marie Eberly

Golden Punch

2 pks orange Kool-Aid
12 oz. frozen orange juice
2 liters Sprite

Mix Kool-Aid according to package directions. Add orange juice and Sprite.

Lime Punch

2 pks lime Kool-Aid
1 quart water
1 can (48 oz.) pineapple juice
1 cup sugar
½ gallon lime sherbet
2 liters ginger ale

Mix first four ingredients. Pour over sherbet and stir to combine. Add ginger ale last.

*An optimist is the kind of person who believes that
a housefly is looking for a way to get out.*

– G. J. Nathan

Homemade "Fizzy" Root Beer

2 cups sugar
1 gallon warm water
1 tsp yeast
4 tsp root beer extract

Combine all, and stir to dissolve sugar and yeast. Pour into glass jugs. Cover tightly, and set in the sun for 4 hours. Ready to chill and serve the next day. Gets nippier with age.

Root Beer Float

Plop 2 dips of vanilla ice cream into each tall, chilled glass. Fill slowly with root beer. Serve with a spoon and a straw. Also good made with Coke or Orange Soda.

Hot Chocolate Mix

Small Batch	Large Batch
4 cups dry milk	8 qt box
1½ cups chocolate Quik	2 lb box
1 cup non-dairy creamer	22 oz jar
¼ cup powdered sugar	1 lb box

Mix all together. Use ⅓ cup of mix to ⅔ cup boiling water. Store mix in a cool place. (I freeze part of it to keep it fresh.)

Vienna Coffee

Combine ½ cup of instant coffee, ⅔ cup of sugar, ⅔ cup of powdered milk, and ½ tsp cinnamon. (Artificial sweetener can be substituted for the sugar, and coffee creamer for the powdered milk if you prefer.) For a great cup of coffee, simply place 2 rounded teaspoons of this mix in a cup of boiling water. This recipe makes about 20 cups of coffee, so store the unused mix in an airtight container.

CAPPUCCINO

1 cup milk
2 tsp sugar
1 cup strong brewed coffee (regular or decaf)

Brew the coffee. Heat the milk to just below boiling. Add the sugar and whip with beater or in blender to make it foamy. Combine with coffee. You can sprinkle with cinnamon or add a bit of vanilla.

FRAPPUCCINO

Fill blender ¾ full of vanilla ice cream (1 quart). Add 3 Tbsp chocolate syrup, 8 ice cubes, ¾ cup strong coffee and ¾ cup milk. Blend until creamy. A delicious frosty milkshake.

STRAWBERRY SMOOTHIE

1 cup orange juice
1 banana
1 cup yogurt
1½ cups strawberries
sugar to taste

Put ingredients in blender and stir until smooth and creamy.

BREAKFAST SHAKE

1 mashed banana
1 cup crushed strawberries
1-2 Tbsp sugar
¼ tsp vanilla
1½ cups cold milk

Mix all together and whip for 1 minute.

The Loser's Diet

I give a sigh and hold my breath and walk before the glass,
The figure that I see therein, its limits has surpassed,
It's time and past, I now decide, for something to be done,
I'll lose some weight and feel just great, this could be rather fun.

While still inspired and feeling brave, I'm headed for the scales,
And as I pass the pantry door, my stomach fairly quells;
But no, I can't, I won't give in, that image 'rose before,
Of me within that looking glass, upon the bedroom door!

I cast a glance upon those scales, while terror fills my eye,
No matter what I tell myself, I know they'll never lie,
I ease my bulk onto the scales, and hold my breath a bit,
The numbers climb and climb until I feel depression hit!

So then I waddle on back out and thru the kitchen door,
I plop down on a chair and think, I need a plan for sure;
To boost my spirits, now I know some coffee's what I need,
A half a cookie would taste good, my stomach loudly pleads.

But oh! a half of cookie is a very meager treat,
I think I'll snitch the other half and make my snack complete;
Now here I sit, my cookie's gone, my conscience starts to prick,
I tell myself this will be it, I'll to my diet stick.

I will not eat another thing until the dinner hour,
I firmly vow within myself to exercise willpower;
I'll throw myself into my work and maybe I'll forget,
The pantry shelves well-stocked with snacks, for diets quite unfit!

I hold out firm till dinner time, tho' fairly caving in,
A diet surely has rewards, already I feel thin;
And when I sit to eat my lunch, the low fat foods I'll choose,
Like vegetables and cantaloupe, they're sure to help you lose.

I leave the butter off my bread, but add a little jam,
For after all it's made of fruit, and that is in the plan;
I trim the fat from off my beef, which leaves it rather dry,
And since there's gravy with the meal, why should I pass it by?

A little dip for pepper sticks, some mayonnaise on the 'matoes,
And just a tiny little dab of creamy mashed potatoes;
I'm tempted when dessert comes past, to think that I can try it,
But no, I cannot let myself forget this wretched diet!

Now dinner's o'er, the dishes washed, I think back o'er my plan,
Some exercise! I says to me, I'll get this flab in hand;
I'll raise my hands up high and then, I'll bend and touch my toes,
Whew! What a job this losing weight, my knees seem prone to bow!

What is some other exercise? I really should do more,
Then like a flash it comes to me, I ease down on the floor;
I put a pillow 'neath my neck and stretch out on the rug,
These situps sure will trim my waist, thinks I while feeling smug.

It feels so good to just lay here and dream about the day,
When I can wear those clothes again that I have hung away;
Of course I know that day won't come if I keep lying here,
I tuck my feet beneath the couch and pull my head up clear.

I flop back down upon the rug and come back up again,
Instead of forty-one or two, I think I'll just do ten!
This exercising business now I'll put far from my mind,
The afternoon sped swiftly by and now it's supper time.

For some perhaps, but not for me, I'll skip this meal tonight,
I fill my glass up to the brim, plain water pure and bright;
I'll just call this my evening meal, who needs to eat so rich?
But as I lick the tablespoons, my family's mouths all twitch.

Now supper's past, the work is done, and night-time's closing in,
I sink into an easy chair and dream of being thin;
I think back how I did today and find no need to grumble,
And as I inwardly applaud, my stomach gives a rumble.

In fact thinks I, I've done so good, I need a small reward,
A tiny little something sweet from out the pantry's hoard;
A bag of chips I find therein, a box of donut holes,
And when I see that fluffy cake, my tummy really rolls.

A tiny sliver of the cake, a handful of the chips,
They have no added flavors, so they need a little dip;
Those donut holes! I am so large, and since they are so small,
I eat one more and then one more, until they're nearly all!

And so this was a common day where diets are concerned,
We try awhile and then give in, for self-control we yearn;
But all we dieters alike, I think this line oft' borrow,
Why should we even try today, when we can lose tomorrow?

– Written by two sisters who prefer to be anonymous

By Gone Days

To the gray house near Dry River was a place we liked to go,
You'd receive a hearty welcome and this I fully know.
Never would you leave there without a snack or two—
Be it breakfast, lunch, or supper, nothing but the best would do.

There would be such good aromas when passing by this way,
"Oh; It's coming from the bakery!" someone would be sure to say.
'Twas a place to stop and visit with your friends all working there,
Sometimes it would get lengthy – we hope they didn't care.

One was sure to get remembered at "Birthday Time" each year
With a party, gift, or greeting, we were getting spoiled I fear—
The trips we got to go on were a highlight for us all!
West Virginia and Chincoteague Island are some I can recall.

Remember then the Christmas season, loss of sleep, but lots of fun,
You all hardly ever knowing when your day's work would be done.
Just a few of many memories, and I think of them a lot,
Working there has been a pleasure – it will never be forgot.

Rosanna (Rhodes) Martin

Memories

Our work place in Rushville was a place that was nifty,
    Overnight would be the stay for the girls under fifty.
Usually there was laughter and always plenty of food,
    Never was there a dull moment, you could sing if in the mood.
Trying were the times when you flubbed up really bad,
    Reassurance was promptly given, and you were no longer sad.
Yearly came the Christmas season with all the extra baking,
    Very seldom would anyone catch us without goodies in the making,
Then sometimes our work lasted late into the night-
    It was often after midnight when we'd turn out the light.
Going to the market was done early in the morn,
    Ethel or Marjorie usually went no matter how weary and worn.
Yummy things to eat were made 'most every day,
    And a lot of steps were involved to send it on its way.
Keeping everything clean required efforts from us all,
    Each day the floors and dishpans beckoned with a mighty call.
Silly could the helpers be that came from far and near,
    Happy were the times we spent in a place we all hold dear.
Of all the fond remembrances and everyone's different ways,
    Precious memories are our keepsakes of our bygone working days!

– Brenda (Shirk) Knicely

The Shenandoah Valley

Oh wilt thou tell, bright light of day,
While on your daily round;
Is any spot more lovely that
Your searching beam has found
 Than the Shenandoah Valley?

   With warm embrace the Blue Ridge east,
   The Alleghenies west,
   Protect the vale from fierce storms
   Safe sheltered in their breast.
    Blest Shenandoah Valley.

Like ladies with their lavish frocks
Of many rainbow hues,
The ridges wear greens, purples, white,
Reds, oranges, yellow, blues,
 To dress the Valley.

   Mole Hill, Giants Grave, Dry River too,
   Bold Massanutten Peak,
   Tide Spring-intriguing ebb and flow–
   Add to the names unique
    In the Shenandoah Valley.

Wildflowers by rambling country roads
Creeks, rivers sparkling bright,
Lush patchwork fields and cattle-ed hills
Reflect thy favored light
 On the Shenandoah Valley.

   But deep beneath her limestone crust
   In vaulted, ethereal seams,
   Your rays can never penetrate
   The caverns' awesome scenes
    Underneath the Valley.

Surely the shameful Civil War
Caused weepings on your round,
As raging battles senseless spilled
Men's blood upon the ground
    Desecrating the Valley.

          And often when you sink to rest
          In peaceful western bed
          Exquisite sunset colored quilts
          You gently o'er us spread
             With benediction on the Valley.

Serenest moon, on silent trail
Of radiant, silver glow,
Where doth compare with beauty rare,
Oh tell me—do you know—
    More than the Shenandoah?

          Coyotes howl, the whip-poor-will
          And owls add soft refrain,
          Night creatures shyly venture out
          To catch the ling'ring strain
             Serenading the Valley.

"Daughter of the Stars," the Indian said
This Valley's name shall be
And nightly from dark velvet sky
These sparkling gems agree
    Above the Shenandoah.

          I pray some day the Son of Light
          Will take us ever where
          That naught on earth has beauty worth
          To Heaven's scene compare,
             Not even the Shenandoah Valley.

                – <u>Frances</u> (Rohrer) Good

    But as it is written, Eye hath not seen, nor ear heard,
      neither have entered into the heart of man, the things
which God hath prepared for them that love him. – I Corinthians 2:9

Holy God, Thou art within every seed,
and fruit and harvest;
Help us to see Thee within
our lives as the source
of all that is good
and true and loving.
Guide us in the paths of righteousness,
and make us grateful
for your presence.
— Amen

I found this prayer in the recipe collection
of Grandma Marie Rohrer after her passing.

Grandma's Pies

When I sit back and close my eyes,
I still remember Grandma's pies,
All in a row on baking day,
Her handiwork there on display.

I still recall the spicy smell,
Her kitchen that I loved so well.
I wish I could go back once more
And see her standing at the door.

Then she would cut a slice for me,
And join me with her cup of tea.
Oh, how I long for days gone by,
For one more slice of Grandma's pie.

But cherished memories remain,
When I walk down memory's lane,
Of Grandma's pies and Grandma's love,
A blessing sent from God above.

— Author Unknown

Index

Cakes and Frostings

Candy and Snacks

Cookies and Bars

Desserts

Garden Salads

Main Dishes and Meats

Relishes, Sauces, Dips and Miscellaneous

Soups and Sandwiches

Vegetables

How to Order

Country Home Cooking

To receive additional copies, or to send this book as a gift; return an order form below with your payment. If you wish to enclose a signed gift card, we'll mail it with your book.

Make Checks Payable To:

Country Home Cooking
7382 Mt. Clinton Pike
Harrisonburg, VA 22802
540-867-0007

- -

Please mail _____ copies of Country Home Cooking at $20.00 per copy plus $5.00 for shipping and handling per book. Virginia residents add $1.00 sales tax.
Enclosed is a check or money order for $ _____.
Mail book to:

Name _____

Address _____

City_____ State_____ Zip_____

- -

Please mail _____ copies of Country Home Cooking at $20.00 per copy plus $5.00 for shipping and handling per book. Virginia residents add $1.00 sales tax.
Enclosed is a check or money order for $ _____.
Mail book to:

Name _____

Address _____

City_____ State_____ Zip_____